Shanghai Homes

GLOBAL CHINESE CULTURE

GLOBAL CHINESE CULTURE

David Der-wei Wang, Editor

Shanghai Homes

Palimpsests of Private Life

Jie Li

 COLUMBIA UNIVERSITY PRESS   NEW YORK

A subsidy from the Harvard FAS Tenure-Track Faculty Publication Fund helped offset publication costs.

Columbia University Press wishes to express its appreciation for assistance given by the Chiang Ching-kuo Foundation for International Scholarly Exchange and Council for Cultural Affairs in the publication of this series.

Columbia University Press
Publishers Since 1893
New York   Chichester, West Sussex
cup.columbia.edu
Library of Congress Cataloging-in-Publication Data
Li, Jie, 1979-
Shanghai homes : palimpsests of private life / Jie Li.
pages   cm. — (Global Chinese culture)
Includes bibliographical references and index.
ISBN 978-0-231-16716-1 (cloth : alk. paper) — ISBN 978-0-231-16717-8 (pbk.) —
ISBN 978-0-231-53817-6 (electronic)
1. Dwellings—China—Shanghai. 2. Chinese—Dwellings—China—Shanghai. 3. Shanghai (China)—Social life and customs. 4. Shanghai (China)—Civilization. I. Title.
GT366.S525L52   2015
392.3'60951132—dc23
2013050042

Columbia University Press books are printed on permanent and durable acid-free paper.
This book is printed on paper with recycled content.
Printed in the United States of America

COVER PHOTO: © Paul Rushton / Alamy
COVER DESIGN: Milenda Nan Ok Lee

References to websites (URLs) were accurate at the time of writing. Neither the author nor Columbia University Press is responsible for URLs that may have expired or changed since the manuscript was prepared.

For my grandparents and Anton

CONTENTS

ACKNOWLEDGMENTS

OVER THE PAST DECADE and a half, I have accumulated many debts of gratitude to those who helped me draft, build, remodel, and furnish *Shanghai Homes*. After leaving Shanghai for New York at the age of eleven, I revisited my grandparents' alleyways only in high school English classes, encouraged by my creative writing teacher, Douglas Goetsch, to excavate memory shards from childhood and polish them into vignettes. In college, courses with Leo Ou-fan Lee and Eileen Cheng-yin Chow inspired me to remap my family's experiences onto Shanghai's broader cultural landscape and cosmopolitan history. As enthusiastic and judicious mentors, they helped me conceptualize a creative blueprint for an undergraduate thesis and scaffold a critical framework.

My extended family members and former neighbors provided the most important building materials for this book, enlivening it with their voices over several summers. I thank them for entrusting with me their family and personal histories and can only hope that this book has done their stories justice. Among the many grandmas and grandpas, aunts and uncles who so patiently answered my repeated inquiries in person, over the telephone, and through correspondence, I am especially grateful to two alleyway neighbors, Aunt Duckweed and Grandma Apricot. Both gifted storytellers with detailed and sensuous memories, they could recreate the sights, sounds, smell, taste, and touch of the spaces they had inhabited as well as conjure up long-gone characters.

Video was an important part of my fieldwork, and I thank Richard Gordon, Carma Hinton, Dick Rogers, and Irene Lusztig for teaching me how to capture and edit everyday life and oral histories.

After completing a first version of *Shanghai Homes* as a senior thesis in 2001, I received supportive and critical comments from friends and teachers: Rabia Belt, Wilt Idema, Ying Qian, Adam Storeygard, and Honza Vihan. Kiku Adatto's inclusion of this thesis in her course syllabus for "Culture and Society" in the subsequent decade brought new readers to it every year. Meanwhile, as Shanghai alleyways were demolished, old communities dissolved, and the memories of my elders faded, the portraits of individuals, families, and neighborhoods in the thesis—albeit flawed and incomplete like an old family photo album—seemed ever worthier of preservation.

To refurbish an undergraduate thesis into a book was a bit like renovating an old house into a museum, a process requiring updated fieldwork, archival research, and almost complete rewriting. For their faith in an unorthodox manuscript between a family memoir and an academic study, I am deeply grateful to Jennifer Crewe and David Der-wei Wang. Insightful and detailed comments from Eugene Wang and an anonymous reviewer pushed me to clarify my methodology, solidify engagement with secondary scholarship, and improve the book's illustrations. A postdoctoral fellowship at Princeton's Society of Fellows in 2012–2013 gave me both the serenity of mind and the intellectual stimulation needed to complete the final manuscript revisions. Inspirational conversations with Mary Harper, Susan Stewart, Carolyn Rouse, Janet Chen, Aihe Wang, and Winnie Wong deepened my thinking on addressing audiences across different fields and disciplines. I am particularly indebted to Denise Ho, Hanchao Lu, Ying Qian, and Yomi Braester for their perceptive and thoughtful comments on the final manuscript. I would also like to thank Yang Xu for helping me with many illustrations and Annie Barva for her superb copyediting, as well as Leslie Kriesel and Jonathan Fiedler for their patient editorial assistance.

Writing a book about homes and private life intensified my appreciation of my own family and our shared memories. A *zhiyin* throughout the years, my husband, Daniel Koss, has always been the first reader and candid critic of every fragment and complete draft. I would not have written this book without his affection for its characters and stories. My mother, Wang Yaqing, and father, Li Bin, planted the seeds from which my intellectual passions have grown, supported the research and writing of this book at every turn, and lovingly furnished it with their hand-drawn illustrations. My four grandparents—Li Baoren and Zhu Yuehua, Wang Zhengwen and Yao Zhanghua—first illuminated for me the human vitality and personal meanings of a baffling and tumultuous century. It is to them that I dedicate this book.

ILLUSTRATIONS

DRAMATIS PERSONAE

Residents of Alliance Lane

GRANDMA APRICOT: Resident of Alliance Lane from childhood to old age, first in No. 111 with her grandparents and parents from 1938, then in No. 83 when she married a neighbor in 1949—moving out of the alleyway only upon its demolition in 2006.

WAIPO: My maternal grandmother, who came to Shanghai from the countryside as a silk worker, married Waigong, moved to the third floor of No. 111 after "Liberation," and had four children: my mother, Aunt Yahua, Uncle Strong, and Little Aunt.

WAIGONG: My maternal grandfather, who came from a declining land-owning family and became a silk worker and "proletariat" in Shanghai.

AUNT DUCKWEED: My mother's downstairs neighbor, who lived with her parents and siblings in the front bedroom of No. 111 from the 1950s to the 1980s. Her mother, Grandma Front Bedroom, lived there until 2000.

PRINCIPAL ZHANG: Vice principal of the local middle school who lived with his wife and four children on the ground floor of No. 111 from the 1950s to the 1980s.

NEIGHBORS: Mother Mao (Moth); Mother Yang; Mother Huo, her daughter Peace, and granddaughter Ping; Uncle Prosper; Uncle Little Brother; schoolteachers White Hair and Black Hair.

Residents of Lane 1695 Pingliang Road

NAINAI: My paternal grandmother, who was betrothed to Yeye as a child bride, moved to Shanghai in 1947, volunteered for the neighborhood committee, and had five children: Aunt Treasure, Aunt Pearl, my father, Aunt Bean, and Uncle Lucky.

YEYE: My paternal grandfather, who attended St. John's College in the early 1940s, worked as accountant for the Textile Bureau, and was labeled a Rightist in 1957.

NEIGHBORS: Grandma Yang (model worker); Old Wu; Old Wang.

Shanghai Homes

INTRODUCTION

YEYE,[1] MY PATERNAL GRANDFATHER, always tied a long string of keys to his waist that jangled as he walked. One might think he were the concierge of a grand palace, but the keys merely fitted the many rusty locks on doors, cabinets, and drawers in his decrepit old house. One summer day in 2000, when I was a rising college senior, Yeye unlocked the drawer next to his bed and took out a yellowed, brittle document with transparent tape patching over torn edges. After being unfolded several times, the palm-size booklet expanded into the size of a tabloid newspaper (fig. 0.1). It turned out to be his own 1943 diploma from St. John's University, a missionary college in Shanghai that had closed down after the Communist Revolution.[2] What first struck my eyes was not the black, printed text in English bestowing the B.A. degree in economics, but rather a dozen large and small red X's painted tremulously with brush and ink. As Yeye explained, when the Cultural Revolution began in 1966, he feared that Red Guards might search his home and find this "evidence of collaboration with foreign imperialists." So he made red crosses all over it to show that he had already denounced himself. In the end, the Red Guards never came, and the diploma survived to this day.

When I asked Yeye to pose for my camera with his diploma, he shifted between two poses: first as a proud new graduate holding the diploma to his right side and then as a target of "struggle sessions" in the Cultural Revolution—holding it before his belly like a heavy placard dangling from

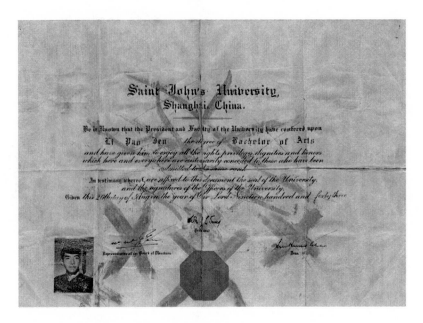

FIGURE 0.1 Yeye's St. John's diploma as a palimpsest. Photograph by the author.

his neck (fig. 0.2). Both poses looked absurd, and Yeye laughed so hard tears came out of his eyes. This was when I recognized his diploma as a palimpsest bearing markings from different eras and thus holding incongruous meanings and contradictory sentiments: pride and shame, hope and fear, humor and pathos. Behind the camera, I could see simultaneously Yeye's wrinkled face in the year 2000 alongside a snapshot of his young countenance in 1943, crossed over by red dashes from 1966, and I realized that this must be what history meant to him—the marking and remarking of the same paper, the same face, the same place.

This book is built on the concept that an old house, inhabited by various families over several decades, is a layered ruin of their private lives, woven into but not subsumed by larger historical events. Even when wars, revolutions, and market reforms effaced and replaced the public monuments and textbooks of old regimes to suit present demands,[3] the past persisted in the form of artifacts and whispers in domestic realms. Besides the diploma, my grandfather's long string of keys unlocked other patina-ridden souvenirs and stories in his cluttered alleyway home. In such intimate spaces, history did not proceed cleanly, with each new era purging the bygone era, but rather accrued into rich sediments of personal memories. Like the diploma, many outdated things, habits, and values endured, giving a sense of continuity to lives precariously stretched across historical ruptures. Certainly, the home is not a time capsule. Its porous boundary with the outside world means that it is constantly readjusting its order and appearance, adding new things and discarding old things. Like a museum of history, it presents a selective assemblage of objects and narratives, but the selection process is seldom as deliberate and systematic as a curated exhibition. Instead, each house is a palimpsest of inhabited spaces, material artifacts, and personal narratives that evolved over time.

Although any old house can be a palimpsest, Shanghai's alleyway homes have collected an especially rich repository of stories. As the city changed from a semicolonial treaty port to a socialist industrial center to a global metropolis, alleyway homes have accommodated more than half of the

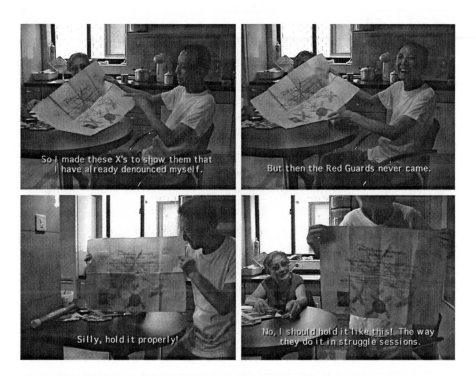

FIGURE 0.2 Yeye tells the story of his St. John's diploma to me in 2000 with Nainai in the background. Video stills by the author.

city's heterogeneous population for more than a century. They have thus become fruitful sites for understanding the accumulated long-term human impact of modern Chinese history's vicissitudes. This is not to say that any given set of alleyway residents could serve as symbols or personifications of historical forces or social categories. Too ordinary to be called heroes or villains, they were neither grandiose makers of history nor its passive victims. Instead of epic tales or national allegories, their stories were the stuff of family trivia and neighborhood gossip. Nevertheless, their irreducible individualities resist collective labels such as *the masses, the people, the proletariat, the bourgeoisie,* or *the intellectuals.* Rather than treating alleyway residents as typical or representative samples of their class, I argue that the strands of their lives are inextricably woven into a larger historical tapestry, giving it color, texture, and nuance often lost in sweeping grand narratives.

To highlight the "wisps of narratives"[4] that touched, intersected, and sometimes contradicted one another, I anchor this book to the physical spaces of two alleyway homes and their respective neighborhoods. First built in 1915 and 1927 by Japanese and British companies, respectively, both alleyway homes were located in the industrial Yangshupu 楊樹浦 District, in the eastern part of what used to be the International Settlement before 1949 (fig. 0.3). Both were originally single-family houses occupied by the managerial staff of foreign factories. The foreign owners and inhabitants of these homes left Shanghai after World War II and the Communist Revolution, and it was around then that my paternal grandparents moved into one of these alleyway homes and my maternal grandparents into the other. In the decades that followed, they raised their children and grandchildren and cultivated intimacies, mostly unsolicited, with a motley cast of neighbors. As more and more people came to occupy these houses, formerly open spaces were partitioned into narrow strips. Sheds and shanties, eaves and screens, wings and tentacles grew all over these neighborhoods, while clotheslines, antennae, and smoke fragmented the sky. In these alleyway homes, residents whispered to one another gossip worthy of novels and witnessed spectacles worthy of cinema through many windows.

Having collected within them the secret passions and disenchanted squalor of several generations, these alleyway homes had been swept off the city planner's map and into the dustbin of history by the turn of the millennium—one was demolished in 2006, and the other is marked for imminent demolition by 2014. Although scholars have associated

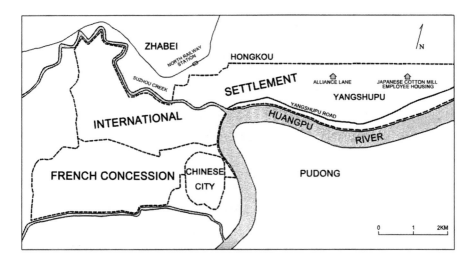

FIGURE 0.3 Location of the two alleyway compounds in this study. Map by Yang Xu.

contemporary urban demolitions with trauma, amnesia, and nostalgia,[5] this book seeks to salvage some of the *specific* memories under erasure in order to discern what exactly ordinary Shanghainese might be "homesick" *for*. It does this by tracing spatial and material transformations, by chronicling the familial and emotional lives of the alleyway homes' changing residents, and by exploring the multifaceted meanings of "home" and "private life." Since the 1990s, the commercialized glamour of Shanghai nostalgia flourished at the expense of the real lives of ordinary citizens. By contrast, this book seeks to take an unflinching look at the hardships of everyday life in the alleyway, showing how nests were built twig by twig, havens carved out inch by inch, and footholds fought for tooth and nail.

Since my parents grew up in these alleyways, where I also spent some childhood years, I bring personal experiences and inherited memories to this project and draw on interviews with dozens of former residents and neighbors, contextual historical research, and ethnographic participant observation. I wish to demonstrate that one's own home and family *can* be a valid source of scholarly inquiry, providing insights otherwise inaccessible via established methods. Such mixed sources and methods provide an entry point for understanding the multiple and inextricable dimensions of "home," from the architectural to the affective, from the literal to the figurative, from the socioeconomic to the psychological.

The Rise and Fall of Shanghai's Alleyways

> Shanghai's longtang—her vast neighborhoods inside enclosed alleys—are the backdrop of this city. Streets and buildings emerge around them in a series of dots and lines.... As day turns into night and the city lights up, these dots and lines begin to glimmer. However, underneath the glitter lies an immense blanket of darkness—these are the longtang of Shanghai.... The darkness buoys up Shanghai's handful of illuminated lines and dots, supporting them decade after decade. Today, everything looks worn out, exposing bit by bit what lies underneath.... What moves you about the longtang of Shanghai stems from the most mundane scenes: not the surging rush of clouds and rain, but something steadily accumulated over time.
>
> —WANG ANYI, *THE SONG OF EVERLASTING SORROW*[6]

The Chinese word for "home," *jia* 家, also means "family," "house," "household," as well as "lineage" or "hometown." Both as clan and as architecture, the traditional neo-Confucian *jia* is like a tree that grows over time to accommodate multiple generations, from venerated ancestors at its roots to unborn descendants, or leaves, on its branches.[7] Beyond the courtyard at its center is a family altar or shrine that doubles as a public reception hall, and to the sides are more private rooms for different family members. As Francesca Bray points out, the family home embodies in microcosm "the hierarchies of gender, generation and rank inherent to the Chinese social order, tying all its occupants into the macrocosm of the polity."[8] Before Shanghai became a foreign treaty port, such "treelike" Confucian family homes grew sparsely and freely in the Jiangnan area as families built houses on lots of land they owned in a time-honored layout. When families expanded, they built additional structures along the central axis so that homes grew with the clan in a more or less organic fashion, sprawling into forestlike townscapes.[9]

After Shanghai became a treaty port in the wake of the Opium War (1839–1842), foreigners came to settle in the city and built homes for themselves in colonial styles.[10] In the 1850s and 1860s, domestic turmoil drove tens of thousands of Chinese refugees into Shanghai's foreign settlements. In response, the British, French, and Americans terminated their former segregation policy and invested in building batches of identical houses in rationally organized rows for rent. As Hanchao Lu suggests, this investment marked the beginning of a modern capitalist real estate market: instead of taking root in familial belonging, these homes were built quickly and in bulk as transferable commodities.[11] Because Chinese compradors and contractors built and managed these properties, most housing compounds still retained the traditional courtyard layout, south-facing orientation, and local decorative motifs. Such a housing compound was called *li* 里 or *fang* 坊, its main alley *long* 弄, and its branch alleys *longtang* 弄堂, which also functioned like a court (*tang* 堂) or communal space. From the street to the alley *long*, the branch alley *longtang*, the individual houses, and the rooms inside each house, the architecture maps out a gradation from the most public to the most private spheres, with porous rather than strict boundaries. Known over time as *lilong* 里弄 or *longtang* 弄堂, most alleyway homes were named after a decorative motif called *shikumen* 石庫門, or "stone portal gate," marking the front entrance of each alleyway and the front door of each house within the alleyway.[12] Derived from traditional gateways to a village or a neighborhood, the *shikumen* gate gave off a grandiose, monumental air, even if the spaces inside each compound and inside each house became divided and subdivided, crowded and congested over the years.

With migration and fragmentation, homes, or *jia*, were no longer trees but nests, and each individual sojourner resembled not so much a leaf fixed to a branch, but a bird that flew about daily for its livelihood. The Shanghainese term for "home" is *wo*, *woli*, or *wolixiang*. *Wo* can be written as 窩 (*wo*, nest) or 屋 (*wu*, room). *Li* is 里, which can mean either "inside" or "housing compound." *Xiang* can be written as 廂 (wing of a house), 巷 (alleyway), or 嚮 (toward). The compound *wolixiang* can thus evoke for Shanghainese speakers the following meanings: "toward the inside of the nest/room" or "room nestled in a wing of a house" or "room nestled inside an alleyway." In everyday usage, it can refer to one's spouse or immediate family. Comparing *wolixiang* to the more generic concept of *jia*, we also find multivalent meanings of family, architecture, and community, yet the Shanghainese term is more intimate and inward looking, lacking the sense of the traditional family as a corporate lineage or as a microcosm of the state that reinforces Confucian hierarchies. Its spatial focus is on the individual room and a side wing, evoking a more private feminine boudoir or nest than a more public masculine ancestral hall.

In the early twentieth century, greater numbers of migratory birds—shop assistants, clerks, schoolteachers, university students, and other petty urbanites—came to Shanghai. Although all alleyway houses were designed for one family per unit, as housing demand and prices grew, many primary tenants remodeled their houses and sublet rooms to subtenants. From the 1920s to the 1940s, second landlords—primary tenants who sublet rooms—became the major players in leasing dwellings in the city. Indeed, making a profit out of homes was quite natural given that many alleyway houses were businesses—shops, restaurants, even factories—sites of labor and commerce as well as of living. Since neither landlords nor tenants could afford to pick their neighbors on the basis of local origin or profession, the diversity of alleyway residents helped to foster the city's unique cosmopolitan culture.[13]

Among those who lived in Shanghai alleyways were writers and film-makers who made those alleyways a site of their literary and cinematic imaginations. In *Shanghai Modern*, Leo Ou-fan Lee writes of Republican-era intellectuals who lived in the *tingzijian* 亭子間, "pavilion room," a small room just above the kitchen and facing the back alley, situated between the first and second stories. While fashioning a "half-inflated and half-parodied self-image of their bohemian existence" in this special "ivory tower," they also documented the lively interactions of other tenants in the Shanghai alleyways in fiction, essays, plays, and films.[14] Alexander Des Forges argues that Shanghai alleyways can be understood as a fundamentally theatrical "arena in which windows look out onto other windows, barriers between one rooftop laundry space and the next are insignificant or non-existent, and the sounds and smells of the city waft easily in even through closed shutters." Some classic films set in the city in the 1930s and 1940s, such as Yuan Muzhi's 袁牧之 *Street Angel* (*Malu tianshi* 馬路天使, 1937) and Zheng Junli's 鄭君里 *Crows and Sparrows* (*Wuya yu maque* 烏鴉與麻雀, 1948) even construct their plots around alleyway spaces, featuring key motifs such as eavesdropping and spying, tenant–landlord relations, and trysts between young lovers with windows facing each other.[15]

Literary, theatrical, and cinematic portraits of Shanghai alleyways, however, focus on the 1930s and 1940s, an era in the city's history that has also received much scholarly attention and nostalgic evocation since the 1990s.[16] By contrast, the decades within the living memories of most Shanghai alleyway residents—the 1950s to the 1980s—find little mention in either academic or popular literature.[17] Yet it was in this period that most Shanghainese turned from the city's sojourners into its natives, and the alleyways turned from a temporary abode to the birthplaces and inherited homes of new generations. Such transformation was due to the fact that the Communists closed down the erratic real estate market, ended immigration into the city, and fixed residents in their places with the household registration system. The new government, instead of delivering the housing utopia it promised, crammed a small fraction of selected workers who used to live in shantytowns into alleyway houses and Western villas.[18] This change ironically furthered rather than destroyed the diversity that defined the alleyway milieu, distinguishing it from both work-unit-based socialist housing compounds and recent commodity housing that segregated residents by class and income.

Thus, an unwritten history unfolded in the socialist period under Shanghai's eaves. Houses formerly built by foreign entrepreneurs came to accommodate their Chinese employees, who later shared the same spaces with former concubines or servants of the old Shanghai bourgeoisie as well as with factory workers from shantytowns. In this city of immigrants, most of Shanghai's residents had deep roots and extensive ties to hometowns elsewhere, mostly in the countryside. Yet the revolution's successive campaigns severed many roots and branches of those extended families. Threads of kinship with former landlords, capitalists, or Nationalist officers became disavowed family secrets. Meanwhile, remnants of commercial and religious activities from the Republican era were exiled from public spaces into the more private spaces of alleyway homes. The increasingly monolithic public culture, the unfree press, and a need for "relentless public performance" all contributed to a desire to "exchange information, tales, rumor, and gossip" in more private conversations.[19] Even though state surveillance also extended into these neighborhoods, alleyway homes still served as a haven for people, things, discourses, habits, and beliefs without proper places in the new regime.

This haven came under the greatest siege in the Cultural Revolution, when home searches were common, when inhabitants themselves destroyed treasured yet incriminating artifacts, and when alleyways became a stage for humiliating denunciations and punishments. Alleyway youths of different class backgrounds, classmates in the same elementary and middle schools, made revolution against one another's parents or rebelled against their own, fell in and out of love, and became scattered all over the country as sent-down youths. The close quarters with multiple families cultivated a tyranny of intimacy and an intimacy of tyranny, for neighbors knew one another's personal histories and could readily use such private knowledge for denunciation to the authorities. In this era of unprecedented state interference into the private sphere, previously repressed private interests and desires manifested themselves in public and theatrical ways. All the same, the entangled personal relationships of inhabitants under the same roofs forged a pragmatic tolerance and a separate peace.

Since Shanghai's economic renaissance in the 1990s, demolition has become the common destiny of most alleyways.[20] Following decades of stagnation and isolation, the municipal government began leasing land to transnational developers, tearing down existing neighborhoods, and relocating old residents to the suburbs to make way for expensive residential and commercial skyscrapers. Losing their way in the new labyrinth of shopping complexes and expressways, many Chinese urbanites succumbed to nostalgia as a way to "absorb a socioeconomic shock."[21] Yet if personal nostalgic sentiments span and blend the Republican, the Maoist, and the post-Mao eras, commodified manifestations of nostalgia heavily gravitate toward only one historical and social layer of the city's palimpsestuous history, namely the 1930s—what Xudong Zhang calls the "classic moment of Chinese bourgeois modernity."[22]

The few alleyway houses being preserved and restored as historic monuments tend to be the former residences of celebrities and "Red heritage sites" of pre-1949 underground revolutionary activities. Most prominently, the alleyway house where the Chinese Communist Party was first founded in 1921 has turned into a memorial museum, but the surrounding neighborhood was razed and rebuilt as Xintiandi 新天地, New Heaven and Earth, a chic leisure and shopping area that recycled the bricks and stones from the old architectural rubble into a nostalgic facade. Xintiandi also hosts the city's only museum devoted to everyday life in alleyway homes. Furnished with impersonal memorabilia that suggest a single-family, upper-middle-class household from the 1930s and 1940s, this museum contains no lingering traces of the *actual* residents who used to live in this neighborhood, mostly poor urbanites and workers. Hence, the officially promoted revolutionary legacy has joined forces with global capital to banish the city's subterranean populations into the suburbs and the socialist past into oblivion.[23]

The disappearance of Shanghai alleyways from the urban landscape brings an end to a rich and unique history of private life written by diverse residents across a century of radical change. Ordinary people do not write their autobiographies in books so much as they inscribe family and personal histories onto a place they call home, and instead of the written word they use images, artifacts, and bodies as their medium. Written and rewritten over time, the resulting texts are often multilayered, obscure, perhaps even secret, for unless private homes are turned into impersonal museum exhibitions, they are accessible and meaningful often only to those who have lived in or near them. These "home texts" or "archaeological sites" have remained as illegible and insignificant to historians as they are to city planners eager to dispose of them. Although it is impossible to halt this amnesiac modernization process, this book shows that even a small cross-section of a Shanghai alleyway, viewed in the twilight of its demise, can give us a kaleidoscopic glimpse into the mentalities and lived experiences of the Shanghainese over the past seven or eight decades.

Excavate Where I Stand

He who seeks to approach his own buried past must conduct himself like a man digging. This confers the tone and bearing of genuine reminiscences. He must not be afraid to return again and again to the same matter; to scatter it as one scatters earth, to turn it over as one turns over soil. For the matter itself is only a deposit, a stratum, which yields only to the most meticulous examination what constitutes the real treasure hidden within the earth: the images, severed from all earlier associations, that stand—like precious fragments or torsos in a collector's gallery—in the prosaic rooms of our later understanding.
—WALTER BENJAMIN, "A BERLIN CHRONICLE"[24]

Given the rich and complex evolution of Shanghai homes, what are some possible methodologies for studying them? Home—as well as its Chinese counterpart *jia* or the Shanghainese term *wolixiang*—is a resonant concept connoting at once a physical place and a psychological haven, an ideal object of universal longing and a specific site of personal memories. Architectural scholars discuss Chinese homes as vernacular architecture; historians study them as part of social histories or women's histories; anthropologists and sociologists focus on changing patterns of family and kinship; and literary scholars study representations of homes in fiction and film.[25] Borrowing from these methods, I adopt an interdisciplinary approach to address the multiple yet inextricably intertwined dimensions of Shanghai homes. I call this approach "excavate where I stand."

Specifically, "excavate where I stand" can be defined with the key words *palimpsest*, *microhistory*, and *familial ethnography*. In contrast to a blueprint or prototype, the palimpsest metaphor treats Shanghai homes as idiosyncratic cultural texts, drawing on literary and visual analysis as well as accounting for their material and spatial, ideological and bodily dimensions. Microhistory is concerned with temporal change and cross-examination of multiple sources, oral and written, specific and contextual. Familial ethnography treats one's own extended family connections as a field site and employs anthropological methods of interviews, participant observation, and thick descriptions.

Homes may begin as blueprints, but as the architects and contractors leave and residents enter, homes turn into theaters for the lives of their inhabitants. "To live is to leave traces," Walter Benjamin famously said,[26] and the trope of the palimpsest engages with those messy traces rather than erasing them to reveal an ideal prototype. In studying traditional Chinese houses, architectural scholars do not usually examine the ephemeral material structures of homes and their individual residents but rather distill more general and enduring architectural forms, shared over generations and across localities.[27] In this sense, a house is "a cultural template; living in it inculcates fundamental knowledge and skills specific to that culture."[28] Yet in modern times Chinese homes, especially in Shanghai, underwent radical transformations and were rarely inhabited as they had originally been intended. Their diverse residents also became the producers of these spaces. Concerned with variation and change, a palimpsest approach engages as much with the symbolic order as with the shambolic disorder of Shanghai homes.

Shanghai alleyways are also palimpsests of voices and noises, past and present. Their diverse inhabitants spoke in multiple tongues, gestured toward various genres, fashioned different personas, and contained recurring themes that can be analyzed with literary techniques. In conversations or contestation, these voices may operate in harmony, in dissonance, or in counterpoint. Like the Chinese rural women interviewed by historian Gail Hershatter, they "talk back to or talk past big state projects."[29] Filled with immigrants from elsewhere, Shanghai's alleyways spoke a Babel of languages: the standard Mandarin of radio announcers;

the "pidgin Mandarin" or accented officialese of neighborhood committee cadres; the Shanghainese vernacular punctuated by different accents; the slang of alleyway youths; and native dialects spoken only within families. Depending on context and personal background, residents of the same alleyways shifted between linguistic registers, mixing vocabularies and genres.[30] Glib or inchoate, comic or poignant, the incongruous mixture of official jargon, urban vernacular, local dialects, and personal accents created a unique palimpsest of sounds, languages, and narratives.

Shanghai homes can also be studied as an accumulating patchwork of moving images. A major inspiration for this book was Hou Hsiao-hsien's 1989 film 侯孝賢 City of Sadness (Beiqing chengshi 悲情城市), about a Taiwanese family's experiences of transition from Japanese colonial rule to the Nationalist regime in the late 1940s.[31] Composed largely of long shots and long takes with a stationary camera, the film proceeds as if someone is flipping through an album of still photographs, reminiscently, and the remembered moment "comes to life." Throughout the three-hour film, "a residue of action and emotion builds" with the repetition of the same views,[32] often delimited by a door or a window frame. It is as if the camera were placed on a piece of furniture, bearing silent and disinterested witness to births, deaths, wars, and peace that passed through its field of vision and hearing.

Considering home in such cinematic terms, I went about my research as if preparing for a film, seeking to reconstruct momentous or plausibly typical domestic "scenes." I asked my interviewees carefully about the "mise-en-scène" of their homes: the setting, the lighting, the choice of "costumes," the placement of the "props," and the "acting" of inhabitants and guests. Beyond sights and sounds, I also searched their and my own memories for the touch, smell, and taste of these domestic spaces. Having used a video camera in fieldwork and interviews, I treated the material I had collected as "footage" to be selected and edited according to the principles of continuity and montage, opting for seamlessness at times and juxtaposition at others. In chapter 2, for example, the Cultural Revolution in the alleyway is told through a montage of different perspectives to complicate both top-down official narratives and popular accounts of victimization.[33] Rather than studying the impact of the revolution on a single individual or family, I show how the same political upheavals had altogether different meanings for different individuals living in close quarters.

This palimpsest approach finds a close parallel in the more established method of *microhistory*. Defined by its small scale and local perspective, microhistory refers to a style of historical writing since the 1970s that intensively investigates a small area and/or a small number of people, especially the details and textures of their lived experiences.[34] Unlike biographies or local gazetteers, microhistory focuses less on the unique importance of an individual life or community than on an historical era and its mentalities that a single person or locality could refract.[35] Since people live their lives in several contexts simultaneously, the microhistorical approach can "preserve this diversity of contexts within the frame of a relatively limited investigation," thus reconstructing "the fabric of society."[36] Microhistorians wish to "see the world in a grain of sand," but a common critique of it is that it "sees only the tree, but not the forest." Yet when the very aim of microhistory is to disturb the homogeneous texture of aggregated statistics, it is not part of its method to substitute a fragment for the whole picture or to multiply one life by a million.[37] Although qualitative findings cannot be used to prove or disprove quantitative results, studying one village or one neighborhood allows us to consider "how the grand narratives of history have interacted with local experience."[38] A microhistory is not the last nail on the coffin of its subject matter, but rather an invitation to examine similarly obscured lives and to open up the Pandora's box of a past era.

The sources of most microhistories are not living informants, but rather archival records created by a judge or detective in the distant past. Yet rather than investigating the subject from a lofty distance, I take on the role of a root-seeking child whose annual homecomings over summer vacations catalyzed a process of defamiliarization and refamiliarization. I became privy to the homes and stories of my interviewees only by virtue of being *personally* implicated in these lives, families, and communities—relationships that predated not only this project, but also my birth. This subject position takes into account how experiences and memories are transmitted from generation to generation, while my repeated inquiries into their pasts also made my elders think more reflectively about their lives.

Although inhabiting these alleyway homes as a child, I was certainly no historian or anthropologist. After moving to the United States, however, I interviewed my extended family and searched my own memories for many school projects, from making family trees to writing creative nonfiction. Answering my inquiries, my extended family (re)collected their old documents and photographs, wrote "memoirs," and took me along to revisit their old neighbors. In university, I began to think of old neighborhoods as field sites, my family members as informants, and their papers and albums as an archive. Anthropology courses taught me methods such as participant observation and thick description as well as concepts such as "native anthropologist" and "autoethnography." History courses taught me to assess the reliability of primary sources and to glean them for evidence. Literature and film classes taught me to pay attention to language, form, genres, myths, and ideologies.

In addition to my one-on-one conversations with close family and friends, these "chief informants" took me to visit relatives or neighbors distant from me but close to them. Such informal gatherings naturally elicited reminiscences of their own pasts and gossip about others they knew in common. First, I tried to map persons onto spaces: who lived where and when, where they came from, what their everyday lives were like, and why they moved away. Second, I sought to inventory material objects (once) kept inside these homes: what was displayed and stored away, how things were ordered, and what they saw, heard, smelled, touched, and tasted on a daily basis. I asked to see photo albums, account books, and other documents, certificates and souvenirs, which often unraveled narratives. My questions also sought to juxtapose historical events and personal plights: What did the Sino-Japanese War, Communist Liberation, the Cultural Revolution, and market reform *mean* for them and their families? How did these historical milestones match up to significant personal happenings, such as marriages, births, and deaths?

Historians skeptical of human memory are bound to ask: "How reliable are these oral narratives?" The possibility to *cross-examine* living informants, as Orlando Figes points out in his study of private life in Stalin's Russia, is one benefit of oral history and repeated fieldwork within a familiar milieu: "Like all memory, the testimony given in an interview is unreliable, but, unlike a book, it can be . . . tested against other evidence to disentangle true memories from received or imagined ones."[39] As Yunxiang Yan notes in his study of the Chinese family under socialism, through repeated fieldwork "the same informant who lies in the first interview may reveal his or her actual experience in the third or the seventh interview."[40] Such repeated inquiries may well bear troubling echoes of the interrogations of the Maoist decades, but when Yeye referred to his written confessions to the authorities as a memory aid to answer my questions, he was also clearly reclaiming his life story from the oppressive circumstances that produced those confessions. Oral narratives, as Gail Hershatter points out, "are as contaminated as any other retrievable fragment of the past. It requires cultivating an interest in and respect for that contamination."[41] Apart from checking oral narratives against the written record and against each other, I also ask what the inconsistencies, anachronisms, and blatant errors in their narratives *can* tell us—that is, how their narrators saw the world and experienced history.[42]

In making homes a site of inquiry, this book writes history not as the succession of public events, but rather as the sedimentation of private experiences. Its focus on families and neighbors reveals the crisscrossing of divergent subjectivities in everyday life often obscured by studies of a given social category. Examining inhabited spaces, material artifacts, and whispered narratives that stretched across generations, we begin to get a sense of how ordinary families cope pragmatically and affectively with compressed, radical historical change. In listening to and putting together the alleyway residents' stories, I found myself most drawn to their emotional moments of private passion, anger, fear, hope, disappointment, and laughter. I wished to uncover what Jonathan Spence calls the "realms of loneliness, sensuality, and dreams" that might help the historian come a bit closer to, say, "what might have been in the mind of Woman Wang as she slept before death."[43] Even while positioning their lives in larger historical contexts, I listened for elements of dissonance, irony, pathos, and humor. I looked for what Hershatter calls "a good-enough story," which "surprises and engenders thought" about "how and where the history we tell . . . is not good enough."[44] Thus, I sought to build a palimpsest of stories that brushed against the grain of well-trodden grand narratives.

This book reproduces many narrative strands in my informants' first-person voices. Although based on transcriptions of recorded interviews and on casual follow-up conversations, these strands are not literal translations of verbatim quotations. The details of many tales came from not only a single telling, but also multiple everyday interactions, such as family dinners and quarrels, neighborhood gossip and offhand remarks, lighthearted jokes and nagging grudges. Even when working with transcripts, I edited fragmented comments into more coherent narratives to enhance readability. Wherever possible, I provide reflexive comments on the construction of these narratives: the context of the conversation, the relationship between teller and audience, and the prior knowledge I brought to these encounters. I do not wish to efface myself as a mediator of their stories—a human and empathetic mediator not necessarily less faithful than a mechanical recorder.

Reconfiguring the Private Realm

Upon returning from a visit to Moscow in 1927, Walter Benjamin wrote: "Bolshevism has abolished private life."[45] The statement may be even truer of Maoism, which, as Peter Zarrow puts it, "was dedicated to destroying the private realm."[46] Besides the collectivization of land and private enterprise, the power and surveillance of the party state extended into every village and neighborhood. The "big family" of the work unit, school, and communes took precedence over one's own kin as private relationships were politicized and "class-ified" under slogans such as "all public, no private" (*da gong wu si* 大公無私) or "struggle ruthlessly against the flash of the private self" (*hen dou sizi yi shannian* 狠斗私字一闪念). Coming under siege was not only private property, but also private families and friendships, private space and time, and the very "bourgeois" idea of privacy. Many individuals had to surrender their private *histories* to public administration and, later in some cases, to public exhibition.

Yet did communism really abolish private life? And what were some of the consequences of trying? Yunxiang Yan's *Private Life Under Socialism*, based on ethnography in a northeastern Chinese village, shows that the Communist dismantling of the traditional kinship system in rural China paradoxically led to the rise of the more private nuclear family. Moreover, later market reforms advanced the rise of the "uncivil individual" defined by ego-centered consumerism.[47] Yet has the privatization of businesses and the enhanced privacy of homes since the 1990s brought about a more enriched private life? As Shanghai residents move from crowded alleyways into more "private" high risers, why have they become more alienated than ever from their families and friends? In an age of material plenitude, why doesn't food taste as delicious, clothing seem as precious, and home feel as intimate, however spacious?

To answer these questions, I should explain more precisely what I mean here by "private life." Private/public distinctions are defined primarily by two criteria: visibility, or what is hidden or withdrawn versus what is open, revealed, and accessible; and collectivity, or what is individual versus what is collective—a distinction applicable to state administration versus market economy as well as to the social realm versus the domestic realm.[48] Major studies of "private life" take the family and the household as the unit of analysis, where the private is defined as a "zone of immunity for individuals, a realm that is, ideally, not open to the scrutiny of the community and not subject to the intrusion of public authority."[49] These studies focus on the emotional and moral world of the family and its constituent members as well as on the evolution of the domestic sphere and standards of "privacy," or the right to withhold access or draw boundaries around the "inner" world of the home.

Scholars have pointed out that the distinctions between public and private spheres in the West do not map exactly onto Chinese history and society.[50] Yet just as public and private spheres have not remained fixed dichotomies but rather have evolved over time in the West, it is useful to historicize such distinctions in China and examine how these spheres have been reconfigured over time. Contributors to the edited volume *Chinese Concepts of Privacy* point out that Chinese debates on the political and ethical implications of the separate spheres and interests of *si* 私 (private, personal, self, selfish) and *gong* 公 (public, open, communal, impartial) go back to the Warring States period, yet such debates as well as modern scholarship focus much more on the public end of the spectrum.[51] In particular, historians interested in the notion of a "Chinese public sphere" explore the tripartite conception of *guan* (official), *gong* (public), and *si* (private) in late imperial and Republican era China, focusing on the issues of both political participation and collective proprietorship.[52]

As a counterpart to *gong* and *guan*, the Chinese word *si* may refer to "private ownership, private interests or selfishness, private as distinct from public service, private as in underhand or secretive conduct, and privacy as a state of seclusion to which access is controlled by the subject."[53] Beginning with the late imperial period, the word *si* had largely pejorative associations with profit (*li* 利) and immoral desires (*yu* 慾), but late Qing moral discourse still considered the private realm legitimate and necessary as a site to cultivate personal and civic virtues.[54] Another Chinese word for "private" has been *nei* 内 (inner, as opposed to *wai* 外, outer). Dorothy Ko argues that the confinement of women to the "inner chambers" was not merely oppressive but might have provided women with dignity and freedom, security and privacy.[55] Analyzing the architecture of traditional Chinese homes and the roles played by women, Francesca Bray shows a moral and political continuity rather than a clear-cut split between home, community, and state in late imperial China.[56]

Under Mao, however, the valorization of the public and the denigration of the private became an intense obsession. Whereas neo-Confucians considered the family to be a state in microcosm, Communists set up a stark dichotomy between the state and the family so that individuals increasingly had to renounce the private family to become a legitimate member of society.[57] As Harriet Evans points out, Chinese Communist discourse reworked the language of "inner" and "outer" spheres whereby women's "liberation" derived from "leaving the home" and engaging in "productive labor." The domestic and private domains took on pejorative connotations in an "ideological project to reorient individual loyalties and aspirations away from the family and toward the party state, in the form of the workplace and collective."[58] As individuals "drew lines of demarcation" from stigmatized family and friends, they were also mobilized into collective units by age and profession. This led to the institutional and psychological atomization of individuals into "selfless bolts" at the disposal of the state. By the Socialist Education Campaign in the mid-1960s, individuals had to struggle not only against their families, but also against their own private thoughts and feelings. And yet, as I argue, private realms remained as imperishable as shadows under the meridian sun.

Although the term *privacy* can simply mean "the condition or sense of being private," this concept cannot quite subsume the notion of *private life* at the core of this book. Privacy refers more to the *boundary* than to the *content* of private life, and it seems natural that the elite have always enjoyed *more* privacy because they can afford to draw a clearer line between the exteriority of the community and the interiority of the home. Those with more square meters to their name can distribute rooms among different family members and between different family activities. They can live farther away from their neighbors without having to share everyday facilities. By contrast, the urban poor must accommodate multiple persons and multiple purposes in the same rooms. Cooking, dressing, and even going to the toilet may be observable affairs, and domestic activities often extend into semipublic spaces such as communal kitchens and alleyways.[59] Insofar as "the private houses of elite and well-to-do families all [draw] a clear line between the exteriority of the community and the interiority of the home,"[60] private space seems to be a class privilege and a cultural luxury.

Yet private life—a feeling of home, a sense of intimacy, and a zone of immunity from community scrutiny and public intrusion—can take forms other than the insulated space of a room or a house. Svetlana Boym has shown how the private in Soviet Russia was reconstituted "in the minor aesthetic pursuits of communal-apartment dwellers and their personal collection of souvenirs, by means of poetic escapes, obsessive scribbling, and a few unofficial guitar songs shared with friends in the crowded kitchen."[61] If we define the private not by degrees of separation but rather by personal meanings invested into texts, objects, and spaces, then even the most dispossessed vagabond is not without a private life, which can hide inside a treasured object in his pocket or take the form of dreams and memories.[62]

In contrast to *privacy*, *private life* is less measurable in terms of "objective" criteria and cannot be easily correlated to the amount of property one owns. As Hannah Arendt points out in *The Human Condition*, the word *private* has its etymological origins in the Latin word for "deprived" and is closely related to *privative* and *privation*,[63] suggesting that even poverty and deprivation can paradoxically enhance its content. An analogous idea in Chinese might be Ouyang Xiu's 歐陽修 (1007–1072) famous phrase *qiong'er hou gong* 窮而後工, or that poverty and adversity give rise to great writing.[64] Vice versa, the ownership of property and the increase of wealth do not necessarily enrich our private life as it may increase our privacy. Finally, the phrase *private life* has a historical and accumulative connotation that the word *privacy* does not.

While wishing to retain the connotations of privacy, domesticity, and intimacy, this book redefines private life as the domain of personal experience—the *personal* meanings invested into texts, artifacts, spaces, and human relationships. The private is what one might consider one's own, although legal private ownership is not the precondition of making a place a site of familiarity or personal memory. A brand-new villa in which no one has ever lived, even if privately owned and allowing for maximum privacy, does not constitute a palimpsest of private life. Moreover, a private artifact is to be distinguished from but may originate in mass-produced commodities. As such, the fast consumption of fashionable clothing or other personal items does not endow that commodity with personal meaning. By contrast, basins, cups, or pillowcases inscribed with slogans from the Mao era may initially serve as evidence for the intrusion of political propaganda into people's private spheres, but their materially impoverished users inscribe their personal histories onto such items through years of diligent use and care. Similarly, all units in an alleyway may have been identical when they were first built as real estate investment, but generations of residents remodeled their exterior and interior to accommodate their idiosyncratic needs and desires. The better part of such personal histories is swept away with the relocation into new residential high risers. In this sense, Arendt suggested, not only do communist revolutions invade the private realm; an accelerated process of production and consumption in a late-capitalist society could lead with even greater certainty to a "withering away" of the private realm.[65]

Rather than valorizing a Western or bourgeois idea of privacy, this book's understanding of private life underscores the plurality of personal histories woven into domestic spaces, artifacts, and narratives. This book seeks to tease out complex familial dynamics and diverse human responses to historical forces—often camouflaged under mass performances of class identities and obscured by the abstract categories of official historiographies. It also shows that private life grows most resiliently in a state of privation. Although the Maoist regime sought to obliterate the private realm, individual interests and repressed desires found outlet in what is supposedly the public realm. That is, by enforcing collectivity and demanding transparency from everyone, socialism also reinforced obsession with individual possessions, escalated the stakes and theatricality of personal conflicts, and eroded civility in the public sphere. The interpenetration of the public and private spheres contributed to corruption and an intimacy of tyranny. Paradoxically, visceral memories of deprivation forged the most intimate bonds between family members, neighbors, classmates, and colleagues. The depth of such human relationships can make kinship and friendship in later times seem pale and impersonal by comparison. This study thus treats Shanghai alleyway homes as a last refuge for heterogeneous private lives submerged in the mass politics of the Mao era and the mass economics of the post-Mao era.

The Chapters

This book investigates three dimensions of private life—private territories, private artifacts, and private narratives of history. Chapter 1, "Foothold," treats the two homes primarily as *housing* to accommodate families and individuals in a crowded city. It constructs a chronology of inhabitants and accounts for every territorial or spatial change from the 1930s to the 1990s, divided into three historical layers that correspond roughly to the Republican era, the socialist era, and the reform era. Built with colonial capital in an industrialized area of the International Settlement, one alleyway compound served as Japanese company housing and the other accommodated Chinese small factory owners and the "Number Ones" (foremen) of larger factories along with their multigenerational and polygamous families. When their foreign owners were repatriated, both housing compounds became "public housing" under communism, and with every political campaign more workers moved into such "bourgeois" neighborhoods. These alleyways thus became contact zones between Shanghai's foreign and Chinese spheres as well as between the city's old and new ruling classes. As overcrowding became exacerbated in the socialist and early reform eras, people sometimes turned on their neighbors, parents, and siblings to secure more dwelling space for themselves, albeit often in the name of the collective. Yet private relationships were a source of compassion as well as of corruption, and one could secure a private foothold in Shanghai only through various forms of collective complicities.

Shifting focus away from *housing* as physical territories with tangible boundaries, chapter 2, "Haven," considers homes to be an assemblage of familiar artifacts, a psychological haven, and a refuge from the outside world. It investigates the changing meanings and values of the homes' material contents—as everyday necessities or aesthetic expressions, status symbols or potential liabilities. After unraveling the palimpsest histories of a few domestic objects—a grain bed, a writing desk, a sewing machine, a handful of photographs, and a radio—this chapter focuses on the Cultural Revolution in the alleyway, especially the attack on the "four olds" and the impact of the home searches. I show that just as the scarcity of goods made material life ever more important, the susceptibility to public exposure only intensified the significance of the private realm, however repressed or camouflaged. Although family members vandalized their most cherished belongings, the very dispossession of an artifact was enough to transform it into a poignant metonymy for a lost private world. After the Cultural Revolution, as materialistic consumption returned with a vengeance, a younger generation of "petty urbanites" such as my aunts and uncles reinvented petty bourgeois privacy in Shanghai homes through interior decoration. This chapter concludes with an elegy for disappearing artifacts and practices from Shanghai homes, worldly objects that both bear witness to an era of privation and yet helped make home home.

Chapter 3, "Gossip," focuses on private narratives of the past in the form of neighborhood gossip and family lore, an undercurrent of private interests, voices, and beliefs beneath the facade of public slogans and collective rituals. Whereas the home is a foothold defined by square meters in the first chapter, a haven defined by the boundaries of privacy in the second chapter, here it is a site of memory and storytelling, a site haunted by ghosts. The first section traces a cultural genealogy of gossip in Shanghai as an everyday social practice, a recurring literary trope, and a form of counterhistory. The second section provides a tour of my own childhood alleyway home and shows in concrete terms how an alleyway's voyeuristic and exhibitionist theater of everyday life gives rise to gossip. The next section reconstructs the lives and legends of a few marginal women who had come to the alleyway through marriage or concubinage, who lost their husbands to the revolution, and who took over despised and underpaid work such as knitting, laundry, and night-soil collection. Not fitting into the official discursive frame of the "bitter past and sweet present," they could only "speak bitterness" in private conversations with their children and neighbors, who relayed the stories to me. This chapter concludes with the "whispers" of Aunt Duckweed, who recounts the domestic drama of her family in a single-room home from the 1950s to the 1980s. In all these cases, my concern is less with factuality as with subjectivity and narratology, with the ways these lives are *told* and *listened to*, the ways such gossip served as a different and more powerful kind of education than schools, mass media, and other ideological training grounds.

The last chapter, "Demolition," reconstructs the decay, death, and afterlife of the two houses in this study and the neighborhoods to which they belonged. Beginning in the 1990s, Shanghai's cityscape underwent great transformations, and its real estate market saw a renaissance that "revolutionized" the living environments of most of its citizens. Such urban renewal, however, meant laying to ruin and eventually erasing old neighborhoods and communities from the city map, a process fraught with corruption, conflict, and inequality and accompanied by greed, outrage, and violence from multiple parties. Focusing on the neighborhood where I spent years of childhood, this chapter chronicles the complex micropolitics of demolition: both the strategies of the relocation teams and tactics of the so-called nail households who refused to budge and were sometimes forcefully evicted. As these palimpsests of private life are torn apart and swept away, many memories flash up for just a moment before they are condemned to eternal oblivion. Finally, having resurrected this book from the attic after the passing of my paternal grandparents, I devote the coda to the final days of their lives and to the things they had kept over the decades in their old house.

1

FOOTHOLD

IN THE HUMAN SEA OF SHANGHAI, a home is above all a foothold in the city, a sliver of territory one might claim for oneself and one's family. Over the past century, the ownership of such territories did not remain static but rather underwent many historical vicissitudes. Mapping out the spaces of two houses and their associated alleyways, this chapter accounts for the changes in their inhabitants, boundaries, and usage from the Republican era through the Maoist and reform eras. Originally commissioned and owned by foreign investors, these homes had hybrid architectural styles that testify to Shanghai's unique history of colonial capitalism, industrialization, and cosmopolitanism. As their foreign owners and inhabitants were repatriated with the end of World War II and the Communist Revolution, these housing compounds came under state possession and became collective property subject to redistribution through successive political campaigns. The former bourgeoisie and the rising class of proletariats became neighbors who observed the tumbling of each other's destinies and a constant reshuffling of the social and political order.

Instead of being passive recipients of state welfare or tyranny, my grandparents and their neighbors enthusiastically flocked to the support of the new socialist regime in 1949, celebrating its success, participating in its construction, and joining its mass movements and surveillance systems. Their private interests found public manifestations, for they either really identified their personal welfare with that of the collective or made clever uses of state policies or political campaigns for their own ends. Sometimes the former activists' enthusiasm backfired, and they would become the targets rather than the makers of revolution, which every now and then swept various waves of Shanghai residents off their feet into the hinterlands.

Most of those banished from Shanghai in the Cultural Revolution returned to the city in the early reform era, whereas other alleyway children who stayed in Shanghai grew into adults, formed families of their own, and competed with their parents and siblings for housing. From the late 1970s through the late 1980s, even once respectable alleyways decayed into slums with all their crooked and precarious illegal structures, which the residents themselves built with materials and labor scraped together from every relation. They also partitioned the interiors of existing structures into many dark corners to accommodate multiple generations—a volatile, reluctant coexistence that lacerated familial bonds and quickened the demise of alleyway homes.

Foundations and Original Residents, 1910s–1940s

Built in 1915 and 1927, respectively, the two alleyway homes in this study hold memories older than most of their living former residents. Despite external patching and internal remodeling over the past century, their architectural forms remained artifacts and relics of the early Republican era. Both lay in Shanghai's northeast industrial zone known as Yangshupu (see fig. o.3), originally a sandy shore until its industrialization and urbanization in the early twentieth century. Running parallel with the Huangpu River north of Suzhou Creek, Yangshupu Road, or Poplar Tree Shore Road, had China's first tap-water factory and biggest electrical power plant by the 1880s, illuminating half of the city. After Japan's triumph in the First Sino-Japanese War (1894–1895) gave foreign industrialists the legal rights to manufacture in Shanghai, the early twentieth century saw the flourishing of factories in this district, especially in the tobacco and textile industries. Despite disruptions by the Second Sino-Japanese War (1937–1945), big mills grew with small alleyway workshops, attracting hundreds of thousands of migrants from the countryside,[1] among them my maternal grandparents and many of their later neighbors.

Whereas many migrant workers built transient bungalow-type, single-story houses and straw shacks for themselves,[2] real estate investors built large-scale alleyway compounds for factory management or for rent to an emerging "middle class" of small workshop owners and foremen (or forewomen), often called Number Ones. Still, the residents of Yangshupu remained acutely aware of their marginal relation to the metropolitan center. As Grandma Apricot, who lived in one of these alleyways from 1938 to 2005, explained to me:

> In my childhood, the Yangshupu area was still something of a frontier, with cotton fields and rice paddies alongside factory smokestacks, loading docks, and hutments built up by workers from the countryside. Our neighborhood thus belonged to what Shanghainese called the "lower corner" [*xiazhijiao* 下之角]. By contrast, the "upper corner" [*shangzhijiao* 上之角] in the city center was much more prosperous and chic, with lots of department stores and big bosses living in garden villas. When we wanted to go shopping in the "upper corner," we would say: "We are going to Shanghai"—we did not consider where we lived Shanghai.[3]

No. 111, Alliance Lane, 1927–1950

In 1927, a British real estate company, Metropolitan Ltd. (Hengye 恆業 in Chinese), invested in the construction of a large *shikumen* housing compound on Ward Road and named it Alliance Lane (Youbang Li 友邦里).[4] This alleyway consisted of 141 units of single-bay houses (3.5-by-15 square meters) mapped densely onto a territory of about 12,700 square meters, with 15,500 square meters of building area (fig. 1.1).[5] If we think of the compound's internal structure as a tree that grew southward, the main entrance was at the "root," through which one walked into the "trunk" of the main alleyway, with "branches" of small alleys on both sides, all dead ends except for two leading to a side street and two others connecting to neighboring alleyway compounds. The northern and eastern rows of houses had shops facing the street on their ground floors, following the dual structure of "outside shops and inside neighborhoods" (*waipuneili* 外鋪內里).[6] The overall layout of the compound thus interwove

Ward Road / Changyang Road

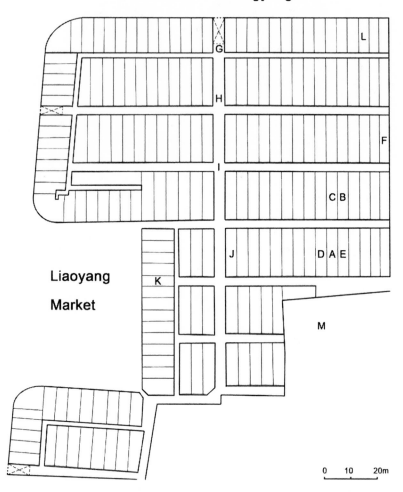

FIGURE 1.1 Layout of Alliance Lane. A: No. 111, the main house in this study (see fig. 1.5). B: No. 83, where Apricot lived after 1949. C: No. 81 (see Mother Mao's story in "Several Lifetimes to a Life" in chapter 3). The ground floor of the row of houses that include B and C were converted into a kindergarten in 1958. D: No. 109 (see Mother Yang's story in "Several Lifetimes to a Life" in chapter 3). E: No. 113 (see "Home Searches" in chapter 2). F: No. 61, which once hosted a Communist radio station. G: Alleyway entrance (see fig. 1.2). H: Position for the stage of struggle sessions during the Cultural Revolution. I: The vantage point from which one might view figs. 1.3 and 1.4. J: No. 91, site of the later neighborhood committee. K: An alleyway school. L: A photographer's studio (see fig.1.2). M: A neighboring alleyway. Sketch by Yang Xu.

FIGURE 1.2 View of the main entrance of Alliance Lane from the street, with a photographer's studio and a "tiger stove" that sold hot water and tea on the left, a paper and tobacco shop, and a barber shop on the right. At the alleyway entrance is a cobbler and a woman using a public telephone. Rather than a photographic representation, this drawing depicts my mother's memory of the most typical everyday shops in her childhood. Drawing by my father, Li Bin, and mother, Wang Yaqing.

commercial openness with residential privacy into an intimate labyrinth (figs. 1.1–1.4).

Built throughout Shanghai from the 1870s to the 1930s, *shikumen* alleyway homes were hybrid in their architectural planning. The individual houses had a traditional courtyard layout, south-facing orientation, and local decorative motifs. Yet whereas traditional Chinese alleys were natural accumulations of residences built as freestanding structures in different times and with varying styles, *shikumen* houses were rationally planned and uniformly constructed in high density to maximize the profit from the rent.[7] Thus, *shikumen* housing became, as architectural historian Chunlan Zhao points out, "a perfect match to satisfy nostalgia for traditional Chinese living and the demand for modern urban dwelling with great concern for economy."[8] Consisting of two stories and an attic, each unit of Alliance Lane had a layout reminiscent of the traditional Chinese house and was designed to accommodate a single multigenerational family (fig. 1.5). When entering the stone portal gate on the unit's south, "frontal" side, one first crossed a courtyardlike sky well (*tianjing* 天井, 6 square meters) into the living room, or guest and ancestral hall (*ketang jian* 客堂間, 24 square meters). At the back of the guest and ancestral hall was a door that opened onto the staircase, beyond which was the kitchen (8 square meters) and back door. Above the kitchen

FIGURE 1.3 View of Alliance Lane's big alleyway and entrance northward from the same vantage point as figure 1.1l. Refer to the section "Alleyway Space as a Milieu for Gossip" in chapter 3 for a more detailed explanation of the social life depicted in this image. Drawing by my parents.

FIGURE 1.4 View of an Alliance Lane alleyway branch eastward from the same vantage point as figure 1.1l. The big doors on the left are the stone portal gates, or *shikumen*, that gave this type of architecture its name. These are the "front doors," whereas the small doors on the right side are the "back doors." Drawing by my parents.

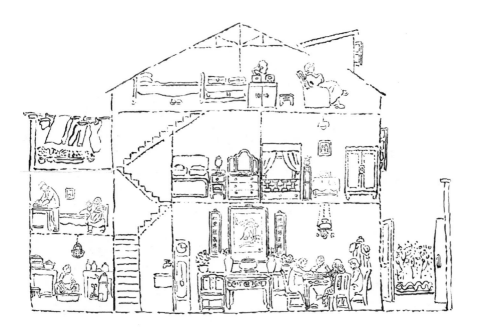

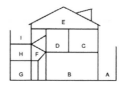

FIGURE 1.5 A cross-section view of an unmodified individual unit in Alliance Lane in the 1940s. This depiction is roughly based on Grandma Apricot's description of her family in this chapter, with the difference that Apricot's family had remodeled the third-floor attic into a proper third story. A: Sky well (*tianjing* 天井). B: Guest and ancestral hall (*ketang jian* 客堂間). C: Front bedroom (*qianlou* 前樓). D: Back bedroom (*houlou* 後樓). E: Third-floor attic (*sanceng ge* 三層閣) with a tiger window (*laohu chuang* 老虎窗). F: Staircase, next to which is a faucet room, which has no ceiling and is also called a "small sky well." G: Kitchen (*zao pijian* 灶披間). H: Pavilion room (*tingzijian* 亭子間). I: Sun terrace (*shaitai* 曬台). Drawing by my parents.

and halfway up the staircase was the *tingzijian* 亭子間, or pavilion room (8 square meters), and above that a sun terrace. The darker and smaller spaces of the kitchen and pavilion room faced north. Because the sun shone into the house from the south in the winter and from the north in the summer, these spaces were cold in the winter and hot in the summer. Along with the attic right beneath the roof, they were considered the back spaces for the family's servants. By contrast, the brighter spaces

FIGURE 1.6 Residents of No. 111 Alliance Lane from the 1930s to the 1950s: Apricot's grandparents, father, and younger brother around 1948. Photograph courtesy of Grandma Apricot.

FIGURE 1.7 Apricot (*middle*) and two neighbors in Alliance Lane around 1947. The girl to her right is Golden Precious of No. 109 (see "Several Lifetimes to a Life" in chapter 3). Photograph courtesy of Grandma Apricot.

of the guest and ancestral hall and the bedroom faced south and were thus warm in winter and cool in summer—they were thus considered the front spaces for the masters of the house. Such a hierarchical spatial arrangement would undergo radical transformations later when multiple families came to inhabit this house.

From 1938 to 1952, three generations of the Wang family (fig. 1.6 and 1.16) lived in No. 111 Alliance Lane. The eldest Mr. Wang was a manager at the nearby British American Tobacco factory.[9] He and his wife had only one son, a Number One at the same factory, who married a female worker under his supervision and had three children with her. Their eldest daughter, Apricot (fig. 1.7), married across the alleyway and continued living in Alliance Lane until its demolition in 2005. Over several afternoon chats in 2000, Grandma Apricot (fig. 1.8) recounted to me memories of her childhood home:[10]

When my grandfather first rented No. 111 from the British Hengye company, he had to pay a one-time takeover fee [*dingfei* 頂費] in the currency of three "big yellow fish," gold bars weighing about 150 grams each.[11] As a manager for British American Tobacco, my grandfather was in charge of buying coal, and coal mines sometimes bribed him to secure his business. I still remember how he poured out a huge sack of money onto our Eight Immortal Table one night for the entire family to count together. Since money was worth less with every passing day, however, my grandmother would exchange all this cash for gold bars. She then buried the gold bars in a flowerbed on the terrace so that thieves and burglars wouldn't be able to find them.

After taking a lease on the house, my grandfather was free to remodel it as he wished. The greatest change was to raise the roof of the attic on the third floor to make it into a proper third story with a big bedroom

FIGURE 1.8 Grandma Apricot at her back door in No. 83 Alliance Lane around 2000. Photograph courtesy of Grandma Apricot.

[18 square meters], a small bedroom [6 square meters], and a tiny storage room [4 square meters]. This was why No. 111 was several feet higher than most other houses in Alliance Lane. My parents, sister, brother, and I lived on this third floor. Downstairs on the second floor, my grandparents lived in the main bedroom of the house, which they partitioned into a front bedroom [*qianlou* 前樓, 14 square meters] and a back bedroom [*houlou* 後樓, 8 square meters]. Since I was their eldest and favorite granddaughter, they let me live in the back bedroom as an adolescent. The window in my room faced north, looking down into both our faucet room [a 2.5-square-meter room that opened off the kitchen] and the faucet room of the adjacent house, No. 109. Since there was no ceiling over the faucet room, this space was like another small "sky well" that gave a bit of light and breeze to all the rooms in the backside of the house—staircases, pavilion rooms, back bedroom, and the backside of the guest and ancestral hall. All of these rooms had windows that looked onto each other.

Downstairs on the ground floor was the guest and ancestral hall, also my family's mahjong room. I grew up with the sound of mahjong and used to play the game even as a child. When the Japanese occupied Shanghai, they did checkups in our neighborhood, so we padded our tables and installed two curtains—black on the outside and red on the inside—to block out the light. If the Japanese found out you were playing mahjong all night, they'd make you eat the pieces. ["That's only hearsay," Apricot's husband interrupted.] In any case, my grandparents carved out the backside of the guest and ancestral hall so that we could play mahjong undisturbed.

When my grandmother invited neighbors over to play mahjong, our two maids poured tea for us and received tips from the winners. Otherwise they were paid in room and board. One maid was responsible for dusting, sweeping, and pouring water into basins for us to wash our faces and feet mornings and evenings. The other washed clothes, bought groceries, and readied vegetables and meats for cooking—the cooking itself was my mother's duty. The two maids lived in the pavilion room. Sometimes a tailor also came to stay with us for a month or two to make clothes for everyone in the family, telling us children many stories from his peregrinations. This was usually before Chinese New Year's, a time augured with vats of pickles under the staircase and in the sky well. The two large square Eight Immortal

Tables made of mahogany would be placed in the middle of the guest and ancestral hall as a sacrificial altar, decked with incense and a pig head, fish and chicken, nuts and fruits. Nobody would sleep on New Year's Eve, for we'd play until dawn to set off firecrackers.

My grandfather and father may have worked for a British company and lived on British-owned property, but my grandmother made sure that we maintained a traditional household. When we had our meals, my grandparents always sat on one side facing the window to the south, to their right sat my father all by himself, and to their left sat my mother and myself. Across from them were the seats of my brother and sister, who preferred to eat with the servants after the rest of us. The best dishes were placed before my father, and my grandmother also put delicacies into my brother's bowl. I was free to eat whatever I wanted, but my mother dared not raise her chopsticks.

My mother was a typical victim of feudal society. She used to be an ordinary worker in the cigarette factory, whereas my father was a Number One. After getting married, she had to quit her job and cook at home. My grandmother was very conservative and forbade her son to take his wife to dancing halls or cinemas. She forbade my mother from leaving the house except to shop for groceries. Only if nobody else were available would she be allowed to join my grandmother at the mahjong table. Her place was in the kitchen and bedroom on the third floor, with a radio and a gramophone her only company since my grandmother did not like to see her associate with other women, let alone other men.

Yet my father remained a fun-loving dandy who liked to enjoy the city's nightlife. He was always dressed smartly in a Western suit with polished leather shoes. Since my mother could not go out with him, he took a courtesan along with him to his friend's drinking and dancing parties, and she soon became his mistress. When my mother suspected as much, she made every excuse to go out and tail my father to find out where the other woman lived. When she made a scene about it one night, my father broke the mirror on her wardrobe, getting his fists all bloody. My grandmother knelt down to beg him not to be so angry and allowed him to bring that woman home as a concubine. To appease my mother, my grandmother took out her own money to buy a new set of mahogany furniture for her bedroom. After a brief ceremony where the concubine kowtowed to my grandparents in the guest and ancestral hall, she moved with a baby into the small room adjacent to my mother's bedroom on the third floor. My father gave out spending money to his two wives every month, but whereas he slammed the portion for my mother on the table, he gave the concubine her allowance with caresses. My mother couldn't stand this and attempted suicide. This time, my grandmother took out her own money again and told my father to rent another place for his concubine, but making him promise to spend four nights every week at home. This was the state of our household before 1949.

Since *shikumen* architecture was by design a fusion of tradition and modernity, the Republican-era residents of Alliance Lane also led hybrid lifestyles—as compradors (intermediaries) whose livelihoods depended on foreign industries, as dandies who danced in jazzy ballrooms with Western clothes, and as Confucian patriarchs and matriarchs who maintained strict domestic hierarchies and imprisoned daughters-in-law in their inner chambers. Even after the alleyway's demolition many decades later, a local housing bureau archivist I interviewed in 2011 summarized his impression of its pre-1949 demographics as "the homes of Number Ones and small capitalists," plus their "wives and concubines." Those who rented homes that faced the street often converted their guest and ancestral halls into shop fronts, and some entrepreneurial residents, such as the family living a few doors down from the Wangs, even rented two adjacent units to open up small factories complete with worker dormitories. A neighboring alleyway on the same block housed one of China's first fountain pen factories, Huafu Gold Pen Company, which later developed China's own famous "Hero" brand to compete with the British Parker Pen during the Great Leap Forward.[12] Besides such middle-class families and their budding capitalist enterprises, Alliance Lane also served as a sanctuary for a number of underground Communists. According to party history, No. 61 harbored one of the first Communist underground radio transmitters in the 1930s.[13] As related in chapter 3, Apricot's sister-in-law in No. 83 had a transitory marriage with a distant cousin from Manchuria who had sublet their pavilion room in the 1940s—she found out later that he had been an underground party member seeking camouflage under the roof of a capitalist. Alliance Lane thus remained a vibrant contact zone between tradition and modernity, residence and commerce, leisure and drudgery, capitalists and communists.

The predominance of single-family homes in Alliance Lane did not reflect the city's average housing standards in the Republican era. A 1937 report from the Council of the Foreign Settlements of Shanghai showed that the average living space in the International Settlement was only three square meters per person and that it was not uncommon for a single *shikumen* unit to accommodate four or five families at a time.[14] In crowded alleyway factory dormitories, each worker occupied merely a bunk as his or her foothold in the city. Such were the living conditions of my maternal grandparents when they first came to Shanghai from their rural hometowns in Zhejiang at the end of World War II to work in a silk filature. They lived and met in a *shikumen* house three blocks away from Alliance Lane. My grandfather, Waigong, lived with nine other young men in what used to be the guest and ancestral hall. Waipo, my grandmother, lived with three other young women in the pavilion room (fig. 1.9). Upstairs in the terrace was the makeshift shack of a young couple working in the same filature. In the front bedroom lived the brother and sister-in-law of the silk filature boss, who lived in a garden villa in some upper corner of the city. Still, he liked to tell his workers—all from the same native place as he or related to him—that he had first arrived in Shanghai with nothing but a bundle of clothes on his back.

FIGURE 1.9 Waipo and Waigong in the late 1940s.

Beyond hopes of upward mobility, both Waigong and Waipo were enchanted by the big city's material civilization, and Waipo would speak even in her old age of the euphoria she felt upon turning on an electric light for the first time or getting her first photograph taken or learning to ride a rented bike—"It was just like flying!" The only joke Waigong knew and kept telling in his old age was about a man from the countryside—we sometimes speculate that it might be himself—coming to Shanghai for the first time and wanting to see the renowned "Asphalt Street." He searched up and down amidst Shanghai's skyscrapers and neon lights, asking for directions to Asphalt Street until someone told him that it was just beneath his feet. "That's what country bumpkins we were," Waigong would conclude his tale, "and that was how backward the rest of China had been."

The silk filature workers had two days of rest every month, and on those days Waigong and his coworkers would walk for hours into the city center—since they wanted to save the tram fare—to gawk at the colonial buildings at the Bund, the waterfront of the Huangpu River, to watch dockworkers unload big ships, to do window-shopping at the department stores on Nanjing Road, to visit the tigers in the Zhongshan Park Zoo, and even to "drink grape juice and eat a biscuit" in a Catholic church. Waigong liked to tell of his first encounters with this cosmopolitan city based on the things he had bought with his first wages, six months after his apprenticeship.

A coworker told me that there was a "big sale" on Canton Road, so I walked through half the city to check it out. Indeed, a man kept shouting "Big Reductions" through a megaphone. That's when I bought my first toothbrush and tube of toothpaste. I had never heard of brushing one's teeth before coming to Shanghai, and I never had a toothache, but in Shanghai it was fashionable to brush one's teeth, and I thought I could make my teeth look white and shiny like in the advertisements for Black Man Toothpaste.[15] Toothbrushes at the time were made out of ox bone and pig hair—plastic didn't exist back then—so it was really worth something.

Later, because there was currency inflation all the time, two other coworkers and I subscribed to a newspaper together, the *Impartial Daily* [*Dagongbao* 大公報], to check out the price of rice and cloth, gold and silver. Since we already paid for the paper, I read through the rest of it too and became interested in politics, in the Civil War raging through the country. Since then, I have never passed a day in the past six decades without reading a newspaper. Newspapers at the time referred to the Communists as "bandits" and the People's Liberation Army as "bandit army." After work, I liked to listen to alleyway neighbors discuss politics in evening chats: "What does communism mean? It means that mine is yours and yours is mine. It means to 'communize property' and 'communize wives.'" "If Chiang Kai-shek and Mao Zedong love to fight, we should lock them in a room and have the two of them fight it out!"

Before Liberation, there were still many foreigners in the city and Chinese who wore Western clothes and drank coffee. We had only heard of coffee but never had a taste, so a coworker and I went to buy some at the Jewish shop. Many poor Jewish refugees lived in the alleyways near our neighborhood—they were the only foreigners we felt sorry for because we learned that they had to escape for their lives halfway across the globe.[16] We rang a little bell at the entrance of the shop and asked for coffee. The Jew took out a small glass jar and rang up the cashier. "Sixteen hundred," he said in accented Shanghainese. At home we dissolved the brown powder in a glass of hot water, but it tasted so terrible we never touched it again, which was a pity, since sixteen hundred was a lot of money.

Soon after stepping onto Shanghai's "Asphalt Street," my country bumpkin maternal grandparents had effectively migrated not only through space but also through time from the backward countryside to the modern city, from their roots in clans and villages to the swirls of national and global history. As their identities changed from farmers to workers, they began to partake in a new material civilization and a cosmopolitan imagination that nevertheless remained anchored to their alleyway milieu. Before turning to the watershed moment of Communist Liberation and its impact on Alliance Lane, I want first to recount the Republican-era history of the other alleyway home in this study, where my paternal grandparents came to live from 1948.

From Japanese Company Housing to Enemy Property, 1915–1948

The Yangshupu area at the eastern part of the International Settlement began its industrial development following the First Sino-Japanese War

(1894–1895), which allowed foreigners to manufacture in Shanghai. From the 1910s to the 1930s, the Japanese came to dominate the spinning and weaving industry in China, with dozens of cotton mills in Shanghai lining the banks of the Huangpu and Suzhou Rivers with towering smokestacks and loading docks.[17] Unlike Western factories such as British American Tobacco that employed Chinese Number Ones, including Apricot's father, Japanese companies assigned Japanese managers to exercise direct control over Chinese workers in order to instill more discipline and to prevent strikes.[18]

To provide a home away from home for its Japanese managerial staff, the Japanese-owned Shanghai Cotton Mill constructed company residential quarters (*shataku* 社宅) at the intersection of Pingliang Road and Linqing Road from 1915 to 1918. Built twelve years before Alliance Lane and in a more peripheral edge of the International Settlement, this compound took up twice as much land (20,586 square meters) but only half as much building area (7872 square meters). This residential compound consisted of 22 rows and 144 two-story units, in addition to a communal bathhouse, a clinic, a club, and a cooperative (fig. 1.10).[19] With a front garden and backyard for every house, this "new-style lane" (*xinshi lilong* 新式里弄) was lined with flower shrubs, bamboo fences, and luxuriant trees (fig. 1.11)—including four cherry trees in the community garden. Such open and green spaces gave this alleyway a more foreign and classy air than the average *shikumen* compounds such as Alliance Lane. Distributed to employees by rank rather than leased for a profit as *shikumen* housing was, such housing was a unique precedent for work-unit housing that became prevalent in Chinese cities after the 1970s.

The houses themselves were built out of wood and brick, their facade reinforced with a layer of cement and decorative pebbles. Inside, each unit was equipped with a gas stove and flushing toilet, modern conveniences rarely available in *shikumen* alleyways. With about 50 square meters of living space, the overall design of the interior followed a Japanese model. The south-facing front door opened into the *genkan* 玄関, or an entryway for the removal of shoes before stepping up into the living room (*ima* 居間, the size of six *tatami* mats[20]) and tea room (*cha no ma* 茶の間, three *tatami* mats), which were built on a platform raised half a meter above the ground level. Two steps down from the tea room was the kitchen that adjoined the toilet and the backyard. A staircase in the living room led up to the second floor with a north-facing six-*tatami* bedroom and a south-facing eight-*tatami* bedroom that opened onto a balcony, three more

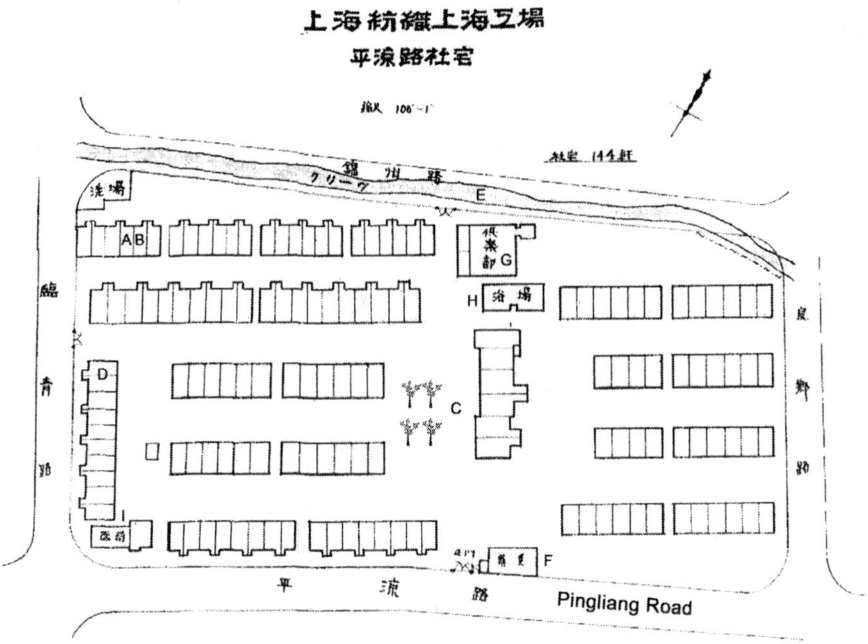

上海紡織上海工場
平涼路社宅

縮尺 1/600

社宅 144戶

鎮州路
クリーク

E
A B
俱楽部 G
H 浴場
D
C

醫務
室 F
清
野
路

平　涼　路
Pingliang Road

FIGURE 1.10 Layout of the Japanese Shanghai Cotton Mill Employee Housing on Pingliang Road. A: No. 183, the house in which Yeye and Nainai lived from 1947 to 2011. B: No. 181, housing awarded to a model worker in 1956. C: Communal garden with four cherry trees, later the site of nuclear bunker. D: No. 53, site of the neighborhood committee after 1952. E: A creek, filled in 1958 to build a factory in the Great Leap Forward (for more on A–E, see "After the Communist Revolution" in this chapter). F: A cooperative shop under the Japanese, later converted into a doorkeeper's lodge with public telephones. G: A club under the Japanese, converted in the 1950s into an elementary school. H: Bathhouse. I: Clinic. Courtesy of Shanghai Municipal Archives.

FIGURE 1.11 Front view of a row of Japanese company housing with front yards. The house on the right is No. 183, where Yeye and Nainai lived from 1947 to 2011.

FIGURE 1.12 A cross-section view of an individual unit of the Japanese company housing. A: Front yard. B: Living room. C: Tea room or dining room. D: Kitchen. E: Toilet. F: Backyard. G: South-facing bedroom. H: North-facing bedroom. The depiction of the people and furniture draws inspiration from archival photographs from Chen Zu'en's *Social History of the Japanese Diaspora in Shanghai* (2009). Drawing by my parents.

tatami in size. All interior spaces were separated through removable *shōji* sliding doors (fig. 1.12).

A Japanese map of Shanghai from 1932 prominently marks this and a few other *shataku*s along with a Japanese elementary school in the same neighborhood, showing a small but significant presence of a diasporic Japanese community in this area.[21] In 1927, the Japanese expatriate population was about 4,000 in the Yangshupu area and 26,000 in all of Shanghai, the latter number increasing to 100,000 during World War II.[22] Joshua Fogel points out that, like Western expatriate communities in

Shanghai, "Japanese life there was designed to resemble home," and many Japanese were "oblivious to the fact that they were in a foreign country."[23] Chen Zu'en writes in detail of the way the Japanese community in Shanghai maintained their own culture in terms of food, clothing, customs, religion, and education. Some cotton mill residential compounds had their own shops, schools, kindergartens, clinics, Shinto shrines, and other cultural facilities, and the outdoor communal grounds provided space for open-air film screenings and baseball games.[24]

From the 1910s to the 1930s, however, the Japanese community in Shanghai keenly felt and aggressively retaliated against waves of anti-Japanese boycotts and rare armed attacks, and it called for the Japanese government and military to "punish China." These tensions exploded in the Shanghai Incident of 1932—resulting in more than 6,000 Chinese dead and 1.2 million turned refugees—as well as an all-out war between Japan and China by 1937. By the end of this war eight years later, more than 70,000 Japanese sojourners were sent back to Japan from Shanghai along with more than a million Japanese prisoners of war.[25]

In December 1945, *Life* magazine photographer George Lacks photographed Japanese men, women, and children waiting for expulsion from Shanghai and repatriation to Japan (see fig. 1.13 for one of these photos).[26]

FIGURE 1.13 The postwar repatriation of Shanghai's Japanese residents in 1945. Photograph by George Lacks in *Life* magazine. Courtesy of Getty Images.

Which faces in the anonymous crowd pictured in the photos, I wonder, could have been the former residents of my grandparents' old house? Perhaps this man crouching on the ground and holding his head? Or that old woman wearing her striped kimono over the large bundle on her back? Or maybe that little girl with short hair and bangs sleeping on a pile of blankets? Everyone wore thick layers of clothing, and most packed their luggage in big cloth bundles. Fine fabric with exquisite embroidery was now just part of the paraphernalia of banishment, waiting to pass through customs. Each person was allowed take with him or her only thirty kilos, five thousand francs in cash, and no precious metals,[27] so in a few photos the Chinese officials are weighing and examining their luggage, leafing through a notebook, prying through someone's sandals, and searching beneath a man's shirt. In another photograph, two female custom officials are examining the bodies of a Japanese woman and child as they take off their outer pants, making sure that these "enemies" do not take their "plunder," supposedly stained with Chinese blood and sweat. In a larger Chinese nationalist historiography, these images may be considered redemptive—the rightful expropriation of enemy property and expulsion of colonialists.

The Japanese presence in China certainly had a profound impact on the lives of my grandparents Yeye and Nainai, yet their personal entanglements with the invasion and occupation were much more ambivalent than a nationalist historiography could suggest. Both Yeye and Nainai fled their ancestral homes in Yangzhou on account of the 1937 Japanese invasion of the Chinese mainland. Yeye's parents, fearing that either the Japanese or the Nationalist armies might conscript young men as soldiers or coolies to fight the other side, sent him to high school and university in Shanghai, whose foreign settlements remained free from Japanese occupation until December 1941. Yeye graduated from St. John's University in 1943 (see his diploma in fig. 0.1) and worked as a clerk in a bank in Nanjing for two more years. Meanwhile, Nainai, betrothed to Yeye since adolescence, lived with her future parents-in-law in a coal mine in Shandong from 1938 to 1946 (fig. 1.14). Yeye's father worked there as a land surveyor and was eager to curry favors with the local Japanese occupiers. Nainai recalled that every autumn, when local tenant farmers delivered peaches, peanuts, and other goodies to their house, she would pick the most impeccable fruits from the sacks, carefully brush away the fuzz, and package them in brown paper bags for their Japanese neighbors. The salaries and bonuses from the coal mine not only paid for Yeye's college tuition but also maintained his parents' opium habit for eight years. When the Japanese finally lost the war, Yeye's parents fled again with Nainai, this time from the Nationalist troops, who, they feared, might prosecute all friends to the Japanese as traitors.

FIGURE 1.14 Nainai and her parents-in-law at a Shandong coal mine, around 1940.

In 1946, the Nationalist government established the China Textile Construction Company (Zhongguo fangzhi jianzhu gongsi 中國紡織建設公司) to take over as war spoils three dozen abandoned Japanese textile mills in Shanghai, along with their associated properties. The Shanghai Municipal Archives still hold some meticulous listings of such "enemy property," and here I copy out just a few items left over from the cooperative shop (fig. 1.10F) in the residential compound:

349 pounds of yarn of various colors, 21½ feet of yellow khaki cloth, 83 boxes of dry wheat gluten, 76 pounds of salt, 6 boxes of spicy soy sauce, 82 boxes of dried seaweed, 69 pounds of dry noodles, 162 boxes of "chicken brand" and 190 boxes of "pig brand" mosquito incense, 56 big boxes of matches, 26 enamel basins, 49 boxes of socks, 10 cans of bamboo shoots, 6 boxes of tooth powder, 237 glasses, 20 enamel ashtrays, 11 bags of candles, 181 boxes of chili powder, 3 bottles of peanut sauce, 8 bottles of soda, 235 barbed wires, 7½ dozen boxes of facial cream, 86 cans of curry powder, 25 kilograms of cooking oil, 14 boxes of mahogany chopsticks, 50 hair nets (for women), 200 toothbrushes and various brands of tooth powder, 50 bottles of glue, 230 bars of bathing soap and 1200 bars of laundry soap, 145 dozens of gauze gloves, 40 bottles of bedbug disinfectants, 45 eyeliners, 63 writing brushes, 84 sheet music notebooks, 4 maps, 5 boxes of crab meat, 126 washing boards, 24 bottles of soy sauce, 84 bottles of blue ink and 47 bottles of black ink, 8 tubes of shoe polish, 118 pounds of sugar, 49 bundles of Japanese chopsticks, 10 boxes of crayons, 800 notebooks, 77 dozens of white handkerchiefs, 96 boxes of black children's socks, 200 pairs of inner pants, 42 bento boxes, 220 checkered cloth, 20 kimonos, 24 wool blankets, 11 pairs of rubber shoes, 115 dozen towels, 44 meters of grass green khaki cloth, 500+ meters of other types of cloth, 225 glasses, 5 writing desks, various other tables, chairs, cabinets, folding screens, vats, fridges, and clocks.[28]

Though statistically insignificant in terms of trade or consumer patterns, this detailed, trivial, and contingent list does give us an inkling of the material texture of the former residents' lives inside this alleyway compound at the end of the war. We might surmise that the Japanese women still wore kimonos and rubber shoes, tied up their hair in buns, and put on makeup. They knit sweaters, mended men's uniforms with khaki cloth, and scrubbed their laundry on washing boards. Wearing gauze gloves, they disinfected *tatami* mats against bedbugs, deliberated over different brands of mosquito incense, and lined their gardens with barbed wire. They took their children to school with *bento* boxes containing sushi or curry rice, and the teacher still taught music classes. The men smoked, wore polished leather shoes, and wrote with fountain pens. Besides the Japanese who used such items, the list also gives us a glimpse at the Chinese officials who took over, eager to count the spoils of war rather than leaving it to the mob. Yet the fastidiousness of the record belies the corruption that followed the distribution of "enemy property."

To fill the gap of Japanese management staff and restore production, the China Textile Construction Company began hiring white-collar clerks with high salaries. In 1947, Yeye secured an accounting position in the company's finance department by scoring the highest in its entrance exams, a landmark in his life that would both console and upset him from his political downfall in 1957 until his death in 2011. In addition to this enviable job, Yeye also managed to obtain company housing and hence was able to bring Nainai and their first daughter, Treasure, from Shandong to Shanghai. According to his own account of how he gained such a precious foothold in Shanghai,

> Mr. L [Yeye refers to himself as Mr. L in the memoirs he wrote for me[29]] became a clerk for a cotton mill under the Nationalist regime in 1947. In its previous life, the factory belonged to the Japanese. After World War II, it was nationalized along with all of its properties, which included a housing compound for employees. While the new factory administration was still consolidating its policies, Chinese employees of all ranks used all methods at their disposal to obtain one of the houses. Mr. L also tried to pull strings by bribing the bigwigs, and after treading the tortuous path of exploiting others and being exploited, he finally procured this house from his superiors.

When they first moved into this house in 1947, Yeye and Nainai had found some *tatami* mats on the floor and in the closets, along with a stool that looked Japanese. It did not strike them as ironic, having left their ancestral homes on account of the Japanese, to make a Japanese house their permanent new home. Yet the house soon ceased to be inhabited in the way it was originally intended. The *tatami* mats were removed a few years later

FIGURE 1.15 Decorative perforations of the top frame of the sliding doors between the two upstairs bedrooms, the only visibly Japanese remnants of these alleyway homes after several decades. This image is from No. 181, the home of my grandparents' next-door neighbor, in 2013. Photograph by the author.

because they attracted bedbugs in the summer. Still later, when more and more people came to occupy the house, its open spaces became divided into narrow strips, and a crude and pitiful shack overtook the backyard, once planted with cockscorns, morning glories, rose balsams, and touch-me-nots. On the top frame of the sliding door between the two bedrooms upstairs were perforations in the elegant shapes of bamboo leaves (as seen in fig. 1.15). Many years later, when these became the last visibly Japanese remnants of the house, they were to make my father wonder how a culture capable of such refinement was also capable of so much cruelty, as he had learned in school. It made him wonder if that cruelty would have turned benevolent over time and therefore been forgiven, but history had already passed its verdict, and such thoughts were no more than treason and blasphemy. Bookended by two world wars, the Japanese foothold in this house and in this city was to remain an effaced layer of the Shanghai palimpsest for the next few decades.

After the Communist Revolution (1950s–1970s)

Under socialism, you could foresee your future to the coffin.
—UNCLE MORNING SUN

You never know what's going to happen tomorrow.
—NAINAI

After the Communist takeover ousted the Western imperialists from Shanghai, Alliance Lane, former British property, turned into state property and public housing (*gongfang* 公房). The name of the street it was on changed from Ward Road to Changyang Road 長陽路, the Road of Everlasting Sunshine. After the postwar expulsion of the Japanese residents and a brief stint under Nationalist control, the former Japanese cotton mill housing compound—now called Lane 1695 of Pingliang Road 平涼路, the Road of Serene Coolness—also became public housing under Communist proprietorship. Shanghai's new rulers did away with the real estate market and speculation that drove up housing prices, and then they redistributed homes abandoned by their foreign, capitalist, or Nationalist owners to Communist cadres and model workers.[30] The new government did not seize alleyway housing from residents who stayed on, but declining capitalist or comprador families soon had to share their single-family homes with a newly empowered class of workers.

In the Maoist era, Shanghai's character was to change from a "consumer city" to a "producer city," from a "world city" with a cosmopolitan culture to an "industrial workhorse for a plan-bound economy."[31] To build a socialist city at a residential level, the Communists created new bureaucracies to exert control over Shanghai's inhabitants. The household registration system kept tabs on who lived where and froze the previously fluid boundaries between urban and rural areas.[32] The Housing Management Bureau managed, maintained, and occasionally allocated state-owned housing in collaboration with the authority of various work units. Street offices mobilized housewives such as my paternal grandmother to join the neighborhood committee in making propaganda, spying on residents, and mediating conflicts.[33] These new webs of control fixed most households within the same square meters for several decades and under neighbors' mutual surveillance. Meanwhile, successive political campaigns swept selected groups of people off their feet, shrinking their living spaces, banishing their bodies, and making their fall another carnival for the masses. As a result, the socialist era left behind contradictory memories of security and insecurity, stability and terror.

Seesawing Destinies in No. 111, Alliance Lane

When the People's Liberation Army marched into Shanghai in the spring of 1949, Grandma Apricot's family still had the entire house of No. 111 Alliance Lane to themselves. Besides a few Nationalist officials who left for Taiwan, most tenants of this alleyway stayed on and did not care whether they paid rent to the British property-management company or to the newly established housing bureau under the Communists. They took a wait-and-see attitude toward the Communists and were quite glad to see the end of the Civil War. Grandma Apricot showed me a photograph taken on a family outing shortly after Shanghai's liberation (fig. 1.16) and recounted her family fortunes for the next few years:

Here I am on the right side, dressed in a fashionable *qipao* [cheongsam]. I was sixteen years old and about to be married. My husband lived across from our alleyway branch in No. 83 Alliance Lane [see fig. 1.1B]. We had played together since childhood, and the alleyway was our matchmaker. We chose October 1, 1949, as our wedding date, the same day when the People's Republic of China was founded. It was an extravagant wedding, with a theater troupe and bamboo awnings that reached the alleyway entrance. A procession of men carried my dowry—red mahogany trousseau chests filled with clothes, jewelry, and money, a clock, a radio, new cotton quilts, silk and satin linens, basins and buckets. We feasted our alleyway neighbors for an entire week. Alas, all our wedding pictures were lost in the Cultural Revolution [see "Home Searches" in chapter 2].

In the center front of the photo is my grandmother, the family matriarch. My grandfather's health was failing then, and he died of a heart attack a year later. We held a lavish funeral for him, with a parade of Buddhist monks and Daoist priests and everybody in the family wearing white clothes especially made for the occasion. Still rich then, we did not know how to plan for the hardships to come. I suppose it was a timely death, for otherwise my grandfather might

FIGURE 1.16 Apricot's family on a spring outing to Hangzhou in 1949, shortly after the Communist liberation of Shanghai. *Front row, left to right*: Apricot's father, grandmother, and an old family servant. *Back row, left to right*: Apricot's father's concubine with a baby; Apricot's brother, sister, and cousin; Apricot's mother (holding the Buddha's mouth); Apricot. Photograph courtesy of Grandma Apricot.

have been targeted a few months later in the Suppression of the Counterrevolutionaries like my father-in-law, also a manager at the British American Tobacco factory. I still remember the sound of the gunshot at his execution, and his counterrevolutionary status haunted our family for the next three decades. Following my father-in-law's arrest, the police came to search No. 83 and confiscate his belongings. I moved the most precious items of my own dowry back into that hidden attic on the third floor in No. 111, and that was how I was able to keep my own jewelry and mahogany furniture.

My mother in the picture is the one holding onto the Buddha's lip. The two kids closest to her are my brother and sister. The woman holding the baby is my father's concubine. After my grandfather's death in 1951, my father still earned a regular salary but gave all of it to the concubine. They lived elsewhere in Shanghai, so my grandmother, mother, sister, and brother were the only ones remaining in No. 111. Without any regular income, my grandmother pawned gold bars, jewelry, and furniture items; she dismissed all the servants (including this old man in the picture) and began subletting rooms to other families to collect takeover fees—first the front bedroom, then the back bedroom, then the pavilion room, and eventually the entire third floor.

In 1954, my mother died of pneumonia, so my father moved back to No. 111 with his concubine and their four children to save expenses. By then, all rooms above the ground floor had been sublet to other families, so they stayed in the front guest and ancestral hall, and my grandmother retreated with my brother and sister to the back. Now that my grandmother had no money, the Concubine stripped away her submissive mask, seized control of the household, and treated my brother and sister like the stereotypical evil stepmother, begrudging every meal they ate at home. Unable to stand her abuses, my sister signed up to go to Qinghai when the Ministry of Petroleum came looking for workers. The Concubine remained very nasty to my brother, so once I had a big fight with her and made my father lose so much face in the alleyway that they swapped housing with another family. [See "Alleyway Space as a Milieu for Gossip" in chapter 3.] This was how, by 1956, my childhood home came to be inhabited by five families of strangers [fig. 1.17].

While original residents of Alliance Lane lost money, status, and even family members to revolutionary justice, the Wangs surrendered living

FIGURE 1.17 A cross-section view of No. 111 Alliance Lane around the late 1960s. In contrast with figure 1.5, five families lived in different rooms of this house from the mid-1950s to the mid-1990s. A, B, C: Waigong, Waipo, and their children lived on the third floor, with Waigong napping on the grain bed inside the tiny attic room (A) before his night shift, my mother reading in the small bedroom (B), and a big bedroom (C) with a radio on the dresser and a photo over the Eight Immortal Table (for more on the grain bed, radio, and table, see "Domestic Artifacts as Historical Witnesses" in chapter 2). D: Sun terrace where Waigong built a little shack as kitchen. E: Pavilion room with a woman whose husband was sent to labor reform. F: Staircase with a light bulb for each family. G: Back bedroom with a loft (*erceng ge* 二層閣). H: Front bedroom with Aunt Duckweed's family (see "A Room of Her Own" in chapter 3). I: Communal kitchen. J: Faucet room with four faucets (for more on E–J, see "Alleyway Space as a Milieu for Gossip" in chapter 3). K, L: Guest and ancestral hall, now divided into a front part (L) and a back part (K) with a loft, housing Principal Zhang, Mrs. Zhang, and their four children (also see "Home Searches" in chapter 2). M: Sky well. Drawing by my parents.

FIGURE 1.18 Appareled in the most fashionable "Lenin suit" of 1951, Waigong (*second from the left in the back row*), Waipo (*third from the right in the front row*), and twenty coworkers from the old privately owned silk factory joined a state-owned factory.

space to former country bumpkins and new urban proletariats such as my maternal grandparents. As Waipo recalls,

> Moving into No. 111 Alliance Lane was one of the happiest events of my life. You see, your *waigong* and I were truly liberated by the Communists. As children in the countryside, we grew up with growling stomachs. As teenagers, we came to Shanghai to learn a trade, worked on our feet at an alleyway silk factory twelve hours a day, and never even saw the daylight (fig. 1.9). When our boss heard the Communists were coming to communize property, he gave us three months' wages as a dispersal fee and tried to fire us all, but the Communists helped us get organized and struggle against the boss to get our jobs back. In the early 1950s, many small alleyway factories like ours merged into big state-owned factories, which guaranteed us a lifelong good wage, full medical insurance, and a retirement pension (fig. 1.18).[34] That's when your *waigong* and I felt secure enough to get married, in a collective wedding fashionable at the

FIGURE 1.19 Waipo and Waigong (*third couple from the right in the middle row*) got married in a collective wedding ceremony in 1952. Even though all the couples are dressed in Western clothes, a huge traditional bridal sedan chair decorates the backdrop with propaganda posters and slogans supporting the Korean War.

time and under the new marriage law (fig. 1.19). Our master of ceremony told us to strive for socialist construction and to strengthen the nation, and our wedding march was a battle hymn for the Korean War.

Our factory provided dorms separated by men and women, but no housing for married couples, so we rented a small flat in a hutment, a place with no running water but that got flooded whenever it rained. Our coworker, Master Chen, had just brought his bride from his native Suzhou [see fig. 3.7] and sublet the front bedroom of No. 111 Alliance Lane [fig. 1.17H] as his marriage chamber. He told us that his second landlord was looking for a subtenant for the back bedroom [fig. 1.17G], so we moved in after paying Apricot's grandmother a "takeover fee" of 300 yuan—about two months of our common income at the time. I was sleepless with joy the first night we were here.

As our life improved, the life of our second landlords got progressively worse. They were always making trips to the purchasing station [government-run pawnshops], selling this or that. We bought Apricot's mother's radio since your *waigong* wanted to listen to the news [see "Radio Waves" in chapter 2]. We didn't care for mahogany furniture, but my sister-in-law bought her set cheaply from another family in decline, while Master Chen, now our next-door neighbor, bought his set from a Suzhou village where landlord property was confiscated. The fortunes of the rich and poor were indeed reversed overnight! Then again, our second landlords had no idea how to live frugally. In our shared kitchen, we saw how they used oil like water, and when they ran out of money, they would sublet another room.

A year after moving to Alliance Lane in 1954, I was pregnant with a second child, and my mother came to visit us from the countryside. There was not enough room for all of us in the back bedroom, so your *waigong* had to go sleep in the factory dormitory. Apricot's grandmother had not yet sublet the third floor and the ground floor, so when we met on the staircase, I said to her: "You have so much space, and we so little!" The old lady immediately offered us the spacious 18-square-meter big room on the third floor [fig. 1.17C] at the price of 350. She also allowed us to use the 4-square-meter third-floor back room [fig. 1.17B] as long as we paid its monthly rent to the state.

A few months later, Apricot's grandmother wanted to sublet that little room to another couple with three children, but we wouldn't let her—imagine two families on the same floor separated by nothing but a thin wooden wall! We got into a big argument and had to go to the Housing Bureau to settle the matter. By then, subletting was technically illegal, and because we had been the ones paying the rent for the past year or so—and maybe also because we were proletariat and they were bourgeois—the Housing Bureau allocated the room to us. But the Housing Bureau did not know about another room hidden behind the right wall of the contested room, a tiny attic whose ceiling slanted down to the floor [fig. 1.17A]. To smooth over hurt feelings, we paid another 150 yuan privately to Apricot's grandmother for the right to use the attic as well. After we took over the entire third floor of No. 111, Apricot's grandmother also offered Master Chen and his wife the back bedroom, but they haggled with her, so she sublet it to another worker couple. After this, household registration became fixed, and Master Chen would regret his momentary stinginess for the rest of his life. [See "A Room of Her Own" in chapter 3.]

In the 1950s, Alliance Lane turned from an alleyway of upper-middle-class tradesmen, nationalist officials, and small capitalists into a neighborhood of mostly worker families. Yet if some original residents moved away, some of their family members—wives, concubines, children, or siblings—often retained residence in one of their old rooms. Former servants of rich families occasionally became the permanent neighbors of their erstwhile masters. Old alleyway factories, collectivized into state-owned enterprises, became the property of specific work units, which allocated them as housing for model workers. Intellectuals and once underground Communist Party members also occupied various rooms in the alleyway. Residents came from different walks of life and different parts of China: my grandparents came from Shaoxing, whereas Pavilion Room Uncle came from Ningbo. Grandma Apricot's own parents were native Shanghainese, but her husband's family was originally from Shandong. Back Bedroom Auntie quarreled loudly in her Subei dialect with Front Bedroom Auntie, who spoke Suzhou dialect with a sharp pitch. The alleyway's population did not become less diverse and certainly remained more heterogeneous than any other type of housing in China, past or present.

Whereas Alliance Lane's first generation of residents in the Republican era often had one house per multigenerational family, residents who moved here under socialism were mostly nuclear families occupying single rooms with three or four children on average (fig. 1.20). This meant turning the kitchen, faucet room, staircase, terrace, as well as the back alleyway itself into communal spaces shared between several families—not to mention the sharing of many walls, windows, and doors. The architecture that previously sheltered the privacy of bourgeois families was thus transformed into a complex labyrinth of mutual surveillance, where everybody had a view of or was within hearing range of the intimate spheres of a number of others. Most neighbors forced to share communal spaces maintained a negotiated and reluctant coexistence, while the sights and sounds of each family's private lives fermented an endless stream of gossip (see chapter 3).

Overcrowding was also rampant in Republican era Shanghai, yet most of the city's population consisted of sojourners who considered their stay in the city temporary.[35] In the socialist era, originally transient sojourners in the city, now without social or physical mobility, became permanent residents, and most children born in the alleyway also grew into adulthood in the same spaces with the same neighbors. For instance, the Zhangs on the first floor, the Chens on the second floor, and my grandparents on the third floor of No. 111 Alliance Lane remained neighbors for a few decades.

FIGURE 1.20 A worker family consisting of Waigong, Waipo, and their three children in 1957: my mother, the eldest; Aunt Yahua; and Uncle Strong (baby).

The friendship between some of the neighboring children in these families, such as between my mother and Aunt Duckweed, at times exceeded the affections between siblings. Since the back bedroom and the pavilion room were truly unbearably small, however, their residents changed every decade or after an arduous, Kafkaesque process of petitioning the Housing Bureau.

A Model Worker Moves Into Lane 1695

Let us now take a short bus ride from my maternal grandparents' Alliance Lane home to the old Japanese residential quarters on Pingliang Road where my paternal grandparents lived beginning in 1947 to learn how the Communist Revolution changed their neighborhood. We will first knock on the door of their next-door neighbor, Grandma Yang Lingying in No. 181, who was awarded this house after earning the title of a citywide model worker and membership in the Communist Party in 1953. According to Grandma Yang, all the homes in this compound were once reserved exclusively for "the bourgeoisie," by which she meant the Chinese clerks, technicians, and managerial staff of nearby cotton mills after the expulsion of the Japanese in 1945. She was among the first proletariats to live here. Aunt Treasure, my father's elder sister, who used to play with Grandma Yang's daughters at their house, recalled that Grandma Yang's model worker certificates (one of them shown in fig. 1.21) were

FIGURE 1.21 Grandma Yang Lingying's Model Worker Certificate from 1956, the year she moved to No. 181 of the former Japanese housing compound. Image courtesy of Grandma Yang Lingying.

always framed and prominently displayed on the wall. "I used to be very jealous of them—it was as if they were born aristocrats because of the honor bestowed upon their mother." Though facing the same shortages as everybody else, Grandma Yang and her husband were able to make ends meet much more easily than many of their white-collar neighbors, who got by with only the husband's salary, because of the relatively high wages both of them earned as workers.

In the Shanghai Municipal Archives, I found a report from 1954 on Grandma Yang's "model achievements," such as breaking new production records with minimal waste as well as working for seven successive years without a single instance of absence or lateness. A short biography recounted her impoverished childhood, when she helped her shoemaking father and petty merchant mother eke out a living by smuggling goods across creeks and barbed wire. At the age of thirteen, she began working in a Japanese cotton mill that came under Nationalist control after 1945 and supposedly suffered greatly under both regimes: "Not until Liberation, under the leadership of Chairman Mao and the Communist Party, did Comrade Yang Lingying truly leap out of the bitter sea and saw light. She saw with her own eyes the arrest of counterrevolutionaries, and the Number Ones also had to bow their heads. Workers would never be humiliated. With the abolition of the unreasonable body search and with the stabilization of prices, her family, though still relying entirely on her income, was enjoying an ever better life."[36]

The mass movements of the early 1950s, according to the report, further sharpened Grandma Yang's political consciousness. Even though working hours were reduced and wages were fixed, she was determined to work hard for the good of the new nation. All of this qualified her candidacy for Communist Party membership.[37] It is not written that tangible material benefits accompanied emblematic rewards, but it would be unreasonable for this nominal new "master of the country" to continue living in abject conditions where her family could barely straighten their backs.[38] Hence she was awarded this house and, when her family moved out of the hutment, her factory sent a parade of drums and gongs along, as though she were a living advertisement for the new socialist state. Though hardly an articulate speaker, Grandma Yang had to give "thank you, dear Party" speeches in public, and in our interview fifty years later she still made a point to say: "We really felt emancipated when Liberation came."

As much as Grandma Yang's move from the hutment to the new house was made a symbol of the liberation of workers, her case could by no means represent the change in living conditions of all workers. "The confiscation and redistribution of housing occupied by foreigners or 'counterrevolutionaries' did not greatly improve the situation," Marie-Claire Bergère points out in her economic history of the city. "Shanghai did not contain enough bourgeois residences to lodge all the city's inhabitants living in shocking conditions."[39] In the decades from the 1950s to the 1970s, the municipality, starved of funds, constructed only a few "workers' new villages" (*gongren xincun* 工人新村) and satellite settlements in the city's suburbs that barely kept up with the city's rapidly increasing population.[40] In the Yangshupu area, a housing project called "20,000 Households" (Liangwanhu 兩萬戶) was completed in 1953 and hailed as a great socialist achievement. Modeled after Soviet communal apartments, these new constructions were cement two-story apartment houses without ornamentation. Shared between four families, each apartment was about 50–70 square meters and equipped with a kitchen and a flush toilet.[41] Though far from luxurious, these apartments were much better than what most people in Shanghai had at the time. Alas, as their name suggests, they could accommodate only about twenty thousand families. "Our entire factory of three hundred people had only two Liangwanhu apartment slots," Waipo recalled. "It was so competitive—you had to be at least a model worker and living in the worst possible shantytown." Nonetheless, the lucky few such as Grandma Yang became the representatives of the working class, and the workers' new villages were showcased to schoolchildren and visiting foreigners as a socialist housing utopia.[42]

Even in the 2000s, Grandma Yang's house retained a facade of respectability in the neighborhood. Fixed to their door was a red plaque that read "Five-Good Family," an honor bestowed upon harmonious households that also got along with their neighbors. Yet the model worker certificates were no longer to be seen. When I asked to have a look in 2000, she took out a roll of paper from above her wardrobe and spread the certificates out for me. When asked why she didn't hang them on the wall, Grandma Yang replied that they were "outdated." When putting them away, she explained in a whisper that in the Cultural Revolution the factory cadres who chose her as a model worker fell from power and became the "targets of proletarian dictatorship," so the certificates could have brought trouble because they were signed by leaders labeled as "capitalist-roaders."

Fortunately, she had good relations with the factory's rebel faction, so they struggled against her only briefly and left her in peace. Like many other families in the 1970s, her children were sent down to the country-side and her husband to the hinterlands with his entire factory for almost a decade before they could return to Shanghai. After her retirement in the 1990s, the cotton factory also went out of business and disappeared from the cityscape, so these certificates truly became the relics of another age. In place of them, Grandma Yang displayed pictures of her deceased parents and her own "silver wedding" photos (see the photos hanging in fig. 1.15)—images that would have been considered feudal or bourgeois under socialism.

A Housewife Joins the Neighborhood Committee

When Grandma Yang Lingying first moved next door in 1954, Nainai, my paternal grandmother, was the security defense chief (*zhibao zhuren* 治保主任) of the newly established neighborhood committee (*juweihui* 居委會), volunteer work for the alleyway (*lilong gongzuo* 里弄工作) that she treated like a full-time job. Since her betrothal to Yeye at the age of fourteen in 1935, Nainai's life had been largely confined to the domes-tic sphere. Throughout the Japanese occupation, while Yeye attended school in Shanghai, Nainai waited on her parents-in-law in Shandong from dawn to dusk (see fig. 1.14). Her daily chores included cooking meals and "nourishing treats" such as white fungus with lotus seeds, dusting and mopping all the rooms, washing her mother-in-law's feet and clipping her toenails, and serving her in-laws opium until they fell asleep. Yeye came to Shandong briefly in 1941 to consummate their mar-riage, and Nainai gave birth to their daughter Treasure a year later. She recalled that when she cooked an egg for herself during her pregnancy, her mother-in-law scolded her, but her father-in-law treated her like a daughter, teaching her embroidery and calligraphy in his spare time. After moving to Shanghai with Yeye on the eve of the Communist Revo-lution, Nainai gave birth to four more children between 1948 and 1956 (fig. 1.22) and was one of a million housewives in Shanghai whom the Communist Party was eager to mobilize.[43]

Until 1949, the state had relatively little presence in Shanghai's neigh-borhood life,[44] but the Communists spread control to the grassroots by

FIGURE 1.22 A family photograph of Yeye, Nainai, and their children in 1957: Aunt Treasure (*middle back*), Aunt Pearl (*middle front*), my father (*right*), Aunt Bean (*left*), Uncle Lucky (baby).

establishing "offices of takeover commissioners" that later evolved into street offices, usually in charge of ten or twenty neighborhood committees, which in turn governed a dozen resident groups (*xiaozu* 小組), each consisting of about thirty to fifty households. Neighborhood committees both acted as an agent of the state and represented the local community to the state—it was the party's way of turning residents without affiliation to work units into subjects of state control and resources available to political maneuvering.[45] Furthermore, as Wang Zheng points out in her study of housewife mobilization in Shanghai in the early 1950s, women's participation in neighborhood work broke down boundaries between the male public (*wai* 外) and female private (*nei* 内) spheres, bringing "state issues directly into individual households." She further argues that "the success of state penetration of urban families . . . was inseparable from the feminization of this public arena."[46]

When Nainai's neighborhood committee was established in 1951, the local policeman in charge of household registration sought her out after talking to the neighbors, who reported that she had no job but good people skills—in other words, she "excelled in linking herself with the masses." Although she had to care for several young children, including a disabled daughter, Nainai was flattered by the invitation and joined up with great enthusiasm. Working outside the home truly gave her, once a child bride, a sense of "liberation" under communism. Nainai first served as a group leader of her neighborhood committee and was in charge of summoning her block of residents to weekly meetings, where, she told me, "cadres read newspapers and gave speeches." When nobody came to the election of people's representatives, she took the ballot box to people's homes. She also participated in sanitation campaigns, going from household to household to see if neighbors had properly disposed of rubbish or dusted their furniture. Before thunderstorms, she made rounds in the alleyway to tell everyone to shut their doors and windows. On holidays, she helped organize celebration parades and make posters—she once mobilized a group of residents to march several kilometers to People's Square, shouting slogans the whole way, though she could not remember what exactly it was all for—"I was just very activist and wanted to take a leading role for everything." Carrying out her tasks diligently, Nainai was soon promoted to the position of security defense chief, the person entrusted with assisting "the People's Government in preventing treason, espionage, theft, and arson, in liquidating counterrevolutionary activity, and in defending state and public security."[47] In practice, this meant interacting with residents and reporting suspicious activities to the local police. Every week she would check up on all the neighborhood's "Four-Type-Elements" (those labeled as landlords, rich peasants, counterrevolutionaries, and "bad elements" convicted of stealing or other minor crimes) and inform the police of their activities—for example, "they have left the alleyway on such and such dates and hours."

With a model worker and Communist Party member as her next-door neighbor, Nainai always tried to outdo Grandma Yang in her activism for the party. Had Nainai a proper job in a state-owned work unit, she too would have become a model worker. Instead, she treated her neighborhood committee work with the passion of a career, found a stimulating public life beyond her domestic chores, and began to adopt the "officialspeak" of Mandarin that persisted as a habit even in her old age when talking to anyone outside her immediate family. Although Nainai prided herself on her good neighborhood relations, her position alone earned her the mixed feeling of circumspection, affection, and occasional disdain from her neighbors, who tacitly regarded all neighborhood committee members as busybodies and spies. "The security defense member of our residential group used to live upstairs from us," Grandma Apricot of Alliance Lane told me in a hushed tone. "Every time we needed to say something in our own house, we had to whisper or go outside for fear that she would inform the police—not that we were doing anything bad, but you could never know how she would interpret it, being such a 'revolutionary' and all."

A "Rightist" Family Surrenders Living Space

While Nainai became an activist in the neighborhood, her husband, my *yeye*, also enthusiastically answered the party's bugle call at his work unit, the Textile Bureau. In the Three-Anti Five-Anti Campaign in 1952, he became the head of a three-person work team to investigate the accounts of a factory-run convenience store and search for signs of corruption. After combing through their account books, Yeye and his work team jotted down the names of suspects and interrogated them one by one for days. As he wrote for me,

> I was so determined to find a culprit, I would tell the person I was interrogating that others had already exposed him and that it would be better to confess to receive a lighter punishment. I did this with everyone and finally, one by one, they "admitted" to having stolen from the factory. I asked them how much, and at first everyone named a minor sum around 10 or 20 yuan. Of course we weren't satisfied with that, so we interrogated them some more and they started naming wild numbers in the hundreds, thousands, and ten thousands. This got us very excited. I began daydreaming about joining the Communist Party and becoming a cadre. But when I reported the results of my investigation to my boss, he furrowed his brows and said: "This can't be right. The convenience store is not even worth 10,000 yuan, how could they have stolen 12,000 yuan?" Dumbstruck, I went back and interrogated those poor clerks again, but none of them would lower the named amount. In the end, my boss came down to speak to them in person, and suddenly they were all innocent again. That was how I lost my big chance.

A few years later Chairman Mao launched the Hundred Flowers Campaign to encourage everyone to speak their minds and offer constructive criticism to the Communist Party. Yeye once again answered the party's call and wrote up criticisms of bureaucratism and official privileges, but instead of being patted on the back this time, he found himself in deep trouble:

A few weeks after I submitted my criticism, the party secretary summoned me and asked me to "admit" that my words had been antisocialist and anti-Communist. I sensed something was wrong and just kept nodding. In the end, he said: "Why don't you write a self-criticism?"

Then meetings were convened: first large mobilization meetings issued directives from above, and then we were divided into smaller group meetings. The group leader asked everyone to expose one another. Then somebody spoke up: "I heard someone complaining about such and such." I can't remember what he said, but I knew he was talking about me, so I got up and read my self-criticism—verbally smacking myself around. Fortunately, it was still civilized back then, not like during the Cultural Revolution, when they made you stand on a chair and "ride the jet" [with your body bent ninety degrees and your arms folded back like broken wings].

First time round, they told me my confession wasn't profound, so I went home and wrote some more. I didn't sleep for days and just kept on digging up guilt from the bottom of my soul. They passed me finally after seven or eight drafts—my writing skill had really been tempered from those days! Denunciations happened in the past too, but they were never very consequential. Being the fool that I was, I thought that this was going to be the same old—after my self-criticism, the leaders would forgive me, and the waves would calm. But after a week or so, everybody stopped talking to me and giving me work. I sat by myself in a corner and had nothing to do all day. I used to read and approve documents. Now they didn't want my approval of anything, so I knew things were serious this time.

After being in limbo for two or three months, I finally received the verdict. A notice was posted on the bulletin board: 'XXX, XXX, XXX, due to their Rightist speech, will be demoted five to eighteen grades down the wage scale." So they cut my salary by a third and sent me down to the countryside for "thought reform."

This was how Yeye came, in his words, "to wear the hundredweight Rightist cap" by the autumn of 1957. The label meant political stigma, social alienation, and economic deprivation not only for its bearer, but also for his family. Besides a sharp decline in the family's standard of living, Nainai lost her position in the neighborhood committee, my father could no longer serve as the student body president despite getting the highest number of votes, and Aunt Treasure was repeatedly rejected by the Communist Youth League. The whole family blamed Yeye for their grievances and tried to "draw a clear line of demarcation" (*huaqing jiexian* 劃清界限) from him. Even in her old age, Nainai adopted the party line when speaking of this: "Just because your *yeye* was a Rightist did not mean that I was a Rightist as well. He was the one who made the mistake, not I. My job was to help him return to the ranks of the People, to help him ideologically so that he would not make mistakes in the future. Your *yeye* was also more careful after that. When he spoke, he tried to speak along the lines of the Communist Party. We would never do anything that ran counter to the party."

Yeye's fall as a Rightist dealt a particularly hard blow to Nainai, who had been preparing for her application for Communist Party membership. Soon after the verdict came down for him, a small poster appeared on the wall next to his front door: "Family of a Rightist should go labor in the countryside." Yeye was already in the countryside, so the poster was clearly directed against Nainai: "It must have been posted by the neighborhood committee cadres. 'Family of a Rightist should go to the countryside' was all that it said, with no criticism of me personally at all. I think they just needed to draw a superficial line between themselves and me so that they wouldn't be accused of befriending me." Since nobody would sit next to her at neighborhood committee meetings, Nainai stopped attending. For all of her earlier revolutionary activism, she was now a target of the revolution. After that, Nainai's favorite aphorism became "the palm cannot see the back of the hand"—you never know what will happen tomorrow, so better not act too smugly today. At once a reminder to herself and a warning against the hubris of others, it suggested at once the future's unpredictability and a sense of fatalism induced by this precarious mode of existence.

Rightists with more severe offenses were sometimes sent to labor reform camps in remote areas of the country, and it was not uncommon for their spouses to file for divorce in a time when divorce remained rare.[48] Yeye's punishment was "light" in that he was sent to the Shanghai suburbs for labor reform:

> Unlike my colleagues at the work unit, peasants treated me kindly, especially after they saw how hard I worked, unlike those cadres sent there for a few weeks to "experience life." The cadres made it a sport to call me over to confess my "thoughts for the day," to repeat and repent my "crimes." However sincerely I did this, they would say: "This crafty Rightist surely knows how to pretend."
>
> I was not used to physical labor, but after a few weeks I could carry sixty-five kilos of manure in one go! My appetite also improved, and I slept soundly at night. Having sunken to the bottom, my feet finally touched ground, and I was free of worries. Later, along with another Rightist, a female comrade, I was assigned the task of delivering vegetables from the suburbs to Shanghai's markets on a wheelbarrow. Walking three or four hours back and forth everyday, we had many conversations about our common plight. If she didn't already have a fiancé and I didn't already have your *nainai*, who knows what might have happened!

Although not permanently banished to the countryside, Yeye felt that he was no longer entitled to an entire two-story house and so, in a display of how well his thoughts had been reformed, yielded his living room on the ground floor to the Housing Management Bureau to be allocated to other needy families. This "voluntary" surrender of space shows that the party had not only a political interest in designating these new "enemies of the people," but also an economic interest. Instead of building additional housing, the government could simply coerce politically problematic individuals to give up housing to proletariats.[49]

To accommodate another family in what used to be their living room, my grandparents added a wall parallel to the staircase to create a narrow passageway to access the back side of the house, including the dining room, kitchen, bathroom, and backyard. The kitchen and bathroom became shared spaces. It was also in 1957 that Yeye's parents came to live with him in Shanghai after his father's retirement from the Shandong coal mine. The elderly couple lived in the back bedroom, while Yeye, Nainai, and their five children lived in the front bedroom.

When I asked Nainai to give an account of the various neighbors they had over the decades, she introduced every family by naming their class status—party members, clerks, workers, officials, and so on—suggesting that she must have been intensely aware of her own status. In the early 1960s, their downstairs neighbor—a worker and a party member—asked to take naps in my grandparents' bedroom during the day because she had night shifts and found her room to be too noisy. My grandparents dared not refuse, so she paved straw mats on the floor upstairs and slept on them in her underwear. During her naps, Yeye dared not go into his own bedroom, and Nainai even took it upon herself to sit in the front yard and tell passersby not to make noise.

The most difficult downstairs neighbors they had were the Wus, another worker couple with four children, who lived there from 1964 to 1974. According to Nainai,

Since they didn't want to have more children, Old Wu got some surgery that frustrated his sex life. This gave him a bad temper, and he often beat his wife—she always had a black eye or a broken ankle. When he got drunk, he would also smash things and bully us. Then the Cultural Revolution began, and Old Wu joined a housing rebel group. They made rounds in the alleyway and pressed all the black elements [anyone with a bad political label] to give up part or all of their housing to the proletariats. One day they started shouting in our backyard: "Rightist Elements Should Free Up Housing for the Revolutionary Masses!" So your *yeye* said, "Let them have our dining room." I wouldn't allow it—we had only three rooms for nine people. How could we give up one more? Besides, if we gave up part of our house, our neighbors might also be pressured to give part of their house—then they would truly hate us. But your *yeye* insisted and argued with me. The housing rebel group leader heard him and praised him for his "good thoughts," and so we had no choice.

Whereas in 1957 Yeye had given up his living room to the state, in 1966 he yielded his dining room to his downstairs neighbors with a vested interest in denouncing him so that they themselves could live more comfortably. Claiming to represent the entire proletariat class, Old Wu and his fellow rebels *used* revolution as an excuse to advance their private interests. When any member of the so-called proletariat could denounce a member of the so-called bourgeoisie—skipping over bureaucratic mediations in the Cultural Revolution—families bearing bad class labels became extremely vulnerable. With little legal protection of their person or property, they relied on the community's compassion and decency to help them through difficult times. Even in their old age, Yeye and Nainai always used an apologetic, ingratiating tone when speaking to people from outside the family. The most important lesson about life they wished to pass on to their children and grandchildren was "Don't offend anyone!" Neither the cadres nor the masses, neither neighbors nor colleagues— after all, you never know how their private grudges might find expression in the next mass campaign.

New Collective Spaces

As "private" housing was repartitioned and redistributed with every politi- cal campaign, new communal spaces were also created in every neigh- borhood, fashioning new experiences of collectivity. In the Great Leap Forward of 1958, urban communes were formed out of existing neighbor- hoods in imitation of rural communes, consisting of community canteens, kindergartens, and alleyway workshops that employed primarily house- wives.[50] The purpose of these new spatial arrangements was to "liberate the women's workforce," as the slogan went, so that instead of doing domes- tic chores at home, housewives would engage in productive and collective labor. Like many products of the Great Leap Forward, most such experi- ments in the collectivization of life and labor were rashly implemented and transitory: the canteens soon reverted back to neighborhood committee meeting halls, and many alleyway workshops closed within a year or two. The alleyway kindergartens, however, had a somewhat more lasting legacy.

By the late 1950s, my mother was one of sixteen children in house No. 111, more than a hundred children in her branch alleyway, and possibly two thousand children in all of Alliance Lane. Since many children had two working parents, the neighborhood created a kindergarten out of the entire first stories of the row of houses from No. 63 to No. 91 and hired former housewives to be its teachers (fig. 1.23). This meant demolishing a row of stone portal gates and the partitions between their sky wells to

FIGURE 1.23 Alliance Lane kindergarten teachers around 1960. Photograph courtesy of Uncle Prosper.

collectivize that space into a long playground, separated from our back alleyway by a long cement wall just over a meter tall. Instead of looking onto the minicourtyards of fifteen private families, the backside of our alleyway branch—our kitchens, pavilion rooms, and terraces—all faced the communal space of the kindergarten playground.

Born in 1952, my mother was among the first generation of children to attend this kindergarten, and I among the last. She fondly recalls the fan her teacher constructed out of old cloth, cardboard, and bamboo, a dozen flapping pieces strung together with a rope that dangled from the ceiling, so that every pull of the rope created a cool breeze to help the toddlers fall asleep during afternoon naps. Born in 1958, Aunt Duckweed, who lived in the front bedroom downstairs from my mother, recalls sitting in a row with other children and being fed a bowl of rice porridge in assembly-line fashion. Among the last generation of children to attend this kindergarten in the 1980s, I still remember the wall beside my bed because I had trouble sleeping and would always pick at the white stucco just above the part painted with a steely green, eventually digging a hole in it. I would see the same green-and-white walls in my primary school, in hospitals, in my mother's work unit in Northeast China, and in Waipo's silk factory. Later, I was to learn from the writer Joseph Brodsky and the filmmaker Jia Zhangke that a colored line on the wall tinted the collective memories of others who lived through socialism in China and the Soviet Union. As Brodsky writes in his memoir *Less Than One*,

> Those stuccoed walls of my classrooms, with their blue horizontal stripe at eye level, running unfailingly across the whole country, like the line of an infinite common denomination: in halls, hospitals, factories, prisons, corridors of communal apartments. The only place I didn't encounter it was in wooden peasant huts. This décor was as maddening as it was omnipresent, and how many times in my life would I catch myself peering mindlessly at this blue two-inch-wide stripe, taking it sometimes for a sea horizon, sometimes for an embodiment of nothingness itself. . . . They were not colors themselves but hints of colors, which might be interrupted only by alternating patches of brown: doors. Closed, half open. And through the half-open door you could see another room with the same distribution of gray and white marked by the blue stripe. Plus a portrait of Lenin and a world map.[51]

When asked in an interview why there is a green tinge throughout his film *24 City (Ershisi chengji* 二十四城記, 2008), on the memory of workers in a state-owned factory in Sichuan, filmmaker Jia Zhangke replied: "This color comes from my memory of life in the late 1970s and 80s, when many families in northern China painted the lower parts of their interior walls in green as high as one meter. To a child who was short, as I was, that green was the color I met everyday. Moreover, the color not only appeared on the walls of homes but also in all kinds of workplaces. Everywhere, in hospitals, offices, classrooms, all sorts of public places had their walls painted this color. When you went into state-run factories, you would see the green color on those machines and walls."[52]

The green paint on the walls of collective spaces served as a backdrop to the equally omnipresent red banners used to implement state policies in the alleyways, schools, and work units. While a member of the neighborhood committee, Nainai used her own money to buy the red cloth for the propaganda banner. All the schoolchildren of the neighborhood wore red scarves and during the Cultural Revolution red armbands. Even in the 2000s, old women wearing red armbands patrolled the entrances to alleyways as a kind of informal neighborhood watch.

Besides these colors, another marker and creator of collective space during the socialist era was the loudspeaker, installed in every factory, school, and kindergarten, broadcasting revolutionary songs or speeches at regular hours to weave mass propaganda into the fabric of everyday life. Especially in the Great Leap Forward, my father recalls, the loudspeaker of the local factory across from his house sang even during night shifts: "We the workers have the power! Oh yes, we the workers have the power." The song evoked terror for my father's family because they were the "targets of proletarian dictatorship," whereas my mother's worker parents, Waigong and Waipo, hummed it with nostalgia. Even in my own childhood in the 1980s, Waigong continued his old habit of doing morning exercises on the terrace to the calisthenics music from the loudspeakers of the kindergarten below.

While children were collectivized into kindergartens, housewives were also mobilized into the labor force during the Great Leap Forward, and every Shanghai neighborhood created a few alleyway workshops (*lilong gongchang* 里弄工廠) or manufacturing teams (*shengchanzu* 生產組) that employed more than 100,000 new workers by the end of 1958.[53] The propaganda film *Women of the Great Leap Forward* (*Wanzi qianhong zongshi chun* 萬紫千紅總是春, 1959) tells the story of how the housewives of a *shikumen* alleyway were "liberated" from the conservative attitudes of their husbands and mothers-in-law to work in newly founded sewing, embroidery, and toy-making workshops. In a subplot, one woman who bought a new sewing machine remained unwilling to join the sewing workshop until she was besieged by pangs of guilt upon seeing others rushing to finish an order of children's winter jackets.[54] In contrast to this film's plot, Nainai sold her only jewelry—a gold ring and necklace—to buy a sewing machine with the hope of joining a sewing workshop to supplement the family income (also see "Nainai's Sewing Machine" in chapter 2). The sewing workshop in her alleyway never materialized, however, so Nainai joined a road-paving team instead:

> Other women I worked with were the bourgeois wives of doctors and engineers; they were neither used to nor willing to do this kind of physical labor, so none could eat bitterness the way I could. Since

I worked the hardest, they made me the leader of Team No. 8, though they couldn't officially write my name because I was a Rightist family member. We lugged wheelbarrows filled with pebbles and paved them on the ground before machines came to spread the asphalt. The other women in my team called me "Rice Bucket" because I was also in charge of bringing them meals. How young I was then, with boundless energy! If I got tired, I would just take the plank off my wheelbarrow and sleep on the ground. Everybody was covered with dust from head to toe, but our team outperformed every other team, and the cadres praised us at the celebration when the road was finished.

From confinement to the home by order of her mother-in-law in the 1940s, Nainai would even sleep on the streets by the end of the 1950s in order to "build socialism" and provide a meager but necessary supplement to the household income. Decades later, the road she had worked on expanded into an arterial thoroughfare whizzing with traffic and, like roads everywhere, without memory of its builders. In 1969 and 1970, Nainai and other housewives later also volunteered their labor for public projects such as digging nuclear bunkers in the community garden after the Sino–Soviet split. While uprooting the four Japanese cherry trees to make room for bunkers, Nainai recalled, she and fellow diggers were covered in fallen petals. By then, dystopian fears of a third world war had supplanted the utopian visions of the Great Leap Forward, giving urgency and sanctity to those dark burrows in the ground dug with foolhardy labor. During simulated air-raid siren drills, Nainai learned to shepherd residents to an assembly area and assist firefighters by unfolding water pipes.[55] To commend her activism and service, the neighborhood committee rewarded her with an enamel basin that she continued to use into her old age.

Sent Down to the Countryside

The Maoist organization of individuals into collectives transcended and divided families, handling them like machine parts that could be dismantled and reassembled. Industrial workers such as my maternal grandparents took three rotating shifts at the factory and had to attend endless meetings, but they considered themselves lucky and never took their foothold in Shanghai for granted. "Back then they sent you to the countryside for the slightest trifle," Waipo told me and gave the example of the nanny they hired to take care of my uncle in the late 1950s. When taking the baby out for a stroll, she was caught stealing a piece of fabric and immediately sent to a labor reform camp. Waipo could recall three other coworkers at her factory banished from Shanghai: one was a Rightist; another had inadvertently set the factory dormitory on fire while smoking in bed to drive out mosquitoes; and a third "spread rumors" of people starving to death when he returned from his native village in 1959. When giving an account of neighbors who lived in the same house or adjacent ones, she similarly recalled several women whose husbands were labeled some kind of counterrevolutionary and were hence always absent (see "Several Lifetimes to a Life" in chapter 3).

Apart from a form of punishment for political or social deviancy, many "volunteers" were also summoned to leave the city for the countryside for political reasons. By 1962, thanks to Yeye's "good behavior" during thought reform through labor, his Rightist cap was lifted, and he received a small raise—so excited was his entire family over this that they shed tears of gratitude at the "mass assembly to take off the cap" (*zhaimao dahui* 摘帽大會). Yet the cap remained in the hands of the "revolutionary masses," and if ever he did or said something wrong again, they could put it right back on his head. In the same year, rumors had it that Chiang Kai-shek planned a counterattack of the mainland, and a campaign was under way to disperse the urban population. Feeling the pressure at his work unit, Yeye signed up as a "volunteer" to move his entire family to the country's interior provinces, but Nainai refused to leave Shanghai and threatened him with divorce. For all her overt demonstrations of revolutionary spirit in the neighborhood, Nainai was not ready to sacrifice her family's foothold in the city with the best welfare provisions in the country. Finally, Yeye withdrew his registration with trepidation. Fortunately, the liberal political atmosphere of the time allowed this instance of disobedience to pass without dire consequences.

In the late 1960s and the early 1970s, the Going Up the Mountains and Down to the Countryside movement would banish at least one child per urban household into the countryside with few exceptions.[56] Having to send remittances back to their country relatives ever since coming to Shanghai in the 1940s, Waigong and Waipo were all too conscious of the stark disparity between urban and rural conditions. When finally reconciled to the inevitability of sending their sixteen-year-old daughter, my mother, to the countryside, they suggested that she marry a cousin in Waipo's native village in nearby Zhejiang. Yet my mother was still more captivated by the revolutionary romanticism of slogans such as "In the spacious sky and earth lies a great career to change the countryside's backward appearance." Together with her classmates, she registered for the Heilongjiang Production and Construction Corps and went to the Great Northern Wilderness to be "tempered in the revolutionary furnace," to "take roots in the countryside," and to be "reeducated by the lower and middle peasants," as the popular slogans of the time went. This brought worry as well as relief to my grandparents because my mother's choice of going so far away meant that their other children could stay in Shanghai.

Unlike my mother's "proletariat family," a "Rightist family" such as my father's was under pressure to send more than one child to the countryside to show loyalty to the party. In 1968, my father joined the first group of Shanghai youths to go to the Great Northern Wilderness—the head of the rooster that is the shape of China's map. Aunt Treasure, his eldest sister, who had just graduated from university, volunteered to go to the rooster's tail in Xinjiang. His younger sister, Aunt Bean, went to Jiangxi in the early 1970s. Whether with idealistic fervor or pragmatic resignation, they and more than a million other Shanghainese youths left home without knowing whether they would or could ever return.[57]

By 1972, the revolutionary broom even swept apart the family of Yeye and Nainai's model worker neighbor. Grandma Yang's husband, Grandpa Zhu, had to move along with his entire sewing machine factory to Shaanxi as part of the Third Front, a massive program to create industrial base areas in southwestern and western China after the worsening of Sino–Soviet relations.[58] When asked about it three decades later, Grandpa Zhu recalled: "We had no choice but still considered it a great honor to go. Chairman Mao said he could not sleep at night if we didn't build up the Third Front, so the slogan for us was to 'give Chairman Mao a good night's sleep.' Living conditions there couldn't compare with Shanghai, but the locals treated us like aristocrats, and the local cadres all sent their children to work in our factory with the hope of finding Shanghainese sons- and daughters-in-law. We worked Sundays, too, to save up vacation time, but even then we could come home only for two weeks every year."

With the end of the Cultural Revolution, most urbanites once sent down to the countryside returned, sometimes with new spouses and children. Yet the joy of rehabilitation, return, and reunion quickly dissipated into a battle of egos on the ruins of revolutionary idealism. Self-sacrifice in the name of the motherland or for the sake of their families sometimes soured into feelings of betrayal, senses of entitlement, and penurious calculations over limited resources. In Shanghai, the housing shortage became especially acute as the generation born in the 1950s now needed to make their own nests.

A New Generation Comes of Age (1970s–1980s)

Aunt Pearl's Shanty: An "Illegal Structure"

After learning of Shanghai's famed variety of international building styles,[59] I began paying special attention to the architecture of my native city over many summer returns. Yet rather than the neoclassical and art deco buildings on the Bund, the traditional Chinese gardens and temples of the Old Town area, or the futuristic skyscrapers that sprang up in Pudong, what has continued to catch my eye and imagination was the one type of architecture with no distinct style at all—the so-called illegal structure (*weizhang jianzhu* 違章建築). Often built in a former backyard or a terrace with wood, brick, or cement, their roofs might consist of tiles, metal plates, or plastic boards—whatever construction material was available to their builders. These shacks and shanties were often superimposed on top of uniformly designed houses like patches of homespun cloth on a factory-made dress, sometimes so densely spread that the original fabric was no longer visible. Though eyesores in the landscape, these illegal structures accommodated an overspill of the city's population, who would remember them as home.

By the 1990s, in the former Japanese company housing on Pingliang Road an illegal structure had been built in almost every backyard and front yard. These architectural wings and tentacles gave the once classy white-collar neighborhood the squalid look of an urban slum. One of the pioneers of this transformation was the shanty in my grandparents' backyard, which they built in 1974 for Aunt Pearl, their second born (fig. 1.24). Aunt Pearl was ten months old when Shanghai was besieged by the Communists in May 1949. At this juncture, she had a fever that did not subside for days, and since most hospitals in the neighborhood had shut down, she did not receive adequate treatment for what Yeye and Nainai only later learned was polio. With the left side of her body completely paralyzed, she could not walk and was considered unfit for school, so she learned to read and write on her own,

asking Yeye and her siblings to teach her whenever they had a moment to spare. Her disability also rendered her unfit for employment, so she was only able to find odd jobs here and there through the neighborhood committee—sewing buttons and buttonholes on Mao suits, knitting the fingers on white factory gloves, and making little paper bags for roach poison—all work that could be done at home. Once she also tried to get a job in an alleyway workshop, but the man in charge wanted to watch her go to the toilet on her own to prove her self-reliance. "How could people be so obscene?" Nainai would still recall this incident many years later with clenched teeth.

FIGURE 1.24 Aunt Pearl in the early 1970s.

Thus deprived of a public life, Aunt Pearl spent almost the entire thirty-six years of her life at her parents' home. After Yeye and Nainai lost all their territory on the first floor except the kitchen and the bathroom in 1966, Pearl had to be carried up and down a steep flight of stairs on a daily basis, so Yeye and Nainai repeatedly petitioned the Housing Management Bureau for permission to build a shanty in the backyard (fig. 1.25). Finally, an official at the bureau gave his verbal consent, but their downstairs neighbor Old Wu had planted a fig tree in the backyard and refused to cut it down no matter how Nainai tried to bribe or plead with his family. In the end, they built the shanty around the tree, so that it had an L shape, with the tree in the missing corner and just enough room for a bed, a desk, and a homemade wheelchair. As no contractors were available, my grandparents themselves bought building materials from a construction site and dragged carts of bricks and cement to their backyard. Old Wang, a neighbor who was a bricklayer, undertook the task of building the shanty, in part because, according to Nainai, Pearl had knitted several sweaters for his wife: "Such a good man! He refused to take our money, so we bought construction material and repaid him that way."[60]

FIGURE 1.25 In 1974, Yeye and Nainai constructed a shanty for their polio-stricken daughter Pearl in the backyard of the house (also see fig. 1.26F). Drawing by my parents.

After a few months, Old Wu moved off to a new apartment. Before a new family moved in, sympathetic neighbors helped my grandparents saw off the tree so the missing corner of the shanty could be filled in. In addition, Old Wang installed a faucet and a small sink low enough for Pearl in her wheelchair. Because the sewer pipes were buried right beneath the shanty, it also occurred to him to dig a hole into the sewer and cover it with an iron lid, so that Pearl could empty her chamber pot on her own and clean it with tap water a few steps away. "He knew that I would not be around forever to take care of her," said Nainai.

Despite such small conveniences, the shanty was a miserable place to live. It was freezing in winter and could be heated only by boiling water, which would leave behind a damp cold at night that penetrated the bones. The room also flooded in thunderstorms and constantly smelled of sewage. Aunt Pearl tried to make the best out of what she had. Her door and windows were always wide open during the day for ventilation, and if the weather happened to be nice, she would sit outside to knit, read, or chat with the neighbors. When Yeye and Nainai were able to buy her a better wheelchair that she could steer herself, she often spent her days at a nearby park and made a few friends, including a man who harbored romantic intentions toward her. Yet in 1982 Aunt Pearl was diagnosed with leukemia. As her illness became quite advanced, she would wheel herself into the park with a small packet of tea and chew on the leaves to alleviate the pain. "A neighbor saw this and told me," Nainai recalled. "Pearl herself never complained, and it was not until after her death that I noticed how soggy her beddings were. She had lived in all that mildew for all those years!"

In the last two years of her life, Aunt Pearl did not have any peace at home, as described in the next section. After her death in 1984, Yeye moved into the shanty with Nainai, yet Aunt Pearl remained an ominous presence in the room—in the form of a three-by-five color photograph on the cupboard, which had attained the status of a deity for Yeye and Nainai, who ate, slept, and quarreled for the next decade and a half under her eyes.

How Yeye and Nainai Lost Housing to Their Children

In the 1950s and 1960s, Yeye and Nainai had surrendered the first story of their house to outsiders because of his Rightist status, but in the late 1970s and early 1980s they had to yield the second story of their home to two married children. With seven adults and two children sharing less than 30 square meters, the house turned into a war zone. One Berlin Wall after another—as Yeye called them—were built to separate the three families—which should have been one extended family—from each other, yet hot battles still erupted in this cold war.

In 1979, like half a million Rightists across the country, Yeye was "rehabilitated." In the same year, most sent-down youths were allowed to return to their native cities—as long as they remained unmarried in the countryside.[61] Yet Aunt Bean, my grandparents' third daughter, not only married a man from the Jiangxi countryside, but also had a three-year-old son with her husband, Uncle Zhao. In 1978, Uncle Zhao was admitted to a university in Shanghai, so Yeye and Nainai let their son-in-law share their back bedroom with their youngest son, Uncle Lucky. At that point, Yeye's parents had recently passed away, and both their eldest daughter and eldest son had jobs elsewhere without plans of returning to Shanghai. In order to unite Uncle Zhao and Aunt Bean in the same city, Yeye retired early and gave his job to Aunt Bean by the policy of *dingti*

頂替 (replacement).[62] Ordinarily, only someone with an urban household registration could take over his or her parent's place in a work unit, but since Yeye was recently rehabilitated as a "wrongly labeled Rightist" and his superiors felt indebted to him, they made an exception for his daughter. This way Yeye wouldn't bother them about the two decades' worth of salary deductions as a result of his Rightist status. After returning to Shanghai, Aunt Bean, Uncle Zhao, and their son lived in the back bedroom of my grandparents' house, but Yeye and Nainai expected Uncle Zhao to be allocated a new apartment after finding a job and so did not admit him into their household registration booklet.

Three years later, in 1982, Uncle Lucky found a girlfriend and wanted to get married. In theory, they could apply to their work units or the municipal housing bureau for housing, but the queues for both were impossibly long.[63] Holding on to what he himself later called "the feudal notion that daughters should marry out but sons should stay home," Yeye admitted Uncle Lucky's fiancée, Aunt May, into his household registration booklet months before the wedding. Only afterward did family discussion begin over how to divide up two bedrooms between two young couples and one old couple. Aunt Bean and Uncle Lucky both wanted the south-facing front bedroom, which was bigger and sunnier than the north-facing back bedroom.

In the end, Yeye and Nainai gave the front bedroom to Uncle Lucky, who decorated it anew with Westernized furniture and new electric appliances (see "Petty Urbanites" in chapter 2). Uncle Lucky also carved out a 3-square-meter windowless room for Nainai, and Yeye moved into a 2-square-meter closet beneath the stairs (fig. 1.26). Sensing that her presence in that cubbyhole—only a thin wooden board away from the marriage chamber of her son and his new bride—might be more than a nuisance, Nainai promptly moved into the shanty with Aunt Pearl. Yeye and Nainai initially believed that their sacrifices would satisfy everyone, but their daughter and son-in-law were furious at their favoritism and showed their discontent everyday.

The toilet and the kitchen (about 8 square meters with two taps and four gas stovetops) were now shared between four households. Nainai tried to avoid the throng by cooking lunch and dinner in the morning, but this hardly alleviated the tension. As with all communal kitchens and hallways in Shanghai homes at the time, every family conquered space with things—stools and boxes, pots and pans and basins. Private property

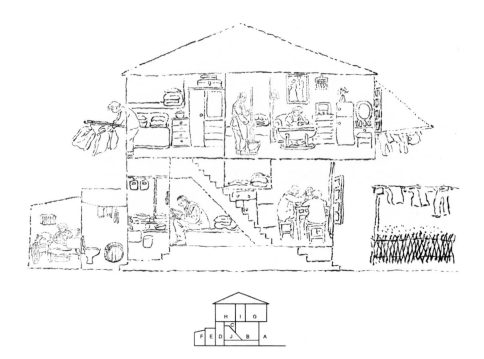

FIGURE 1.26 Cross-section view of No. 183 Lane 1695 in the early 1980s (compare with fig. 1.12). After being labeled a Rightist, Yeye gave up the living room (B) to the Housing Management Bureau in 1957 and then also the dining room (C) to the worker family downstairs in 1966. The kitchen (D) and the toilet (E) became communal spaces. In 1974, Yeye and Nainai built a shanty for Aunt Pearl in the backyard (F, see fig. 1.25). In the early 1980s, Yeye and Nainai gave the north-facing back bedroom (H) to their married daughter Bean and the south-facing front bedroom (G) to their married son Lucky, who carved out a small section (I) for Nainai, while Yeye lived in a closet underneath the staircase (J) (also see "Petty Urbanites" in chapter 2).

placed in communal areas was often not worth very much to their owners, yet endless battles were fought over them. As Svetlana Boym writes of the Soviet communal apartment, "in circumstances of extreme overcrowdedness and imposed collectivity there is an extreme—almost obsessive—protection of minimal individual property."[64] In those days, every door and window, every drawer and cabinet were clamped with bolts and locks. One family's junk sleeping in the dusty corner of a narrow stairway would become another family's stumbling block—until it faced a rude awakening one morning as it got smashed to pieces.

For about three years, Yeye lived like a mouse in the triangular closet under the stairs that resembled a single compartment in the second-class wagon of a night train. At the foot of his small bed was just enough leg room that he could slouch at his desk, a wooden plank the size of a lap-top, and above this he had nailed another piece of wood as his bookshelf. Every morning and evening, his son-in-law would take his bicycle through the narrow passage adjacent to his cell, bumping it against the wooden partition. This created an earthquake for Yeye, for the single light bulb above his head would shake to and fro, and the crashing sound, magnified through reverberations, made his heart thump wildly. "Could you please not bump your bicycle against my wall?" Yeye asked his son-in-law one day. "I can't help it—this passage is too narrow." So Yeye demonstrated by taking Uncle Zhao's bicycle and walking with it from one end of the passage to the other and back without making a sound. Sometimes Uncle Zhao also came down to the kitchen in the evening for this or that, and his momentary singing would always interrupt Yeye's reading for the rest of the night, but Yeye dared not raise his voice for fear that his son and son-in-law would start another brawl.

After six years of domestic warfare, Uncle Lucky managed to immigrate abroad with his wife and daughter in 1990, so Yeye and Nainai moved out of the shanty back into the house proper. In 1992, Uncle Zhao's work unit finally allocated him and his family a two-bedroom apartment in the newly developing Pudong, but, even so, Aunt Bean asked Yeye to keep her son Afu on his household registration booklet to enhance his chances at the university examinations. Since Afu was also registered under his father's new apartment, granted on the basis of a three-person household, he was illegally registered in both places, yet the excuse given—that Yeye and Nainai needed their grandson to take care of them—won over the neigh-borhood committee's sympathies. Aunt Bean reassured Yeye and Nainai that as soon as Afu was admitted to university, they would take his name off the household register, and so Yeye and Nainai complied. Meanwhile, Aunt Bean and Uncle Zhao bought new furniture for the new apartment and left all their old furniture in the back room. Six years later, although Afu had already graduated from college, he remained registered under my grandparents' household. Yeye and Nainai feared that Afu would get married and then inherit the house after their deaths. So once again they asked his parents to cancel Afu's household registration, but Uncle Zhao answered them with "This is not your house. It's state housing!"

In 1998, the municipality allowed inhabitants of certain state-owned housing to buy their living spaces at a discounted price. This way, they would be free to sell their apartments at a higher market price.[65] With the stakes raised, Yeye and Nainai decided to take the issue to court. They wanted to sue their daughter and son-in-law for parent abuse and house usurpation, but their lawyer advised them to sue their grandson instead for his illegal double household registration. Yeye and Nainai won, and the court ordered the cancellation of Afu's registration in the old house and the removal of the furniture. "The day they removed their junk from the back room," Yeye told me, "was one of the happiest days of my life."

From Marlboro Cigarettes to an Apartment: How Waigong and Waipo Secured Housing for Uncle Strong

My maternal grandparents, Waigong and Waipo, had three daughters and a son. By 1983, they had successfully married their first two daughters to men with housing elsewhere. Daughters could marry out, but where would the "marriage chamber" of their only son come from? An ordinary worker at a moribund state-owned blanket factory, Uncle Strong did not stand a chance of receiving any housing allocation. The natural solution, of course, was to do what Yeye and Nainai did—let the married son have half or most of the apartment—yet Waigong and Waipo found this option unacceptable. As a forecast of what would happen if they did let their son share their house, however much they loved him, Waigong repeated an aphorism from his grandmother: "Parents say: Won't my children grow up yet? Children say: Won't my parents die yet?"

Waigong and Waipo were no better connected with the housing authorities than Yeye and Nainai. They did, however, have a better understanding of what must be done to establish such connections. In 1984, Waipo heard from a distant relative about a privately constructed house (*sifang* 私房)[66] for sale at 1,500 yuan—about the same amount she and Waigong had in their lifelong savings. It was a single-story house with just one room and a loft, crudely built by the owners in a nearby hutment in the 1950s. Although Uncle Strong did not even have a girlfriend at the time, Waigong and Waipo paid for the flat without bargaining. Soon after the transaction, the hutment was marked for demolition in an urban-renewal project, and all registered residents were going to be allocated new apartments. This would have been a dream come true except that Uncle Strong had not yet moved out of his parents' household. Now that the household registration for the entire hutment was frozen,[67] he would be entitled to no housing at all after the demolition.

Fortunately, my sociable *waipo* learned that the man in charge of relocation for that area happened to be the son of the woman who delivered milk to our alleyway every morning. Waipo found out his address from her and went with Waigong and their savvy journalist son-in-law to ask for help:

> We bought expensive foreign cigarettes from the Friendship Store—Marlboros, they were called—and knocked on their door.[68] Asi, the milk delivery woman's son, was playing poker with his brothers. They didn't even look at us when we talked to them. Luckily, your aunt's husband worked as a journalist and had all sorts of connections—he had business cards and privileged access to all kinds of stuff. From his demeanor, Asi gathered that he was no ordinary man, and he finally came around and accepted our cigarettes. Then we also brought them these hard-to-get concert tickets and moon cakes for the Mid-autumn Festival. After several more kissing-up trips like these, he finally agreed to help.

Meanwhile, Uncle Strong moved some furniture as well as some pots and pans into the hut they bought. They cooked and ate dinner there on a coal stove once or twice a week; Uncle Strong slept there on weekdays; and Waipo started random conversations with the neighbors. All this served to prove themselves as the hut's legitimate residents. Not that the neighbors had any power, but my grandparents thought it wouldn't hurt to have the good opinion of the masses.

After three years' worth of hassles—Waigong worried so much he lost all of his hair—Uncle Strong was relocated to a room in a workers' new village built in the 1950s with a communal kitchen and bathroom shared between four families. This was not bad considering that without Asi's help he could have been given nothing at all or at most a pavilion room. Thereafter, my grandparents thanked Asi every year by taking him gifts and inviting him to their New Year's feasts. "It was as though we were eternally in his debt," Waipo often sighed and shook her head.

The story of how Waigong and Waipo procured housing for Uncle Strong intertwined three distinct modes of exchange in the Chinese urban political and cultural economy of the 1980s, as outlined by anthropologist

Mayfair Yang: the state redistributive economy, the gift economy, and a resurgent petty-commodity economy.[69] When Uncle Strong's work unit failed to provide him with housing under the state redistributive economy, my grandparents resorted to the resurgent petty-commodity economy, which allowed them to *purchase* a privately owned flat. When city planners decided to tear down the shantytown and allot its residents new apartments, my grandparents used the gift economy to fully secure their son's claim to a new apartment.

Thanks to their shrewd maneuvers of these public and private modes of exchange, Waigong and Waipo were able to maintain a separate peace in their own kingdom on the third floor of No. 111 Alliance Lane. In the late 1980s, my parents went abroad and left me in my grandparents' care for three and half years. On Sundays, Waigong would kill a chicken and cook a big feast for a family gathering, when my aunts and uncles and cousins came over for dinner. This was how my grandparents liked to see their married children, as cordial guests and temporary sojourners.

Alleyway Homes as a Microhistorical Stage

Having traced the territorial and demographic changes of the two alleyway homes, we might envision these spaces on a theatrical stage on which a century of history unfolded.[70] The various residents and sojourners are the dramatis personae who enter and exit, climb or descend, emerge into the spotlight or retreat into the background. Every historical era is another act, with changes in lighting, backdrop, and musical score. The basic structure of the set stays the same, yet the characters rearrange their positions on the set and sometimes rearrange the set itself. When they proliferate, they divide and subdivide the stage into multiple stages that juxtapose comedy and tragedy, melodrama, romance, and farce. At the same time, the characters are spectators of one another's lives as dramas of upward mobility and familial decline crisscross at staircases, as scenes of drudgery and leisure, separation and reunion, tyranny and liberation reflect off of each other through the windows and across the alleyways.

Act 1, Republican Era. Against the backdrop of smokestacks from the British American Tobacco factory and a Japanese cotton mill, a three-story *shikumen* house on stage left and a Japanese-style house with a garden on stage right. In the former, three generations of the Wang family conduct their lives according to traditional Confucian hierarchy, with occasional melodramatic outbursts. Typical scenes: on the ground floor, Apricot's grandmother hosts a mahjong game with neighbors while maids pour tea; in the pavilion room, a tailor makes clothes and tells stories to three children; on the third floor, Apricot's parents fight over a concubine. In the other house, a Japanese nuclear family perform everyday routines in pantomime on *tatami* mats and with *shōji* sliding doors, until their radio broadcasts the Showa emperor's surrender, whereby they pack and exit in a rush. Enter Waigong and Waipo, adolescents dressed like country bumpkins who work from dawn to dusk in a silk filature in a *shikumen* house while marveling at Shanghai's urban civilization. Meanwhile, Yeye in a Western suit and Nainai in a *qipao* move into the Japanese house with a little daughter, speak of finally having a home after almost a decade of refugeehood.

Act 2, Communist Liberation. With footage of the People's Liberation Army parade on Nanjing Road as the projected backdrop, the Wang family in the *shikumen* house holds an elaborate wedding for Apricot. As the projection changes to a mass rally against counterrevolutionaries that ends with the sound of gunshots, old Mrs. Wang sublets rooms in the *shikumen* house to four worker families, including Waigong and Waipo, who ascend first to the second and then to the third floor. Lights slowly dim over this motley crowd in a flurry of washing, cutting, and cooking in common areas. Spotlight stage right on Model Worker Yang's family as they move with gongs and drums next door to Yeye and Nainai. A bustling scene from Nainai's neighborhood committee work is suddenly interrupted by Yeye's soliloquy—his confessions of thought crimes as a Rightist. He changes into peasant clothes and carries two buckets of manure on a shoulder pole offstage, while another worker family moves into his living room. On the cue of revolutionary songs, processions of women, children, adolescents, and workers carrying red banners cross the center stage in turn, taking along with them various members of the two alleyway homes.

Act 3, Late Socialism. Smog over the industrial skyline. Muffled loudspeaker sounds. Wearing a dark-blue Mao suit, Yeye carries his paralyzed adult daughter Pearl down the steep flight of stairs. They cross a narrow passageway into the backyard, where Nainai and two neighbors build a shanty for Aunt Pearl to live out her remaining years. Aunt Bean, a sentdown youth, returns and moves into the back bedroom upstairs with her husband and son. Uncle Lucky remodels the front bedroom for his chic new bride. Stage left, Waigong and Waipo carry packs of foreign cigarettes to curry favor with housing officials with the hope of procuring an apartment for their son. Throughout the act, everyone coming onstage adds another piece to the set, be it a wooden partition, a piece of furniture, or an electric appliance, so that the two houses are increasingly fragmented and cluttered even as they are being renovated and modernized. No sooner does a quarrel subside than another commotion escalates, and in the midst of all this Yeye tries to read inside a closet under the stairs.

2

HAVEN

CHAPTER 1 TREATED SHANGHAI HOMES as *housing*, physical territories marked by tangible boundaries—a roof over one's head, a floor beneath one's feet, and walls on all sides to shut out the wind. It also discussed home as landed property to which different individuals and families laid claims in the Republican, Maoist, and post-Mao eras. Yet it is not just bricks and concrete that make a place "home," nor any certificates of ownership or other entitlements to housing as scarce resource or valued commodity. This chapter, by contrast, considers Shanghai homes to be psychological havens grounded in material artifacts, familial and familiar domains that provide an antidote to the teleological progress of history. Like Noah's ark floating in the apocalyptic flood of war and revolution, Shanghai alleyway homes assembled within them miscellaneous menageries of characters who inscribed their precarious and resilient life histories onto domestic objects. Also like Noah's ark, many Shanghai homes only came into being through historical ruptures that uprooted individuals and families from their native places and extended families. Making a home in Shanghai redefined the meaning of home for them, while the Communist Revolution reconfigured the boundaries between private and public spheres.

Focusing on the material contents of homes and their emotional reverberations, the central inquiry of this chapter concerns revolution and private life in Shanghai alleyways from the 1940s to the 1990s. It was in the socialist period that the city turned into "home" for most of its population, yet this era also saw an unprecedented intervention of political power into neighborhoods, families, and individual psyches. Through a succession of mass campaigns starting in 1949, the Communist Party sought to abolish the private realm along with private property through new bureaucracies of surveillance, public confessions and denunciations, and a new theology of selflessness. At the same time, however, these relentless campaigns banished much public culture from the Republican era into private spaces, so that until the home searches of the Cultural Revolution alleyway homes became a sanctuary for people, things, discourses, habits, and beliefs without proper places in the "new society." Past service to the old regime became family secrets, religious prayers became clandestine practices, and a Westernized education and overseas connections became disgraceful liabilities. Beyond the privatization of so-called feudal or bourgeois remnants, invasive mass movements created indelible shadows in the individual psyches of participants, victims, and bystanders, who continued being haunted by nightmares and pricks of conscience for decades to come.

The first section chronicles the palimpsest histories of an assortment of patina-ridden objects found in the two alleyway homes of my grandparents—a grain bed, a writing desk, a sewing machine, a handful of photos, and radios. The second section focuses on the besieged privacy of homes during the Cultural Revolution and on how this "unprecedented" mass movement played out in the more intimate spaces of the alleyway. The third and fourth sections discuss the reinvention of petty bourgeois privacy in the early reform era and a pervasive sense of nostalgia for the alleyway lifestyle in the age of its extinction.

Domestic Artifacts as Historical Witnesses

Homes are assemblages of artifacts familiar to the eyes, ears, nose, tongue, and fingers, providing a sense of comfort and continuity, solace and security in an uncertain world. They are what the Shanghai writer Eileen Chang calls the "placid and static" aspects of human life, the prosaic, earthbound, and harmonious background for uplifting and dynamic struggles.[1] Embedded within these domestic objects are both historical layers and personal recollections of a family's roots and routes. Some objects have traveled over great distances; some have been passed down from generation to generation; some are mementos of the deceased; and others are relics of a bygone world. As historical time and geographic space crystallize into material forms, such artifacts can be fruitful sites to glean the accumulated human impact of modern Chinese history.

Even more than the physical dimensions of these homes, artifacts played a major role in constituting the private realm in Shanghai alleyways. After all, when individuals had no particular place to call their own, personal belongings could take on great symbolic value.[2] A personal artifact can be a souvenir for a space and time lost to its holder or a metaphor for a yet unrealized future, even if the object itself was originally mass-produced. The souvenir, according to Susan Stewart, "moves history into private time" as it "reduces the public, the monumental, and the three-dimensional into the miniature [and] that which can be appropriated within the privatized view of the individual subject." As such, it also evokes a "narrative of origins" that "seeks to reconcile the disparity between interiority and exteriority, subject and object, signifier and signified."[3] Before market reform accelerated the turnover of everyday artifacts into expendable commodities, many items that furnished Shanghai alleyway homes had a long lifespan and bore witness to the radical upheavals of their owners' lives. The following vignettes centering on household objects seek to tease out their palimpsests of public history and private experiences.

The Grain Bed in the Attic

Inside their tiny attic on the third floor of No. 111 Alliance Lane, Waigong and Waipo kept a "grain bed" as broad and deep, clumsy and sturdy as a coffin, except that it was painted auspiciously red (see fig. 1.17A). The oldest piece of furniture in their home, this grain bed was originally a part of Waigong's paternal grandmother's dowry, which came together with a rice paddy.[4] Every autumn tenant farmers would bring two loads of grain harvested from her rice paddy and pour them into the bed. This would have been enough to feed her until the following harvest, but Waigong's grandmother never ate from this bed and always saved the surplus grain to sell in the spring, when the price was highest, and then deposited the silver dollars at a local medicine shop that promised a high interest rate to its shareholders. After all, why should she eat from her own dowry when her husband, Waigong's grandfather (fig. 2.1), also owned land and a "hundred items shop" in town?

When Waigong was eight years old, his paternal grandfather's shop burned down, and the family had to sell land to pay back creditors. The old man died soon afterward, and the family fell into decline. Waigong's

father tried out a few small businesses, but they all ended in failure, and it became a challenge to feed the many mouths in the family. Still, Waigong's grandmother managed to put away *her* grain inside *her* bed, no matter how her son and daughter-in-law resented her hoarding and her mean struggle for self-reliance. A skinny boy with a big appetite, Waigong looked forward to the annual feasts at the grave-sweeping festival, when the entire clan gathered to make offerings to their ancestors, who had bequeathed land that rotated between the descendants for this very purpose. It was as if the ancestor had planted a tree upon his death, and the roots continued giving nourishment, however meager, to its branches.

FIGURE 2.1 Waigong's grandfather around 1940. The grain bed in the attic (see fig. 1.17A) was his wife's dowry.

Throughout Waigong's adolescence in the 1940s, his mother took him and his siblings to *her* mother's house in the nearby countryside to "eat for a couple of weeks" since his maternal grandmother had her own rice paddies as part of her dowry. Her husband had died early but had bequeathed quite a bit of land to their two sons, whom Waigong called Big Uncle and Little Uncle. Big Uncle's eldest daughter had been promised at birth to a well-to-do Shanghai family, but the local bandit leader wanted to have her and threatened to burn down their house, so Big Uncle had to acquiesce. The wedding took on the appearance of a happy and bustling affair, and Big Uncle learned to accept the bandit as his son-in-law. Later, the local government got wind of this and sent a squad to confiscate goods from this "family of bandits." Waigong happened to be visiting and watched a dozen men with swords charge into Big Uncle's house and carry entire trunks out of the house, crossing the mountains like a wedding parade. Big Uncle saw them from a nearby hill and was so upset he almost jumped into the next well but instead returned home with his tail between his legs.

Since the land could no longer provide for his immediate family, Waigong came to Shanghai in 1947 to work in a silk factory. In subsequent years, he participated in worker strikes and soon came to identify with the Communist Party. In 1950, when Waigong returned to visit his family in the countryside, he learned that both Big Uncle and Little Uncle had been executed. It wasn't just because they owned land. Rather, Big Uncle had a stomach problem and had sought medical help in vain, so when he heard that an infant's flesh could cure him, he paid for a stillborn baby and ate it. This scandal came out during the public tribunal, and he was denounced as a cannibal. Big Uncle also offended many people in his village with his stormy temper and gave his children vicious beatings. Many years later, when Big Uncle's son was already an old man, he would still curse his father for not dying sooner and for preventing him from becoming a party member however hard he tried. Little Uncle, in contrast, was executed not as a landlord but as a counterrevolutionary because he had held a minor secretarial position in the local Nationalist government. Since Little Uncle was not even ranked high enough to go to Taiwan, Waigong could not understand why the Communists had to execute him. Perhaps to fulfill some kind of quota? In any event, Waigong's maternal grandmother watched with her own eyes the execution of her two sons and dared not even put their bodies into coffins.

As for the paternal grandmother with the grain bed as her dowry, when the Communists first came to her town, rumor had it that all private shops would be collectivized, so the old woman lined up with dozens of fellow shareholders overnight in front of the medicine shop where she had invested her life's savings. When the shop failed to open in the morning, they stormed it only to find that the owner had fled overnight through the backdoor, leaving behind nothing but a yard full of dung cakes. The following year her rice paddy was confiscated and redistributed to her former tenants. She slept on the hollow grain bed for another decade, her body shriveling into a brittle pile of bones that knocked against the hard camphor wood. Waigong sent her 10 yuan a month out of his Shanghai worker's salary until her death in 1959.

After burying his grandmother, Waigong inherited her grain bed and arranged for a local refrigerator factory to ship it to his Shanghai home. Whenever he had a night shift at his silk factory, he would eat an early supper by himself, drink a bowl of Shaoxing wine with a sleeping pill, and then climb into the attic to nap on the grain bed while Waipo tried to hush more than a dozen children in a house with squeaky stairs. Inside the grain bed, Waipo stored out-of-season clothes, yarn, and quilts and gave in to her hoarding instincts even while such things out-

FIGURE 2.2 Waipo and her mother in 1963.

lived their usefulness, filling the attic with the pungent smell of mothballs and turning it into a rustic cabinet of curiosities. Among other things, she stored there the original quilts that she and Waigong had first carried on their backs when they first came to Shanghai, like snails carrying their own shells. Waipo's mother (fig. 2.2) had personally grown the cotton that made up her quilt, the same way *her* mother had grown the cotton for the quilt that she had used for a lifetime. Despite hiring itinerant cotton fluffers to loosen the lumps every few years, Waipo said her mother's quilt became so hard in her old age "you could bump your nose against it and get a nosebleed." On fine days, Waipo would climb into the attic, open the grain bed, and take the quilts out into the sun so that they would be warm and dry by evening. Sitting on this grain bed with crossed legs on rainy afternoons, my mother in the 1960s and I in the early 1990s passed many hours of solitary reading and daydreaming.

After the demolition of Alliance Lane, the grain bed was among the few pieces of "antique" furniture my grandparents decided to save, for it served as a memento of their country roots, of a feudal system that had come to a violent end in land reform, of the hubris and *vanitas* of worldly attachments.

Yeye's Writing Desk

Smelling of fountain pen ink, rice glue, and old paper, Yeye's writing desk (fig. 2.3) with its many little drawers was one of the few signs of his university education. He spent most of his time at home huddled over this desk, reading or writing under a lamp that he had himself cobbled together—with exposed wires, a naked light bulb, and a cardboard lampshade. Before him would be a bottle of blue fountain pen ink, a jar of rice glue,

FIGURE 2.3 Yeye at his writing desk around 1967. Drawing by my father.

and an enamel cup imprinted with the name of his work unit and filled with very dark tea—simmered with the cheapest dregs of tea leaves. In the back of the desk, Yeye kept a modest collection of books, mostly from his university days. He was careful to wrap each in brown paper camouflage, so that classical Chinese novels and the books of English literature seemed indistinguishable from propaganda pamphlets and Chairman Mao's *Selected Works*.

At this desk for half a century, Yeye wrote many confessions to the authorities, letters to his children and relatives, and memoirs in answer to my questions about his past. Inside its drawers, he locked away backup copies of such writings along with the household registration booklet, marriage and birth certificates, a few family photographs, and his university diploma and transcript. Like everyone who worked for a state enterprise, the first time Yeye had to write his "autobiography" was after Liberation, giving a basic account of his family background and social relationships as well as the schools he attended, the organizations he worked for, and so on.[5] In political campaigns throughout the 1950s and 1960s, Yeye rewrote different versions of this autobiography, filling in more details on his ideological transformations or on targeted individuals in his social network. Despite attending St. John's, a Christian college known for its cosmopolitan alumni, Yeye confessed that he had been a loner without much economic or social capital to make friends with other bourgeois members of society. This way, he was fortunate enough to steer clear of most counterrevolutionary relationships.

Yeye had to spill a bit more ink, however, on his two cousins, S. and C., who were brothers. Orphaned as children, the two boys came under the custody of Yeye's parents, their uncle and aunt, and grew up with Yeye in a big courtyard dwelling in Yangzhou that housed the family's soy sauce business. When the Japanese invaded the city in 1938, Yeye's parents abandoned their ancestral home and moved to Shandong, where Yeye's father had a job as an engineer in a coal mine. They took along their future daughter-in-law, Nainai, and sent their son Yeye to school in Shanghai, yet they forsook responsibility for their nephews, then still adolescents. The two brothers in turn lost each other in the chaos of war and became soldiers of different armies. Over the years, S. was promoted as an official in the Nationalist army, whereas C. received training as a doctor in the Communist New Fourth Army.

In May 1949, C. came to Shanghai with the Communist troops, settled at a People's Liberation Army hospital, and reconnected with Yeye. Soon afterward, Yeye received a letter from S., who was now hiding out with his wife in her native countryside without a means of livelihood. Yeye advised S. to come to Shanghai and seek refuge with his brother C. The two brothers were soon reunited at Yeye's home, and as a high-ranking Communist official, C. managed to secure a job for S. as a pharmacist in a local Shanghai hospital. When my father was in kindergarten in the early 1950s, S. often came to visit with his wife and daughter, and all the children played together on the *tatami* mats of Yeye's "Japanese house." Yeye and Nainai also took their children to visit S. at his nearby home, an attic in a hutment with steep, dark, and rickety stairs. When my father began elementary school, however, such mutual visits stopped, and later he learned that Uncle S. had died in a labor reform camp in the faraway northwestern province of Qinghai during the Great Leap Forward.[6] Nainai still bumped into S.'s wife at the local food market in the 1960s, but she always hurried away without saying hello.

"She probably blamed your *yeye* for her husband's death," Nainai said. "When your *yeye* wrote reports to the party, he *had* to admit that his cousin used to work for the Nationalists, but how could your *yeye* not confess when he wore a Rightist cap on his head, and how was he to know that writing things down could kill S.? Besides, didn't his own brother, C., denounce him already?" When I asked Yeye about S., he sighed and did not want to talk. Instead, he rummaged through his desk drawers and found a document from 1967—the draft of his reply to an investigation team that formed around C., at the time accused as a capitalist-roader (*zouzipai* 走資派) like many high-ranking Communist cadres in the Cultural Revolution. This 1967 document testified that, contrary to Nainai's memories, Yeye had already "denounced" S. in the early 1950s, *before* he himself was labeled a Rightist: "The Three-Anti Five-Anti Campaign of 1952 raised my political consciousness, so I decided to report the reactionary historical background of S. to the party organization of my work unit. Before writing the report, I discussed the matter with C. by telephone. He expressed support for my correct action to stand firm and denounce S. I do not know how and why the party organization of S. investigated him, but I heard that he was sent to a labor reform camp in Qinghai and died there of illness."

How reliable is this 1967 document, yet another confession exhorted by the authorities who were now investigating not S. the former Nationalist officer, but C. the Communist bureaucrat? Was Yeye telling the whole truth? Does the telephone conversation with C. show that C. himself was ready to denounce his brother and was therefore loyal to the party? Yeye wrote apologetically for *not* having denounced S. earlier and for having helped him seek refuge in Shanghai in 1949: "My political consciousness was too weak at the time, and I only acted on familial sentiments." Yet is there not a shadow of remorse and anguish as Yeye's angular handwriting spells out S.'s death?

A decade after being labeled a Rightist, Yeye was already an expert at writing confessions. While becoming ever more silent and alienated from his family, he searched his memories and poured his heart into various reports written for the authorities. During the Cultural Revolution, it was not just the party but also his own children who put him on trial and forced him to confess his thought crimes. Huddling over his desk all night long, Yeye wrote down six points such as this one: "Some time ago, I bumped into a former colleague in the accounting department where I used to work before being labeled a Rightist. He expressed regret that I no longer worked in his office and humored me with some compliments of my 'good work' from before. I replied with the saying: 'A hero talks not of his past bravery.' I thought I was being self-deprecating, but upon careful reflection I realized that this slip of the tongue shows subconscious resentment of the People's judgment and that I have not thoroughly reformed my thinking."

After Yeye wrote up this confession, his daughter and son—Aunt Treasure and my father—dutifully submitted it to the neighborhood committee's rebel group as the fruits of their revolutionary action at home. Fortunately, the rebel group leader was a kind man who felt sorry for Yeye and told his children, much to their relief, that their father's thought crimes did not amount to counterrevolution. As a result, this confession did not enter Yeye's dossier and remained hidden away inside his desk drawer.

Although Yeye willingly submitted to the tyranny of his children and constantly denounced himself, he also found secret comfort in their revolutionary activism: the children had grown up and could fend for themselves. Collectively, they acted out a public theater of revolutionary loyalty that camouflaged their private sentiments. This curious interface between public and private also manifested itself in the only extant

FIGURE 2.4 A family photograph from 1968. *Front row from left to right*: Nainai, Uncle Lucky, Yeye, Aunt Pearl. *Back row from left to right*: Aunt Bean, my father, Aunt Treasure.

photograph of my father's entire family during the Cultural Revolution. It was taken in 1968, before my father's departure to the Great Northern Wilderness and Aunt Treasure's departure to Xinjiang in the northwestern frontier. In it, my grandparents and all five of their children are wearing Mao badges and holding little red books. Standing or sitting up straight in harsh, determined, and "sculpted" postures, they wear the facial expressions of about-to-be-executed martyrs (fig. 2.4). Even though stamped by the public ethos of its time, this photograph came to be hidden away in Yeye's desk as a private souvenir to commemorate the togetherness of a family about to be thundered apart.

After the revolutionary storm abated in the 1970s and 1980s, Yeye wrote many letters to his scattered children at his desk, where he also translated several technical manuals from English to Chinese, assembled a giant transistor radio, and re-recorded his favorite Peking opera episodes on VHS. In the 1990s, writing to my parents and me in America, Yeye would seal the sour, antiseptic stench of rice glue, the rustle of thin, brittle paper, and a sense of caution and paranoia into the envelope. Since his letter often stuck to its envelope, we learned to hold it against the light, feel its seams with our fingertips, and carefully extricate its interior content from its exterior cover. We never asked if it was the clumsiness of old age or a deliberate tactic to thwart potential censors, but it was clear that Yeye had bowdlerized and mutilated his own letters—there was so much cutting and pasting that some pages were elongated like scrolls and others curtailed like memos. It was also strenuous to decipher his handwriting, which mixed traditional Chinese characters with supersimplified characters popularized in the graphomania of the Mao era. Using carbon paper to make backup copies, Yeye chiseled his words with so much exertion, a few strokes often pierced the page. Such mental and physical exertion left its marks on the wooden surface of the desk, whose drawers locked away a palimpsest archive of Yeye's tortuous soul.

Nainai's Sewing Machine

In spring 1958, Nainai sold three gold rings and bought a Butterfly sewing machine. It was the first major purchase she had made on her own, for she heard that her alleyway was starting a sewing workshop, whereby any housewife with a sewing machine would be eligible to join and earn a wage. After Yeye was condemned as a Rightist, his salary—the family's only source of income—was cut by a third and could barely cover the needs of five children and two adults, so Nainai hoped for entry into "productive labor" to ease the household budget. Alas, such an alleyway workshop never came to fruition, and for the next two decades Nainai took on other temporary jobs such as paving roads, serving as a night security guide for the alleyway, and delivering milk before dawn. Meanwhile, she made sure to animate the sewing machine day and night with her hands and feet in order to clothe her five growing children, husband, and two in-laws so that everyone stayed warm, clean, and somewhat dignified.

Nainai learned to sew after losing her mother and two stepmothers by the age of nine. Her father, a tax collector in Hunan, lost his job when the revolutionary army toppled the warlord government and led a peripatetic life with his little daughter. Nainai began to keep house for her father at the age of nine, tidying up his room, serving him opium, and mending his clothes. When she was eleven, she came under the custody of her grandmother in Yangzhou, who taught her some embroidery and tailoring before she was betrothed to Yeye's family as a child bride. In 1938, at the age of sixteen, she fled the Japanese army with her future parents-in-law until they settled down at a Japanese-controlled coal mine in Shandong, where she served them for nearly a decade before coming to Shanghai and joining Yeye. Her wedding with Yeye took place in the midst of the war in 1941 and was a quiet, domestic affair: "The fortune-teller said that a modest wedding would allow me to enjoy filial sons in my old age, so we just bowed to my parents-in-law and did not even set off firecrackers."

Nainai sewed her own wedding dress by hand: a long-sleeved *qipao* made of emerald cotton crepe, with dark green lace frothing at the hem, walnutlike buttons, and chrysanthemum-like ornamental loops. It was meant to be something she might wear again, but Nainai always saved it for she knew not what, until the revolution rendered *qipao*s out of fashion along with Yeye's three Western-style suits, tailor made for his new job in 1948. Lying in the bottom of their storage chests, Nainai's *qipao* and Yeye's suits—along with Yeye's mother's furs and silks with big sleeves and intricate embroidery—saw the light of day only on bamboo laundry poles in the alleyway on sunny days after the rainy season. Whether feudal, bourgeois, or modern, these relics of earlier eras gave way to the simple lines, sturdy fabric, and monotonous colors of the cadres suit, people's jacket, and laborer's corduroys and khakis.

In the years when Yeye underwent labor reform, he also dressed like a peasant and worker. When he returned home from the countryside or the factory, his body and clothes bore traces of mud and manure, grease and dust, and lice and fleas. When it rained, he wore a peasant's straw hat and cloak instead using an umbrella. "He looked just like a peasant with dark skin and red cheeks," Nainai recalled. "I would have to boil his clothes and force him to take a bath." After that, Yeye always looked a bit unkempt, and when scolded by Nainai he would quote Chairman Mao: "Even though their hands were soiled and their feet smeared with cow-dung, workers and peasants were really cleaner than the bourgeois and petty-bourgeois intellectuals."[7]

FIGURE 2.5 Nainai makes fake collars at her sewing machine. Drawing by my father.

While Yeye wallowed in his disgrace, Nainai continued striving for a dignified appearance. The reduction of the household income, the rationing of cotton in the late 1950s, and five growing children required stringent planning by the homemaker. Unlike other families, Nainai never hired a tailor or outsourced the stitching of shoe soles, but with the humming of the sewing machine as the lullaby of her children, she made sure that on every Chinese New Year's Eve everyone in the family had a set of new clothes under his or her pillow and a pair of new shoes under the bed. Much of such "new" clothing consisted of recycled fragments from old clothes—adjusting to the growing bodies of children; with shreds of old fabric serving as inner linings or shoe stuffing. With the sewing machine's help and an intuitive sense of style, Nainai knew how to turn rags into fashion so that even patches over ripped pants became ornaments rather than badges of shame. Like many Shanghai homemakers, Nainai also sewed many "fake collars," detachable collars worn underneath jackets or sweaters to create the illusion of a full shirt or blouse (fig. 2.5): "Economical in its use of materials and easy to wash, the fake collar created a trendy image for those with limited means at a time when both laundry soap and fabric were rationed."[8]

To save money, Nainai bought the cheapest brands of household items, and she would soak the tiny stubs of soap leftovers in water overnight and then sculpt the mixture into a "new" bar of soap. Before going to bed, she would turn the tap on a very slow trickle, so that the water meter would "sleep" without noticing how a whole basin of water accumulated overnight. Loath to waste hot water for washing clothes and vegetables even in winter, her hands became rough and swollen, much more so than female workers of nearby factories and quite unbecoming of the "idle housewife" designation of her official status. Throughout the 1960s and the early 1970s, Nainai patched broken summer straw mats using the sewing machine and slowly built up her reputation in the alleyway, thereby bringing in a modest supplementary income. Even then, she would strain her eyes under fifteen-watt lightbulbs when sewing at night and take her needlework to her night shifts at the neighborhood security cabin.

Yet Nainai's decades of strenuous labor in and out of the house, forsaking leisure and sleep, were never rewarded with a salary or retirement pension. Although she was classifiable as a Shanghai petty bourgeois, her experience of the socialist era had something in common with the rural women of Shaanxi in Gail Hershatter's study. For them as well as for Nainai, domestic labor remained "unremunerated" and "invisible" in the period's public visual representations and written record. In their private memories, however, needlework was "the activity that most epitomize[d] the incessant, ephemeral, and occasionally creative temporality of domestic life."[9] Whether done by hand or by the sewing machine, Nainai's needlework was her way of chronicling the history of this epoch. Whereas Yeye accumulated stacks of paper and writing, Nainai amassed dozens of fake collars, sleeve covers, shoe liners, pillow facings, and leftover bits and pieces of fabric and lace, elastic bands and buttons—all tightly wrapped inside colorful cloth bundles stuffed into the nooks and crannies of her home long after old age rendered her incapable of threading a needle. She was hardly Nüwa, the legendary mender of heaven in Chinese mythology, but what she did mend was an everyday fabric that sustained life on earth.

Photographs on the Eight Immortal Table

In a framed photograph on their wall, Waipo's round face almost touches Waigong's long face (see fig. 1.17C). She wears a silk green scarf that matches the jade-colored picture frame. Her hand-tinted red lips are open, unveiling a row of large white teeth. The curves outlining her eyes suggest coyness, but her flirtation is directed toward and limited solely to Waigong, who looks young and timid, as if embarrassed about his happiness. The season must have been winter, for the radiance on their cheeks comes from the warmth of layers of clothing.

They sat for this photograph seven years after their marriage in the studio just outside Alliance Lane, which for some time displayed this photo in its shop window (see fig. 1.1L and 1.2). Social photographers at the time were to help revolutionize people's aesthetics, to make beautiful images not of the bourgeois "bedecked with jewels," but of "healthy, down-to-earth, and graceful" proletariats.[10] As a handsome pair of young workers in a state-owned silk factory, my grandparents were politically sound, even if Waipo's permed hair and red lipstick made her look indistinguishable from the daughter of a Number One or the former concubine of a capitalist—other types of women living in the same alleyway.

This photograph remained the most conspicuous decoration of my maternal grandparents' home for the next few decades. Highlighting the centrality of their conjugal bond, it looked over an assemblage of other family photos, placed beneath a large piece of glass placed over the square dining table, a simple Eight Immortal Table (Baxian Zhuo 八仙桌) common in the Jiangnan area. On Spring Festivals and Mid-autumn Festivals, families often used such tables as an altar to make offerings to their ancestors, as had been the practice of Grandma Apricot's family in the same house on Alliance Lane from the 1930s to the 1940s (see fig. 1.5B). Yet Waigong, "antisuperstitious" since his childhood, never offered incense or fruits to his ancestors but instead replaced their spirit tablets with photographs of his and Waipo's parents and grandparents, their children, and, later on, in-laws and grandchildren.

The arrangement and rearrangement of these photographs on the Eight Immortal Table and in the family photo album became Waigong's informal ritual to define the scope and meaning of the extended family, while the family photo album took on the quality of a traditional genealogy. In addition to photos, my grandparents also placed under the glass ration coupons, identity cards, and other vital documents that entitled them to the privilege of socialist urban welfare. Since the Communist takeover and land reform, their socialist factory had replaced their clan lineages as the provider of their livelihood. Whereas Waigong's parents and grandparents had "eaten off" of annual revenues from the collectively owned farm fields of their lineage, now Waigong's and Waipo's wages and urban citizenship put meals on the table every day.

Traditionally, the Eight Immortal Table was "a figurative expression of the happiness accompanying the sharing of food and conviviality with family and friends." Even without Waigong's idiosyncratic photographic assemblage, "this table, and not the hearth," remained "at the core of domestic solidarity in the Chinese home."[11] It was there that everyday and holiday meals were prepared and consumed, and in the cramped corners of Shanghai households it also served as a writing desk for schoolchildren, a mahjong table for the likes of Apricot's family, the Wangs, and a kind of reception area for guests. Some tables had four little drawers on four sides, which parents often distributed among the children as *their* personal spaces. Familial conversations and gossip about the neighbors also took place around this table, and in an age before television children learned about the outside world through these conversations around steaming dinners. As a familial center, the Eight Immortal Table of Shanghai homes retained some remnant symbolism of the ancestral shrine (*citing* 祠堂) at the heart of traditional Chinese homes. Its shrunken size and multiple functions made it much more intimate and casual, and the worship of ancestors and religious deities gave way to the consecration of the nuclear family on the one hand and the reception of mass media on the other.

Radio Waves

From the 1930s to the 1980s, before the spread of television, radio waves permeated Shanghai's alleyways and connected its domestic spaces to a broader world beyond. When my maternal grandparents first came to Shanghai as silk workers in the late 1940s, a radio had been their most coveted luxury. They and a dozen coworkers lived in crowded dormitories on the ground floor and pavilion room of a *shikumen* house. Upstairs in the front bedroom lived the sister and brother-in-law of their boss, who often turned on their radio loud enough for everyone to hear. Even half a century later, Waigong could recall the lyrics of a duet called "Rising Higher Step by Step" ("Bubugao" 步步高):

WOMAN:
Since I married you, life went downhill:
Nothing good to eat, nothing good to wear,
No rings or watches, no gold bars or diamonds.

MAN:
Since I married you, my worries have no end.
Today you argue with me, tomorrow we fight again.
Where do I get diamonds if I'm not a corrupt official?

CHORUS:
Who doesn't want a better life?
Who doesn't want to flourish?
Kowtow as you may to the God of Wealth,
Money will not fall from the sky.
Don't look to those who ride in automobiles,
Don't look to those who live in mansions.
Remember, thrift is the secret to wealth.
How can you get rich by spending?
Shanghai is a glamorous place,
Tempting you to fritter away your earnings.
Saving a buck costs no effort;
It's like plucking a hair from an ox.
Today's merriment counts for naught;
Prepare for happiness in your old age.
Tell your kids: snacks are unhealthy,
Better let your parents save up till you marry
To buy a set of mahogany furniture
And a sedan auto to go to and fro.
When parents teach children good habits,
Each generation will do better than the last.
Make and save, rise higher step by step!
Old and young, the family laughs merrily!

Singing of materialistic pursuits and social mobility while taking a jab at corrupt officials,[12] this song playing on the radio expressed the possibility for poor country bumpkins such as my maternal grandparents to become wealthy like their boss. Waigong and Waipo had yet to think of themselves as workers but rather came to Shanghai to "learn a trade." Yet instead of saving money and accumulating capital over time, they achieved social mobility and became the vanguard class through the Communist Revolution in 1949.

By 1954, Waigong and Waipo had moved to a comfortable apartment on the third floor of No. 111 Alliance Lane and purchased their first radio at a discount from their landlady, Grandma Apricot's mother. This very radio, as Grandma Apricot told me, had kept her mother company in the 1930s and 1940s while her mother-in-law confined her to the house (see fig. 1.5E). As commercial radio stations flourished in Shanghai since the late 1920s and became an important medium for advertisement, storytelling, and music, Apricot's mother and tens of thousands of middle-class female listeners, "previously isolated in the insularity of their sheltered lives, became members of a 'listening public' (*tingzhong* 聽眾) of intimate anonymity via the radio."[13] Unbeknownst to them and operating beneath their radar just a few meters away, No. 61 Alliance Lane harbored one of the first Communist underground radio transmitters in the 1930s (fig. 1.1F). The story of such underground Communist Party radio transmitters in Shanghai alleyway homes would become the stuff of revolutionary cinema such as *The Everlasting Radio Waves* (*Yongbu xiaoshi de dianbo* 永不消逝的電波).[14] On the eve of the Communist Revolution in 1949, there were more than sixty public and private radio stations in Shanghai, but they were gradually eliminated and consolidated into the Shanghai Broadcasting Station by 1954.[15] With its transition from a bourgeois to a proletariat home after the Communist Revolution, the same radio in No. 111 Alliance Lane also underwent a shift from a private entertainment center playing petty bourgeois tunes to a portal receiving state propaganda, especially since Waigong was far more interested in listening to national events than to local operas.

Waigong could not remember the radio's brand or its country of origin, only that it was foreign made and that China could not yet make consumer radios. Often tuned into the Central People's Broadcast Station, the radio announced the time every hour: "Beep, beep, beep, beep. . . . The last beep was Beijing Time X o'clock." Every now and then, Waigong would

FIGURE 2.6 Waigong, Waipo, and my mother at home in 1969. *On the dresser:* a radio, a Three-Five brand clock, and a Mao bust.

adjust the family clock, Shanghai's famous Three-Five Brand, to conform to "Beijing Time" (fig. 2.6). His and Waipo's domestic time, too, was organized around the clock of their state-owned factory, which required them to rotate between three shifts every week throughout the socialist decades: a morning shift (6:00 a.m. to 2:00 p.m.), an afternoon shift (2:00 p.m. to 10:00 p.m.), and a night shift (10:00 p.m. to 6:00 a.m.). Such a schedule was to give my grandparents chronic insomnia and "neurasthenia" in their old age,[16] yet this submission of domestic time and bodily rhythms to the needs of the nation became second nature. Waigong and Principal Zhang, who lived on the ground floor, liked doing calisthenics at home (see fig. 1.17M) at the cue of the radio, which began every broadcast calisthenics with a slogan: "Everyone should exercise, everyday on the drill ground, work for the motherland for fifty healthy years." Later in the Cultural Revolution, the slogan changed to "Improve people's physique, raise vigilance, protect the motherland!"[17] Just as "Be Vigilant and Protect the Motherland" was literally written on the radio my paternal grandparents bought in the 1970s and used for the next thirty years, the uplifting rhetoric and music from the socialist decades were also etched into the gramophones of that generation's memories, inextricable from their most personal experiences.

Although the radio mediated state propaganda and regulated the body and the rhythm of everyday life, it was not necessarily an invasion into the private realm. In the front bedroom downstairs from Waigong and Waipo lived another worker family: Master Chen, his wife, and their three children. The middle daughter, whom I call Aunt Duckweed, recalls that her family also had a radio placed on a shelf above their bed, just out of the reach of her naughty brother (see fig. 1.17H). Her father had bought it in the Republican era along with a Parker pen and a Swiss pocket watch, all relics from a more cosmopolitan era before her birth. Made in Japan, it had a left dial for volume and a right dial for tuning. Aunt Duckweed recalled that, rather than the Central People's Broadcasting Station, her family often listened to the Shanghai Broadcasting Station, which had more musical and entertainment programming. They usually turned it on evenings, perhaps for a half-hour after her mother washed the children's face and feet and tucked them into bed or after her father came home from the 2:00 to 10:00 p.m. middle shift at the factory. Because the walls were thin, it was soft and not a blaring sound, and even then the neighbors might complain, but Aunt Duckweed also had intimate memories of listening to the neighbors' radio—muffled, distant, so that even revolutionary model operas sounded like secret whispers. For her, the Cultural Revolution ended one night when she heard soft piano music filtering in from downstairs, and so she pressed her ears to the floor until the end of the piece, and the radio announcer said that this was a nocturne from Chopin.

The radio's electrified and disembodied voices continued to permeate the soundscape of my own childhood in No. 111 Alliance Lane in the 1980s. I woke up every morning to the Central People's Broadcasting Station blasting from a large radio on the dresser and fell asleep every evening to the surreptitious murmuring of Voice of America from a small radio by Waigong's pillow. In the spring of 1989, during student protests at Tiananmen Square and the subsequent crackdown, I figured out that the two stations often reported the same events from opposite standpoints, using different words and tones, and thus projected contradictory interpretations onto the same events. Eager to share this revelation with my grandparents, I pointed out the differences between the two stations by singing their respective theme music and by imitating the voices of their newscasters, but my grandparents were much more alarmed than amused. "Don't you talk nonsense outside," Waipo warned me. "You would bring trouble to our family." Her scolding gave me the first inkling of an undercurrent of private interests, voices, and values underneath the facade of public slogans and collective rituals. Much like the murmuring from my grandfather's radio, which always received interference from official government stations, this undercurrent was interlaced with official vocabulary, and one would have to listen very closely to decipher what it was really saying.

Home Searches: The Cultural Revolution in the Alleyway

As the films of Ingmar Bergman so frequently suggest, the first act of tyrants… is often to replace a materially bountiful world (with its implicit, if anonymous, human wish for the individual's basic comfort) with a starkly empty one in which each nuance of comfort depends on the vagaries of the egoist's own disposition.

—ELAINE SCARRY, THE BODY IN PAIN[18]

You could find anything in the garbage dump those days: jewelry, antiques, valuables people would kill for nowadays—and old black-and-white photographs, torn beyond restoration, beyond recognition.

—AUNT DUCKWEED

Just about every house in our alleyway has been searched.

—GRANDMA APRICOT

In one of our afternoon chats, I asked Grandma Apricot to show me her family pictures from before her marriage. She went upstairs and returned with half-a-dozen old photos: "We used to have a lot more photographs, but most were confiscated during home searches." Many interviewees mentioned the Cultural Revolution when I asked to see souvenirs of their more distant pasts. Not all of their homes were searched, but many felt the threat and so "purified" their homes by hiding or destroying anything that might not have agreed with the times. After all, the new and the revolutionary depended on the annihilation of the "four olds"—old ideas, old culture, old habits, old customs that took refuge in Shanghai alleyway homes until 1966.

Home searches on a mass scale began as part of the Smashing the Four Olds movement in August 1966. In their nationwide destruction of cultural relics and religious idols, Red Guards attributed guilt and doled out punishments to inanimate objects as if they were animate demons blocking the path to the Communist utopia. As Joseph Levenson has observed, "The dead are no longer monuments, but 'ghosts and monsters' to be slain again."[19] Whereas public vandalism served purely symbolic, iconoclastic purposes, home searches turned domestic artifacts into evidence that incriminated their owners: keeping a bodhisattva figure or Bible was a sure sign of superstition; owning a sofa, a piano, or mahogany furniture indicated a decadent bourgeois or feudal lifestyle; listening to a short-wave radio was proof of espionage for America or the Soviet Union; harboring old account books or land deeds was a counterrevolutionary conspiracy to undo the revolutionary redistribution of property.

In Shanghai, at least 157,700 homes (6.5 percent of total households in the city) were ransacked from late August to September 1966.[20] As Red Guards from Beijing came to "light the fire of revolution" in the "bourgeois bastion" of Shanghai, radicalized middle school and university students all over the city were the first to raid homes.[21] Their first targets were often the homes of teachers from capitalist and other questionable backgrounds. Red Guards asked neighborhood committees for the names and addresses of "reactionary" residents. Some were also led to their targets by busybodies who either had a tangible interest or simply delighted in seeing their neighbors' houses searched. Beginning in November 1966, Shanghai workers began forming their own rebel organizations,[22] and every work unit sent their own home-search squads to the homes of "class enemies" who had infiltrated their ranks. Meanwhile, Red Guard posses appeared in random alleyways to round up former landlords, capitalists, Rightists, and other "black elements," parade them around the neighborhood, hold a struggle session or two, search their homes again, and post big-character posters on their doors.[23] Such "revolutionary actions" also inspired spontaneous neighborhood organizations such as the housing rebel group that usurped my paternal grandparents' dining room (see "After the Communist Revolution" in chapter 1).

While the four olds were destroyed in homes, Chairman Mao's face replaced the countenances of family members, deceased parents, and the Bodhisattva of Mercy on the most conspicuous walls and sacred altars of households. This face not only towered above every public square, workshop, office, and classroom but also in this way watched over many private homes (see one such portrait in the drawing of Yeye at his desk in fig. 2.3).[24] Children, even adults, made vows and confessed misdemeanors in front of Chairman Mao's portrait or statue. Some families shouted "Long Live Chairman Mao!" and sang "East Is Red" before every meal. If a parent had passed away, one rarely displayed his or her image at home because most households had only one room and anything not hidden away was visible to guests. Without room for personal expression or commemoration, love for one's family was to be channeled into love for the Communist Party and Chairman Mao, whose face was to be loved, feared, and worshipped. In many cases, of course, these portraits were also ignored: like amulets, they were there only to protect the family from the accusation that they might be disloyal to Chairman Mao. The portrait, to borrow Vaclav Havel's words, "is really a sign, and as such it contains a subliminal but very definite message," which says, "I know what I must do. I behave in the manner expected of me. I can be depended upon and am beyond reproach. I am obedient and therefore I have the right to be left in peace."[25]

Yeye, however, was genuinely afraid of Chairman Mao's likeness. A neighbor gave him a plaster Mao bust around 1968. He moved it from this room to that room, from that shelf to this shelf, for three days and still did not know where to put it. On the one hand, it had to be in a prominent place. On the other, it was easily breakable, and to smash it would be disastrous, if not fatal, for a Rightist, even one "without a cap." He compared the bust to a ticking time bomb that could explode any time in his hands. After many insomniac nights, he finally managed to give it away to another neighbor whose son was going "up to the mountains and down to the countryside."

Chairman Mao's face reigned not only over the domestic space of the household, but also over the personal space of the diary. Photo albums and blank books of the time were often printed with his face on the first page and then filled by entry after entry of confessions addressed to him.

One major campaign to promote Mao's cult of personality was to emulate Lei Feng, a soldier whose posthumously published diary became a canonical text after 1963. Given his example, some wrote their diaries with the anticipation that they would be discovered and perused.[26] "How I hoped that somebody would read my diary," my father told me. "Then they'd see what a true revolutionary I was, even if my father was a Rightist." "It was hard to keep a real diary," my mother told me, "especially when I was sent down to the countryside and living with five or six other people in the same room. I would have to censor myself constantly or write in codes that I myself couldn't even decipher after a while. One day, while working in the fields, I suddenly realized that I had forgotten to lock my suitcase, where I kept my diary, and almost died of fright."

Much as the iconography of the Cultural Revolution seemed to suppress all individuality and private sphere under the omnipresent gaze of the Mao portrait, mass participation also liberated many people from their everyday roles to act in a revolutionary carnival. Whether people joined in revolutionary singing or performed loyalty dances, whether they scribbled big-character posters or denounced a class enemy at a struggle session, the Cultural Revolution gave them an unprecedented opportunity to *express* themselves—to showcase their voices and bodies, their calligraphy and eloquence, their dreams, jealousies, and grievances. The Cultural Revolution, as Ban Wang points out, "created not only its own art, as in the numerous paintings and portraits of Mao and in the revolutionary model plays, but also an 'artistic' way of life, an elaborate pattern of daily living that puts enormous premium on forms—forms of speech, behavior, bearing, and countless other ritualistic details."[27] Although Wang's study focuses on the Red Guard rallies on Tiananmen Square, such an aesthetically driven way of life played out not only in grand public spaces, but also in the more intimate theater of the Shanghai alleyway.

In the following pages, I have assembled a montage of narratives in the voices of my interviewees, occasionally interspersed with my commentaries, on experiences of the Cultural Revolution from the localized perspectives of the alleyway homes in this study. Representing a variety of perspectives, I hope to highlight not just experiences of victimization,[28] but also the distinct roles played by different members of the same neighborhood. Because most of these narratives were initially oral fragments and digressions, I edited, paraphrased, and sometimes added context to them for the sake of clarity and coherence.

Aunt Duckweed lived with her parents and siblings in the "front bedroom" of No. 111 Alliance Lane, directly downstairs from my maternal grandparents. When the Cultural Revolution began in the summer of 1966, she had just turned eight years old:

> One morning, all the mothers and fathers of the alleyway went to work as usual, and a few fashionable young mothers, such as Mosquito's mother two doors down from us, wore tight trousers and pointy-toe leather shoes, but when they returned in the late afternoon, several had the bottoms of their trousers cut open and were not wearing shoes, and some had funny haircuts. Mosquito's mother came home in a pedicab because Red Guards had cut her heels and pants all the way to her thighs. So that's how our alleyway branch learned: "Ah, the Cultural Revolution has started." Many housewives, both envious and disdainful of such fashionable working-women, took pleasure in their disgrace. But a few weeks later, when neighborhood committees began organizing Mao Zedong thought-propaganda troupes, Mosquito's mother began teaching Red Guard loyalty dances to teenage girls in the alleyway, all dressed up in the newest fashion of the time—imitation army uniforms with belts.[29]

For my father (see fig. 2.4, middle in the back row), seventeen years old in August 1966, the Cultural Revolution was an exciting occasion for his generation to take the stage of history. He bought a piece of red cloth and made himself a Red Guard armband, but the "real Red Guards" at his school from "Red" revolutionary class backgrounds called him out as an imposter and the "dog cub" of a Rightist father. Instead, he made revolution at home under the command of his elder sister, Treasure, who was attending Beijing Normal University at the time and had more authority because of her proximity to Chairman Mao.

> When the Cultural Revolution began, Treasure sent home a telegram saying: "Search for and destroy all four olds in the house!" So my mother burned a few old books in the backyard. They were mostly English literature books from my father's university days and a photo book of Japanese war atrocities with a Nationalist flag on the front cover, given by Uncle S., who had been a Nationalist

officer [see "Yeye's Writing Desk" in this chapter]. I tried to throw my grandmother's Buddhist sutra in the pile, but she wouldn't let go of it, so we warned her not to talk about it outside the house. Then we received a second telegram from my sister: "Don't touch anything. Wait for the Red Guards to search the house." So we stopped burning things and waited for the Red Guards to come.

While waiting for the Red Guards, Yeye and Nainai grew more paranoid by the day and hid from their zealous children a few silver dollars from the Republican era and Yeye's St. John's University diploma and transcripts (see fig. 0.1). Loath to destroy these precious documents but terrified at the potential catastrophe of their discovery, as mentioned in the introduction, Yeye tremulously painted a red X across every word or symbol that might be construed as counterrevolutionary to show that he had already denounced himself. In the end, the Red Guards never came.

Sometimes, the more meaningful an object was to someone, the more he or she was forced to destroy it. Aunt Duckweed recalled:

Our next-door neighbor in No. 113 [see fig. 1.1E], Wubajin, was a devout Buddhist. From where we lived we could often smell the incense from her balcony and hear her chant the bodhisattva's name. Though illiterate, Wubajin could memorize an entire sutra word for word. She had entrusted her whole afterlife to the care of the bodhisattva, but now that the four olds were to be smashed, the neighborhood committee leaders called her into an education meeting and told her to renounce her superstition. The next day she took her mahogany wooden prayer mat and smashed it with an axe in front of her threshold for everyone to see. Her hair, which was always so neatly combed into an S-shaped bun, was all ruffled that day.

With a capitalist husband who had abandoned her before the Communist takeover, Wubajin still carried the stigma of a counterrevolutionary family—one further reason to single her out as an example for the entire alleyway. After watching Wubajin axe her prayer mat, her neighbors all followed suit with similar objects in their own homes. Aunt Duckweed's mother, Grandma Front Bedroom, found a small bronze mirror attached to the windowsill, which was supposed to ward off evil spirits.

It had belonged to Grandma Apricot's family, who used to live there, and Grandma Front Bedroom made sure everyone knew that. Waipo recalled:

> Front Bedroom told everyone about the bronze mirror she smashed and eyed our rooms to see if there was anything we should destroy too, but of course we didn't have any four olds. Besides, as workers we didn't have to worry—nobody was going to come search our home. But she did find fault with Peipei's mother in the pavilion room [see fig. 1.17E], who always got into quarrels with her over shared kitchen space. Peipei's father was a Rightist or some other sort of counter-revolutionary in a labor reform camp. Peipei's mother lived alone with her little daughter, so Front Bedroom accused her of engaging in degenerate acts with a lover. After Front Bedroom informed on Peipei's mother, Red Guards turned the small pavilion room upside down and struggled against her in the alleyway along with the real targets of the Cultural Revolution.

By "real targets of the Cultural Revolution," Waipo meant former capitalists and Communist Party cadres accused as capitalist-roaders and overthrown by workers' rebel factions by late autumn of 1966. Waigong also joined his factory's rebel faction because "rebels were the majority—as long as only one faction dominated, things didn't get too violent."

> My rebel group went to search the homes of several former capitalists whose filatures were collectivized into our factory, and because I had a bit more schooling than other workers, they made me take notes. One old man had a whole house for his family in a *shikumen* alleyway. It was elegantly decorated and very tidy when we entered, but when we left, all the drawers were turned inside out and the wardrobe tumbled to the ground. We looked in every corner for his Change the Sky Accounts [Biantianzhang 變天賬]. The search took all night, and in the end we did find some old account books from before 1949 and interrogated him: "If we are now walking a socialist path, why do you keep old capitalist accounts? Do you want to overturn the revolution? Do you want to change the sky and plot a capitalist restoration?" We also found some reams of silk he had stolen from the factory. I wrote down detailed lists of our confiscations and gave their owners a copy so that they could reclaim their goods should their names be cleared.[30]

Aside from having their homes searched, those incriminated in the Cultural Revolution were often publicly humiliated. Red Guards also occasionally convened struggle sessions in alleyways, producing at once terror and entertainment among the spectators. As Aunt Duckweed recalls,

> Struggle sessions took place in the big alleyway, and the "stage" [located at fig. 1.1H] consisted of two square Eight Immortal Tables—the kind you would find in the living rooms of better-off families, who used them to worship ancestors [see fig. 1.5B]. Using stools as stepping-stones, Red Guards herded their targets on stage with a big plaque around their necks. Several times I saw a man give his public confession as follows: "My name is Zhu Number Five. I'm a counterrevolutionary element with tons of gold in my house. Now the Red Guards have confiscated it all!" Then the guy would fall to the ground on purpose and stop moving. It was cruel but also ludicrous, especially because everything was said in Shanghainese dialect, so the crowd would laugh nervously. We all knew they were "bad people," that they deserved this, but we also felt that they didn't seem bad before.

For Uncle Little Brother in the attic of No. 113 Alliance Lane, eleven years old in 1966, the Cultural Revolution was the most carefree time of his life, especially since he was of solid proletariat stock. His father was a steel worker, and his mother was the resident group leader of this alleyway branch: "There was no school; we played all day and got to watch Red Guards struggle against class enemies. There was no television back then, and radio programs were dull, and so aside from a few revolutionary films we already knew by heart, these struggling sessions were our only form of entertainment. We even came early with our stools and placed them as close to the stage as possible to make sure we sat at the front row."

Although various struggle sessions were held against different targets, everyone I spoke to from Alliance Lane remembered two alleyway schoolteachers, White Hair and Black Hair, also nicknamed "White Cat" and "Black Cat" because the words *cat* and *hair* are pronounced the same way in Shanghainese. White Hair had a head of snow-white hair and very fair skin, so some thought she had foreign blood, though others swore that she was Chinese but only held herself like a Westerner. In contrast, Black Hair had hair as black as coal and was rumored to be White Hair's cousin, sister, or niece or not related at all. They had an entire house to themselves in Alliance Lane (see fig. 1.1K) and turned the ground floor into a classroom. Black Hair taught Chinese and math, White Hair English and music—they also owned a harmonium. Until the Cultural Revolution, Shanghai alleyways concealed quite a number of such private schools (*sishu* 私塾 or *minban xiaoxue* 民辦小學), either remnants from the Republican era or new creations to accommodate both teachers and students who could not secure a place in public schools. The government kept close watch yet tolerated these alleyway schools because public schools did not have enough spots for all the children in the city.[31]

I could not find anyone who attended White Hair and Black Hair's school, only someone who hired the latter to tutor his daughter in "American-style English" in the 1990s, by which time Black Hair's hair was also no longer black. Yet everyone remembered the two teachers because of the many struggle sessions held against them in the Cultural Revolution. According to Uncle Prosper, who lived not too far from them,

> Many people in Alliance Lane were targets of struggle sessions, but most of these took place in work units or public schools. White Hair and Black Hair did not belong to any work unit, so they became the default struggle targets of our neighborhood. Each had to wear a sign that read "Reactionary Literati" (*fandong wenren* 反動文人). Their pupils came out to denounce their teachers' fascist methods because they used physical punishments and made the children speak English even during lunch break. The home search squad found gold bars in a well inside their courtyard, where they hid all the tuition they had collected. Looking back now, I think they must have been very good teachers if parents were willing to pay such high tuition. Between the struggle sessions, White Hair and Black Hair had to sweep the big alleyway every morning.

Apart from this alleyway school, the Cultural Revolution also brought a temporary halt to many other small private businesses and services—"capitalist tails" that survived the nationwide socialist collectivization campaign of 1956 and that made alleyway life so convenient for residents. Among such disappeared conveniences was a little "porridge stove" business at the alleyway entrance, where families could cook their rice porridges in the morning without going through the extensive trouble of lighting their own coal stoves (also see "Thrift, Bricolage, and Nostalgia" in this chapter). And as entertaining as some of the alleyway struggle sessions seemed, when people began dying, even people from "good" working-class backgrounds got scared. As Aunt Duckweed recalled,

> Rumors circulated the alleyways: "XXX hung himself in his bedroom. . . . He didn't leave anything behind. . . . They said they could see his ghost with a tongue as long as a snake. . . . A woman jumped into the well early this morning. . . . They filled up the well because there's a corpse in it. . . . They said she committed suicide to escape punishment. . . ." An oppressive silence reigned over those nights, silence broken only by Red Guards and rebels storming a neighbor's house to search for incriminating items or to make an arrest. If you were in any way related to a capitalist, a Communist Party cadre, or an intellectual, your house was almost bound to be searched, so it was best not to keep anything that would put you at risk—gold, silver, antiques, books. They say wherever you hid your valuables—in a thermos cap, in a bicycle tube, in the wall, in the floor, or in the ceiling—the home search squad would still be able to find them.

According to Grandma Apricot, the more widespread home searches became, the less significant they became:

> Somebody wrote a big-character poster against my husband, so his work unit sent over a home search squad. When I came home from work that day, it was already over. The house was a mess, of course, but what could you do? They took away our photo albums, some jewelry, leather shoes, and some peacock feathers I used to decorate the house. Later they returned the jewelry and the shoes because I explained that they came with my dowry and weren't bought with the "black" money of my father-in-law, who had been suppressed as a counterrevolutionary in the early 1950s for his exploitation and ill treatment of workers.

In this case, bourgeois artifacts as such did not incriminate their owner unless they were proven to be the fruits of exploitation by an a priori accused counterrevolutionary, yet in another account by Grandma Apricot the sheer quantity of material wealth was enough to frame their owner, who had previously been presumed innocent:

> An engineer at my work unit was the thriftiest man we knew—all he ate was plain steamed buns and rice, and he wore the same Mao suit day in and day out. It would not have occurred to anyone to search his house if it weren't for his wife. Apparently, he beat her at home, and in a fit of anger she came to the work unit and informed the authorities that her husband was only pretending to lead a proletariat lifestyle at the work unit, that he really lived like a capitalist pig at home, that he took off all of his proletariat clothes at the threshold and changed into the luxurious attire of a young master. Before she could come to her senses, the home search squad struck and discovered a treasure trove—he had such a collection of antiques passed down from his ancestors! Heaven knows how much those things would be worth these days! So they emptied out his house and filled up an entire exhibition hall with the spoils.

Many items confiscated during the home searches were put on exhibition to educate the public about the decadent lifestyle of the bourgeoisie and to serve as the evidence of their exploitation of proletariats. Yet, as Aunt Duckweed recalls, such exhibitions did not always produce the intended effect:

> My mother took me to a few exhibitions at her factory. I saw mahogany furniture, ivory chopsticks, antique china, *qipao*, silk, yarns, and many other refined things I had never seen before. There was a bag of different combs, all very beautiful, to show the "absurdity and shamelessness of capitalist mistresses." These, they said, were the "fruits of the Cultural Revolution." Besides exhibitions, such bourgeois goods also filled second-hand stores, sold for a trifle to whomever was confident enough to buy them. Since my parents were workers and had no counterrevolutionary relatives, my mother bought some yarn—old brand yarn, 100 percent wool, with colors that had disappeared from the marketplace—and three pairs of pantyhose—one for herself, one for my sister, and one for me. She also bought a short-sleeved wool

sweater—a luxury because it was not for shielding one's body against the cold, but for vanity—and two silk scarves. We couldn't wear any of these things outside the house, of course, but it was a pleasure to own them nevertheless. The Cultural Revolution was the first time I realized how high the quality of life used to be in my parents' and grandparents' generation. After all, the things they used were so much more beautiful than anything we had then, which were purely utilitarian.

Soon after liberating Shanghai, the Communists had banned imports of various luxury commodities and closed down many public spaces of consumption, such as dance halls.[32] In the 1950s, the centrally planned economy monopolized all resources and abolished the distinctions between many domestic brand products so that everyday commodities became crude and rudimentary.[33] Although proscribed, earlier commodities still circulated in black markets, but as remnants of the "old world" they were both devalued and invaluable, for what was mass-produced became singular, and what went out of fashion became vintage items. As conspicuous consumption turned into clandestine consumption, these commodities-turned-into-souvenirs either hid within the homes of their original owners or quietly found their way into the homes of proletariats via the pawnshop. The Cultural Revolution exposed them to the eyes of the revolutionary masses, and some connoisseurs took the opportunity to appropriate such items for their own private pleasure.[34]

Aunt Xia, my mother's childhood friend, was the granddaughter of a rich capitalist and lived in a Western-style garden villa around the corner from Alliance Lane. Since her family came from the same clan as Chiang Kai-shek, they were "swept out" of their house during the Cultural Revolution. A decade later she encountered a Ming dynasty vase confiscated from her house in an old classmate's home in the same neighborhood. "I was overcome with emotion," she told my mother. "My entire childhood and the home search that took everything away flashed before my eyes. That's when I vowed to myself that I would get it all back someday." For her, that vase was a vestige of the private world of her childhood and reminded her all the more poignantly of its loss. Originally a status symbol of conspicuous consumption and a bourgeois item par excellence, the vase took on a new meaning as a result of its dispossession.

An Intellectual Family and Clandestine Reading in No. 111

My mother, Aunt Xia, and many other adolescents in the same neighborhood were attending East City Middle School when the Cultural Revolution began. Their vice principal happened to live on the ground floor of No. 111 Alliance Lane (see fig. 1.17K, L, M), two flights down from my mother's home. Principal Zhang and his wife (fig. 2.7), an accountant at another middle school, moved there in 1956 by swapping their apartment in another part of town with Grandma Apricot's father. They had two sons and two daughters, whom they called Big Brother, Big Sister, Little Sister, and Little Brother. Principal Zhang was a Communist Party member, whereas Mrs. Zhang was a devout Christian whose father had been a pastor. She had a harmonium and played hymns on it whenever she was in a good mood. Before every meal, she would lower her head and pray silently for a half-minute. Yet she did not go to church on Sundays and

FIGURE 2.7 Principal Zhang in the late 1940s and Mrs. Zhang and their first son in 1950. Photograph courtesy of Little Sister.

FIGURE 2.8 Aunt Duckweed (*first from left*) and her sister (*third from left*) with Little Sister and Big Sister, daughters of Principal Zhang around 1970. Photograph courtesy of Aunt Duckweed.

never spoke of Christianity to her children. To avoid contact and conflict with the other four families in the same house, she cooked in a small shack in her own sky well instead of in the communal kitchen and rarely used the back door to enter or exit the house. The only neighbor she associated with was Grandma Front Bedroom, who liked to knock on her door for an idle chat and whose daughter, Aunt Duckweed, often came to play with her little daughter (fig. 2.8).

As intellectuals, the Zhangs owned more books than all the other four families combined. Since they had no space for bookshelves, they stuffed their books under the bed and inside the loft. Mrs. Zhang hung picture books on a clothesline above the basins in the hallway for her children and their friends. Aunt Duckweed was among the beneficiaries of this library: "I loved to go to their house," she told me. "When Mr. and Mrs. Zhang were at work, the whole place was ours. I played mostly with Little Sister, but when Big Brother brought back middle school classmates to discuss more grown-up books, I would eavesdrop on their conversations."

Like most middle school teachers, Principal Zhang did not emerge from the Cultural Revolution unscathed. My mother recalled that he was among a long row of teachers seized on stage during several mass struggle sessions at school: "It was a shocking sight: all those respectable teachers were dressed in tatters and forced into jet plane postures—standing on a chair, bending over ninety degrees, and with a student at each side twisting their arms and pulling their hair. They really befit the label 'ox devils and snake spirits' [*niugui sheshen* 牛鬼蛇神]." When I interviewed Principal Zhang in 2000, he told me that the students in his school accused him of being "an international spy" because he once had two foreigner friends: "They found something wrong with all school-teachers and administrators—except my wife, who was so good-natured she never offended anyone. The students struggled against me every day, going from one classroom to another like a circus. They came to search my house, too, but when a Red Guard climbed into my loft and found nothing but old newspapers, he told his companions: 'He's stinking poor, let's go somewhere else.'"

One midnight in the autumn of 1966, the Red Guards at East City Middle School pounded on the front gate of No. 111 and took Principal Zhang away to an ox shed (*niupeng* 牛棚), a temporary prison for the "ox devils and snake spirits." His arrest, Aunt Duckweed recalled, extinguished all signs of life inside his home, and Mrs. Zhang did not even turn on the lights in the evening:

> My mother forbade me to go to their house now that big-character posters in the alleyway told us that Mr. Zhang was a reactionary academic authority [*fandong xueshu quanwei* 反動學術權威] and capitalist-roader. We didn't want any trouble, even though we knew that they were good people. Mr. Zhang did not come home all winter. Meanwhile, the school stopped paying his salary. It was almost Chinese New Year, and Mrs. Zhang could put very little on the table. On New Year's Eve, my mother put some yellow croaker in a basket and dropped it to the sky well from her window by a string—since she didn't want the neighbors to see her associate with an "ox devil and snake spirit" family. She swayed it to and fro until Mrs. Zhang saw the basket and took out the fish.

Less-kind neighbors took advantage of the situation and made the lives of the Zhangs more difficult. Little Sister recalled that whenever she went into the faucet room to wash clothes during the days her father was in the ox shed, the proletariat who lived upstairs in the back bedroom would pretend to wash his hands and block the narrow exit. So she would climb through the small window between the faucet room and the back living room to avoid rubbing shoulders with him.

In the spring, when Principal Zhang was finally allowed to come home, Grandma Front Bedroom asked him: "How was the ox shed?" "The ox shed was just fine," Principal Zhang replied. "We studied the works of Chairman Mao. The only bad thing about it was that they put me together with the 'four elements' [landlords, rich peasants, counterrevolutionaries, and 'bad elements' charged with nonpolitical crimes]." He seemed troubled less by his terrorizers than by being considered in the same league with socialist society's longtime pariahs. In my interview with Principal Zhang as an old man, he recalled his days in the alleyway after returning home from the ox shed with more humor than bitterness:

> The student rebels at my school posted a big-character poster at the entrance of our alleyway branch with the heading "Who is Zhang XX?" and a list of my "crimes." Following their orders, I reported to the neighborhood committee, which was supposed to help my thought reform through labor. They asked me: "What are you?" I said: "Reactionary academic authority." They said: "That's no big deal." So they assigned me the task of sweeping our alleyway branch and cleaning up the sewage in the gutters. I always performed my task at dawn, before most neighbors got up. Once I was poking at a congested gutter when a neighbor walked by. He didn't know of my troubles and asked me: "Principal Zhang, what are you doing?" I told him that my watch had dropped into the gutter, and I was trying to fish it out. I also had to report to the neighborhood committee: "Today I studied Chairman Mao's thoughts. I learned such and such. I remembered things I did wrong in the past. Today, through hard labor, I have fought my selfish whims . . . and so on and so forth." After a few weeks, I stopped sweeping the alleyway and reporting to the neighborhood committee, but no one seemed to care.

Although spared a house search, Principal Zhang, justly paranoid, burned old calligraphy scrolls and some of his books in the sky well. When asked what happened to her mother's Christian faith in this time, however, Little Sister produced her late mother's Bible, which had survived intact (fig. 2.9). The harmonium fell silent for a few years—only the

FIGURE 2.9 Mrs. Zhang's Bible, printed in 1951 in Hong Kong, survived the Cultural Revolution intact. Photograph courtesy of Little Sister.

children occasionally tapped out the rudimentary melodies of "East Is Red" or "Sailing the Seas Depends on the Great Helmsman" with one finger. One day Principal Zhang discovered that his teenage son was reading Tolstoy's *Resurrection* and was so enraged that he grabbed the book and tore it, not only along the spine, but also across every page. His son had a big fight with him and then pasted the book together page by page because he had borrowed it from a friend.

After the initial smashing, burning, and ravaging of 1966 and 1967, many confiscated four olds began to circulate beyond their former boundaries and contributed in unexpected ways to the enlightenment of the revolutionary youth. From late 1967 to the early 1970s, the students who first sealed off the bourgeois and decadent collections of various libraries later climbed over their walls to steal banned Western classics and secretly circulated the books among their friends.[35] Dumas, Brontë, Tolstoy, Goethe, Heine, Pushkin, Balzac, Hugo—all became enchanting, mysterious, and illicit names. Under their spell, many alleyway children did more reading during the Cultural Revolution than at any other time of their lives. Aunt Duckweed recalls:

> The elder son of the Zhangs borrowed banned books from his classmates, likewise my sister, your mother on the third floor, and other middle school age kids in our alleyway. To read more, they also circulated the books among themselves. Of course, one would lend only to those they trust since the discovery of such books likely spelled their confiscation or conflagration. A mean teacher at my school often made the class turn our book bags inside out, so we had to be extra careful. Since a book was often borrowed from a friend who borrowed it from a friend who borrowed it from

a friend, the loan period for a four-hundred-page novel was only a few days. My sister would try to read at every possible opportunity, even when she was washing her feet by the dim light in the corridor. Don't you scorn these fifteen-watt light bulbs; they lit the minds of all the children of this house into adulthood. My thirst to read was no less urgent, but since I couldn't get any books from my primary school, I could only wait till my sister was summoned away to do chores, grab the book from under her pillow, and imbibe the pages whether I understood them or not. These books were battered, often missing beginnings or middles or endings, for they were probably read by more people than any other books in the world. My parents knew that we were reading banned books, but they didn't interfere, for, despite being not very educated, they believed that reading couldn't be bad.

As revolutionary energy burned itself out among all but the most fervent youths, many young people in alleyways used their free time for bohemian pursuits: reading forbidden literature, singing Russian folk songs, and writing love letters. For some time, there had been some vague romantic feelings between my teenage mother and Grandma Apricot's eldest son, whose window faced my grandparents' terrace, so she could listen to his baritone singing and playing on the piano (fig. 2.10). Like many other alleyway romances, this one broke up with the sent-down youth movement, which required every urban family to send at least one child down to the countryside after 1969. After my mother left for the Great Northern Wilderness, Grandma Apricot's son, who stayed on in Shanghai on account of his frail health, still sent her letters and forbidden books, having undone the book's bindings and camouflaged the pages inside newspapers. Yet the party secretary in my mother's brigade, who claimed that he wanted to help her become a party member, routinely opened her letters and discovered Alexander Pushkin's poems interspersed between the leaves of *The People's Daily*. He lectured her on the difference between proletarian class love and individualistic bourgeois romance and asked her if she would destroy them herself or let him destroy them for her. My mother said she would do it herself. The next day she made an ostentatious little fire in front of her dormitory and threw a stack of paper into the flames, which everyone assumed was the book of poetry. "Of course it wasn't—the book wasn't mine to burn," my mother told me. She kept

FIGURE 2.10 My mother on the sun terrace of No. 111 Alliance Lane, overlooking the row of houses across the alleyway. Photograph taken in 1969.

it at the bottom of her suitcase for half a decade and then returned it to the owner after the Cultural Revolution, by which time the two were like strangers.

If "private space" for my mother took the form of Pushkin's poetry hidden between the pages of a party newspaper, then for her younger sister, Aunt Yahua, it was found in a much less risky love token: the Mao badge. Aunt Yahua often visited the home of a female classmate in a neighboring alleyway branch, so she also got to know her eldest brother, who joined the army in 1970. Since military service was only three years and one could return to Shanghai afterward with guaranteed employment, it was considered much better than going down to the countryside for life. To congratulate him and to bid farewell, his friends, including

Aunt Yahua, gave him Mao badges as gifts—as Aunt Yahua explained it to me, Mao badges were simply fashionable back then.[36] Later, this new soldier's mother came to speak to Waipo, telling her that her son received many Mao badges but wore only the one given by Aunt Yahua, so wouldn't Waipo give her daughter to him as a bride? Since Aunt Yahua was only sixteen at the time, Waipo said they should wait until the young man returned from the army, but in the three years he was gone, the two young people grew apart. In this case, petit bourgeois free love, feudal arranged marriages, and the revolutionary cult of Mao merged without apparent conflict or contradictions.

Just as Mao badges were love tokens, revolutionary songs were love songs, and Cultural Revolution era photographs where everyone posed with a little red book in front of Tiananmen Square (the real one or the backdrop in the photographer's studio) were all keepsakes of private friendships, familial bonds, and romantic liaisons.[37] After Yeye burned all his other English books as four olds, he still read the English edition of Chairman Mao's *Selected Works* in order not to forget his English. It was true that revolutionary politics had pervaded and politicized everyday life. Imprinted with icons and slogans of the time of their production, everyday artifacts—from enamel cups to pillows to letter paper to children's games—all served, much like loudspeakers and movie projectors, to spread the government's ideologies to the most peripheral corners of the nation to those who were never interested in politics. Yet when political propaganda assumed the form of everyday objects, the revolution also became trivialized, quotidianized, and privatized by their users. If many who lived through the Cultural Revolution look back to that era with nostalgia, notwithstanding the traumas suffered by their families, it has much to do with the private, sometimes subversive meanings and memories camouflaged beneath and within that era's public signifiers.

Petty Urbanites: Reinventing Privacy in the Reform Era

> The "really existing socialisms" fall prey to a commodity fetishism more extreme than in any capitalist society because it leads to the surrender of human dignity in exchange for these symbolic markers of modern life.
> —ANN ANAGNOST, *NATIONAL PAST-TIMES*[38]

When Uncle Lucky married Aunt May in 1982, he repainted the floor, installed Venetian blinds on the windows, and bought a brand-new set of furniture for their marriage chamber, including a pair of sofas, a color television, a stereo, a refrigerator, and a washing machine (see fig. 1.26G). She brought eight sets of linens, pillows, and quilts to add to her trousseau chest of clothing, hats, and shoes, along with curtains, cups, thermoses, and other useful things with the most fashionable designs of the time. Uncle Lucky bought Aunt May a gold necklace and gave her Nainai's only gold ring that had not been pawned to supplement the family income. They held their wedding in a nice restaurant—she wore a bright red cotton jacket instead of just a red corsage—and more than fifty guests came to the banquet.

A few days after their wedding, Aunt Treasure—Yeye and Nainai's oldest child—came to visit. A true believer in the revolution, Aunt Treasure had volunteered to go "support the borderland" of Xinjiang, considered a peripheral and underdeveloped region in Western China, after graduating from Beijing Normal University in 1968 and never moved back to Shanghai. Since then, she had taught biology at a secondary school in Urumuqi and had to live on rather modest means, but she always took pride in her career, calling herself an "engineer of the human soul." She took one look at her new sister-in-law and did not like what she saw. "I've been home for almost a week now, and she's worn a different outfit every day, with matching shoes too!" Aunt Treasure reported to Nainai. "Do you know how many pairs of shoes she owns? I looked inside her wardrobe. She has eleven pairs of shoes! Why would *anyone* need eleven pairs of shoes? Even the most senior professor at my husband's university doesn't own eleven pairs of shoes. Who does she think she is anyway? Nothing but a bourgeois parasite and petty urbanite!"

The term *petty urbanite* (*xiao shimin* 小市民) was used to describe, "often with condescension, a type of person whose outlook was limited by the community in which he or she lived." Without its derogatory connotation, the term also referred to "the middle class or the petit bourgeoisie," which include "small merchants, various kinds of clerks and secretaries, high school students, housewives, and other modestly educated, marginally well off urbanites."[39] In Republican era Shanghai, petty urbanites were identified with the *shikumen* house and constituted the main audience for lifestyle magazines such as *Liangyou* 良友 (Young companion) and *Shenghuo* 生活 (Life), which taught them "to make the best of their circumstances, to exercise self-control, and to cultivate spiritual composure."[40] Living in mainly nuclear family units, petty urbanites were targets of advertising for various commodities that would enhance their everyday comfort.[41] After the Communist takeover, the term *petty urbanite* was replaced by such Marxist expressions as *bourgeois* (*zichan jieji* 資產階級) and *petit bourgeois* (*xiao zichan jieji* 小資產階級), only to resurface again after the Cultural Revolution.[42] Aside from Aunt Treasure, I often heard Waigong use the term in the 1980s and 1990s to describe alleyway neighbors who wanted to read only "hearsay and gossip" in the local evening paper, whereas *he* read only about national and world affairs in "serious" newspapers such as *Liberation Daily* and *Reference News*.

Every afternoon after school was out, I would hear paper vendors hawk "*Evening News* is here! *Evening News* is here!" as I crisscrossed the narrow streets and alleyways. Certainly the most popular reading material among the Shanghainese of the 1980s and early 1990s, *Evening News* (*Xinmin* 新民晚報) was the newspaper that prided itself on "flying into the homes of common folks" with its colloquial language and concern with everyday life.[43] By the time I reached home, alleyway grandmas and aunties would already be talking about what they had read: the medicinal effects of this or that food, the rights and wrongs of divorce, new revelations about old Shanghai gangsters, heart-wrenching tales of self-sacrificial teachers, or enraging stories of unfilial children. The latest National Congress and international border conflicts did not interest them, for they wanted to read about people like themselves, everyday moral dilemmas, and means of improving their daily lives. After all, they were petty urbanites, whose kingdom was their home and whose world was their neighborhood.

After a decade of weary class struggle and the politicization of everyday life, Shanghai residents began to retreat from public squares and assembly halls into the domestic sphere by the late 1970s, as if to avenge the imposed collectivity and material deprivations in the Mao era.[44] In her study of Shanghainese home interiors in the 1980s, sociologist Deborah Davis found that none but one of the hundred or so apartments she visited "had any decorations with explicit political content." Rather, common decorations were "pictures of parents and children displayed in the respondent's bedroom/parlor,"[45] showing that it was once again acceptable to exhibit private loyalties over public ones. Furthermore, the private space of the home became increasingly delineated from public or communal spaces, as Davis writes of the apartments she studied: "[In the hallways] bicycles were chained to the railings, dusty bamboo couches hung from nails high on the wall, scraps of building materials were thrown into corners, and, as usual, the overhead lamp sockets were empty. However, once beyond the securely bolted doors and over the threshold, I entered a tidy, private refuge."[46]

The callous attitude toward public spaces greatly contrasted with the fastidious care for private spaces. Almost every home I visited in Shanghai and other Chinese cities from the mid-1990s on—from modern apartments inside high-rises to pavilion rooms inside alleys—required the guest to take off her shoes and change into slippers at the threshold. After all, the floors inside were paved with expensive wood or tiles as a part of the whole renovation package. The contrast between the gray, dark, and dirty hallways and the clean and shiny interior was often so great I had the sensation of walking from a monochrome world into a Technicolor realm. At the same time, to ward off burglars, there were usually at least two layers of doors—the outer one with railing—and two or three locks per door, so that entering a home felt increasingly like entering into a high-security prison cell.[47]

Besides the sharper delineation of private homes from public or communal spaces, younger generations also increasingly claimed their own private spaces *away from* or even *within* the homes of their parents. The 1980s saw the construction of more housing than the combined achievements of the three decades before it,[48] but as suggested in chapter 1, when those born in the 1950s came of age, the housing shortage forced many to carve marriage chambers out of their parents' homes. These "new homes" nestled inside old houses created multigenerational households reminiscent of traditional times, but new norms of family dynamics often turned old generational hierarchies on their heads, and a younger generation's reinvention of privacy sometimes came at the expense of an elder generation.

Uncle Lucky and Aunt May were among the first generation to equip their marriage chamber with a color television, a stereo, a refrigerator, and a washing machine in the early 1980s. "Using electrical appliances," Chiara Saraceno points out in her discussion of modern Italian families, "allows greater privacy for family activities, which no longer must take place in public because of a lack of space and facilities."[49] Instead of playing in the alleyway, children could stay home and watch TV; instead of going to the grocery market every day, the family cook could simply reach into the refrigerator; and instead of cooling themselves out in the alleyway on summer evenings, a family could shut their doors and windows and turn on the air conditioner. Along with the improvement in the supply of commodities, the time-saving appliances also greatly reduced the housework burden and left more leisure time to enjoy this newfound private space,[50] while modern entertainment devices, in particular the television, became the new halos of family intimacy. At the same time, television was perhaps a more subtle and effective means by which the state propagated its ideology into the private minds of its citizens.

With the exception of the washing machine, which needed tap water from the ground floor, Uncle Lucky and Aunt May kept all their new appliances inside their bedroom, even the refrigerator. Enshrined at the top of the main wall, above the color TV, was their wedding picture, where the two of them posed in rented white gown and tuxedo. After their first and only child was born, her picture was added to the wall and a crib to the middle of the room. Her toys gradually filled up a corner of the room, which became her personal play space, something neither of her parents ever had when they were children. In this sense, the private-life-invading one-child policy has had the paradoxical effect of making private space possible for that one little "emperor" or "empress." Since both Uncle Lucky and Aunt May had to work during the day, Nainai served as the babysitter. She also mopped their floor, dusted their furniture, and cooked their dinner, which they ate in the shanty where my grandparents slept and then went upstairs to their private haven, where my grandparents would never disturb them no matter how much they would have liked to watch color TV.

I asked my grandparents why they had given up the best room in their house to Uncle Lucky and Aunt May. Yeye sighed and said that it must have been his "feudal bones," for he had wanted to have three generations living under the same roof like good old traditional Chinese households. After all, Yeye's own parents had come to live in Yeye's house in Shanghai from the late 1950s to their death in the late 1970s. In those revolutionary decades, they may not have commanded as much authority as they used to in the 1930s and 1940s, yet no matter how much the Communists had liberated women, Nainai still prepared hot water for her parents-in-law to wash their faces and feet every morning and evening. By the time Yeye and Nainai became parents-in-law in the 1980s and 1990s, however, none of their sons, daughters, or in-laws ever lifted a finger to serve them. Instead, they might consider themselves lucky if their "filial children" brought them gifts of money or food.[51]

Rather than looking to the hardships of life a generation ago, my uncles and aunts looked to the foreigners on television for "life as it should be." In 1990, the American sit-com *Growing Pains* began broadcasting on Chinese TV and became an instant hit, and many watched it as an ethnographic study of the American lifestyle. Besides the democratic domestic relationships that contrasted with Chinese practices of bringing up children,[52] we noticed that the Seaver family had a living room, every family member had his or her bedroom, and everyone knocked before entering anyone else's room. TV drama from Taiwan, Hong Kong, Japan, and Singapore showed similar standards of private space. "I never had a desire for my own room apart from my parents until I saw how people elsewhere lived," Little Aunt's husband told me. He had spent the first twenty years of his life living in the same room as his parents and two brothers, but by the time he married Little Aunt in the late 1990s, the minimal housing standard for middle-class newlyweds in Shanghai rose to include a living room and a bedroom plus a private kitchen and a private bathroom.

This new or Western conception of private life changed not only the spatial standards for Shanghai homes, but also their interior furnishing and appearance. When my parents and grandparents took me to visit their friends and neighbors in Shanghai in the 1980s, every home had virtually the same set of furniture as well as the same basins, thermoses, towels, lights, clocks, and blankets, all mass-produced by the state-owned factories in the area. Perhaps this was why domestic TV dramas set in the socialist era seemed so endearing to Chinese urban residents—after all, everything on television was in your home as well. Yet a decade later in the late 1990s, when I went to visit some of the same uncles and aunties, their homes were suddenly made anew with sofas, coffee tables, beds with mattresses, glass cabinets, family entertainment centers, and even minibars. Many alleyway residents had built illegal structures in their sky wells, backyards, or terraces, renovating their interiors into modern bathrooms with showers, flush toilets, and modern kitchens with shiny white tiles.

In the era of market reforms, Chinese city dwellers began investing substantial time and money to remodel their homes, be they old or new apartments, so that most domestic spaces came to be transformed through the rise of a "decorating culture." Unlike exterior decoration, as Xiaobing Tang points out, "interior design is compelled to address an individual rather than a projected crowd, to speak a more intimate *parole* with accented variations." As a business, interior design cashes in on "personal preferences, encourage[s] hobbies and idiosyncrasies, and profit[s] from the notion of multiple identities." In the late 1990s in Shanghai, this investment changed not only the interior looks of homes, but also the very meaning of interiority: "instead of articulating a spiritual or psychic structure of depth, interiority . . . now describe[d] a new frontier market for customized products of sorts."[53]

By the year 2000, even Aunt Treasure, having retired from her job as an "engineer of the human soul," unabashedly embraced her materialistic consumer desires, having moved to Shenzhen with her husband and son. When I asked her over the phone if she still meant what she had said about Aunt May eighteen years earlier, she said, "Not at all," embarrassed at my asking. "It was just that at the time, when I saw her cardigans and silk pajamas and leather shoes, I remembered how I wore patched trousers and had only two pair of shoes throughout my adolescence—there had never been any luxuries in our house, and we always seemed so poor in comparison to my classmates. . . . But now that your uncle [her husband] is making more money, I also own leather shoes that cost more than 300 yuan." I asked her if she still believed in Communist ideals now that her family also "jumped into the sea" of business. She fired back: "Workers would be out of jobs without capitalists. Your uncle might make ten times more money than his employees, but he also works twenty times as hard. It's much harder to be an entrepreneur than a teacher because you have to juggle many tasks and take risks. Besides, what our country needs most now is economic development!"

Thrift, Bricolage, and Nostalgia for the Alleyway

Many years after coming to the United States, I would still dream of my grandparents' alleyway home, where I had lived intermittently throughout my childhood. In the dreams, it would always be the "Yellow Mildew" monsoon season. Rainwater flowed from the corners of the eaves into the buckets and basins Waipo used to collect the rain on the terrace. The water made deep splashes in the colorful plastic buckets and sharp timbalelike sounds in aluminum basins. Through the rain I could hear the cooing of pigeons, the prayers and laughter and weeping of Grandma

Back Bedroom and her fellow worshippers, Waigong tuning his transistor radio, a neighbor singing a revolutionary model opera, a mother scolding a child. . . . The rain muffled some voices while making others more distinct than ever before, but I paid no heed to them, for I would be sitting inside the tiny attic room with the slanted ceiling and reading a book by the pale light from the tiny window that looked onto the oceanic waves of alleyway roofs.

Beginning in the late 1980s, more and more Shanghai residents moved out of alleyway housing into newly constructed high-rises. When I left Alliance Lane at the age of eleven to go abroad with my parents in 1991, it was already no longer as populated as it used to be, and by 2000 even Waigong and Waipo "bade farewell to their night stools [chamber pots]" and moved out of their old alleyway. It took little time for everyone to grow used to a comfortable modern lifestyle with private, white-tiled bathrooms and kitchens, hot water faucets and flushing toilets, and large rooms stuffed with consumer goods bought in bountiful supermarkets. Indeed, no one I talked to earnestly wished to return to the crowded alleyways in the Socialist era with its material and spiritual deprivations. And yet the alleyway, with its destruction through urban renewal, came to inhabit the nostalgic dreamscapes of their former residents, as if planted within those labyrinths were the enigma of what it meant to be home.

The usual explanation for alleyway nostalgia is the lost social or communal intimacy with neighbors as each family's and individual's threshold of privacy thickened. The rise of urban crime introduced iron grids on everybody's doors and windows, making modern middle-class homes private prisons of an isolated and alienated existence.[54] Yet there is also a less noted factor: the declining worth of things through the rise of consumerism, so that everyday artifacts—however varied and individuated— became disposable and forgettable because their consumers never had the need to invest them with their own labor and creativity, sentience and memories. By contrast, material scarcity, best represented by the rationing system of the socialist era, gave rise to an art, habit, and value of thrift and bricolage shared among all my grandparents and other elderly persons who lived through that era.

Although my maternal grandparents produced reams of silk every day at their factory for export from the 1950s to the 1980s, they were subject to the same rations of fabric that made clothes "new for three years, old for three years, mended and patched for another three years." Siblings wore one another's hand-me-downs, and a piece of fabric had several lives, from a dress or shirt to sleeve covers or patches on pants—from one's pride to one's shame. After being soiled and laundered, sunned and mildewed, it would be turned into a rag to wipe the table, a mop for the floor, or stuffing for the soles of winter cotton shoes, so that at the end it knew the multiple body parts of various family members as well as many surfaces of a home.

Starting in the mid-1990s, by contrast, my grandparents began accumulating within their wardrobe and storage chests what they called "classy garbage," perfectly "new" and "fashionable" clothing abandoned by their children and grandchildren. Initially they were able to give such clothing to their relatives in the countryside, but by the mid-2000s nobody wanted them. Still my grandparents hoarded these things and wished to give value to them through use—a Sisyphean task given that the synthetic fabric popularized in the 1980s did not easily get worn out. Donned in clothing that they themselves obviously did not buy, for some time my grandparents joined an army of old people on Shanghai streets who appeared to dress in their children's hand-me-downs.

Everyone who spent childhood in a Shanghai alleyway until the 1990s probably remembers the location of the family's cookie tin, usually placed beyond a child's reach on top of some wardrobe or bookshelf, or of some snack basket that dangled tantalizingly from the ceiling. The tin often had a bright picture of chubby boys and girls or animals, though the color was faded, and the tin was chipped and rusty. Our next door neighbor's cookie tin was misshapen and patched with bandages because it had tumbled from its height many times when the children climbed on top of stools to knock it down. Inside the tin would be goodies such as roasted peanuts, popped rice, cookies, or other baked goods, usually from Chinese New Year or the Mid-autumn Festival or, in the case of my grandparents, from their country relatives.

Until the widespread use of gas stoves in the 1980s, alleyway mornings and evenings were filled with the choking smoke of coal stoves. To prepare the fire in the coal stove, you built a little castle in the air with newspapers at the bottom, pieces of firewood in the middle, and coal briquettes on top. While the fire passed from the match to the paper to the firewood to the coal, you had to fan the stove with all your might—amid smoke and crackle, coughs and tears, as if struggling with a dragon—until the coal briquette finally caught fire and turned glowing red. As the paper and wood turned into ashes, you carefully poked the briquettes from the top so that they fell gently rather than with a thump that put out the fire. Once the stove was lit, you put a big kettle of water on boil, which filled three or four thermoses to be used throughout the day, not only to drink but also to add a splash of warm water into the basin to wash your face, feet, or laundry. Next came the rice—once it boiled, you placed an iron plate over the fire, left a crescent opening, and rotated the pot slowly to even out the heat on all sides. You then wrapped the cooked rice inside an old quilt to keep warm. Now you could take off the iron plate and fan the stove to make a big fire for the stir-fry of a few dishes, meanwhile trying not to splatter scalding oil on your neighbors. After cooking, you could either put out the fire or "seal" the stove with the iron plate, whose tiny hole allowed oxygen to flow in and keep the fire "hibernating" until the next meal. If it was winter, you placed half a kettle of water on the stove— you'd be grateful for this bit of heat when washing with this water later.

Food grains, fabric, coal, and other everyday necessities were subject to rationing from the mid-1950s to the mid-1980s throughout urban China,[55] shaping the collective memories of my less politicized family members and neighbors so much that they thought of the socialist era as the "rationed decades." Since the actual supply of goods often fell even shorter than the promises of ration coupons, it became necessary for several family members to rise at the crack of dawn to wait in various queues to obtain the best quality of what there was. The use of bricks and baskets as placeholders often led to noisy quarrels and entertaining spectacles, and everyone had to curry favors with the sellers and put up with their pride and prejudice. Loaded with dirt and decay, vegetables took enormous amounts of time and effort to prepare before they could be cooked; meat or chicken, affordable only on special occasions, came in measly portions that were cut again into tiny pieces. Hence, every meal was a rich stew of toil and calculation, resentment and love, consumed through whatever choreography of chopsticks that corresponded to the unique dynamics of each family.

Not only were Shanghai residents thrifty and inventive with their rations, but, many of them former farmers, they were also sensitive to nature's cycles along with its gifts and threats of sun, rain, and wind. They collected the sun's heat and dryness in their blankets to kill the mildew that built up over the rainy season. To save water they collected the rain to mop their wooden floors until they shined, or they recycled their face-washing water to wash their feet, their rice-washing water to wash the dishes, their laundry water to wash their night stools. To save electricity they turned on the light only when it got really dark, went to bed early, and rose with the crack of dawn. Before the widespread use of air conditioners, they found spots to "catch" every breeze that blew through their homes or alleyways. In the winters, they would warm themselves by the coal stove while heating a kettle of hot water, which they would fill briskly into the thermos lest some of the heat escape. They planted flowers and scallions wherever there was a bit of space and sunshine, and they kept cats, birds, goldfish, cicadas, and chickens.

In contrast to the Marxist idea that objects are inanimate and that human obsession with things leads to a fetishization of commodities and an indifference toward other persons, Elaine Scarry writes of artifacts as projections of human sentience, projections of their makers' aliveness in a world that is always in danger of being "unmade." Subjectivity is thus not effaced but, on the contrary, constructed and reconstructed in the production and consumption of manmade objects.[56] In *The Human Condition*, Hannah Arendt distinguishes between "the labor of our body" (a repetitive, endless process) and "the work of our hands" (fabrication of worldly objects). She claims that with the division of labor "the industrial revolution has replaced all workmanship with labor," for the modern acceleration of machines forces us into a quicker rhythm of repetition and brings about an abundance that transforms use objects into consumer goods: "The ideals of *homo faber*, the fabricator of the world, which are permanence, stability, and durability, have been sacrificed to abundance, the ideal of the *animal laborans*. We live in a laborers' society because only laboring, with its inherent fertility, is likely to bring about abundance; and we have changed work into laboring, broken it up into its minute particles until it has lent itself to division where the common denominator of the simplest performance is reached."[57]

Although most residents of my grandparents' neighborhood were factory workers who adapted their bodies to the rhythm of machines to maximize productivity, the shortages they faced in their everyday lives forced them to learn crafts and skills not ordinarily required of industrial laborers in order to make their homes with their own hands. Comparable to the cogs and wheels of machines in their public lives, they all were *bricoleurs* in their private lives, with different family members and close neighbors serving as carpenter, mason, plumber, electrician, seamstress, and shoemaker as needed. Aunt Pearl's shanty and wheelchair, Nainai's milk delivery cart, and Yeye's transistor radio were all works of bricolage. Exposed wiring, mismatched colors, uneven beams, and coarse edges of the shanties, lofts, and rickety staircases pointed to the imperfect and idiosyncratic work of amateur hands. Out of necessity, my grandmother's generation of women imprinted their needlework on every piece of fabric worn by their families, for most people still wore handmade clothing and shoes from the 1950s to the 1970s, often treating them with greater care than their own bodies. When boys in the alleyway climbed and jumped from heights, their mothers scolded them not so much because they pitied the wounds on their children's knees and elbows, but because their shirts and trousers might be soiled and torn.

Even mass-produced, machine-made commodities took on greater sentience when they were difficult to replace due to a family's limited finances or unavailability in the stores and especially when they came unmade and were then remade. Precarious yet precious were those bowls once broken and put back together by a bowlsmith using tiny nails, or those straw mats torn and mended, or the lamp that had been rewired to a new light switch, or the television whose white noise turned into proper images only with the skillful turn of a toothpick. As my grandparents aged, they felt ever-greater empathy for old, worn, and broken things in their households, referring to them as having but "half a life," just like themselves, for little did they seem to recognize that it was the work of their own hands that gave these inanimate objects a "life" at all.

3

GOSSIP

Their deaths were but a grain of salt dropped into the endless sea of gossip, adding some flavor. But soon, the gossip trade will be the same as before—tasteless and meaningless.

—LU XUN, "GOSSIP IS A FEARFUL THING"[1]

Gossip is always shallow and vulgar.... It is somewhat like the trash of speech... and yet, it is only in such shoddy scandalous material that something true may be found. These true things lie behind dignified appearances. They are things one would be afraid to tell oneself, and so one tells others.

—WANG ANYI, *THE SONG OF EVERLASTING SORROW*[2]

THE WRINKLES AROUND my grandmother's mouth grow outward from her lips like a chrysanthemum. This is because she pouts so much. She pouts when she eats something delicious and when she eats something unsavory. She pouts when prices rise and when prices drop. She pouts when she hears about somebody's death and when she hears about somebody's riches. Waipo's pout can express both pity and envy; it is a signal of life's delectability and bitterness. Waipo often took me to visit neighbors and relatives in their alleyway homes, climbing dark rickety staircases and eating half-rotten apples. I don't remember the content of their conversations, only laughter, sighs, and head shaking. Oftentimes Waipo's mouth puckered up and her eyebrows tied into a knot, as if she had just eaten a sour plum. The chrysanthemum around her mouth simultaneously expressed compassion and severity, disapproval and resignation, belief and skepticism. At once a hyperbole and an understatement, it held for me all the mysteries of the adult world.

The history of any alleyway should be written as an anthology of gossip exchanged among its residents. Circulating through whispers from mouth to ear, it was the most important medium through which many alleyway residents learned of the goings-on in the world and circulated their own tales to an audience of discerning listeners. Using the Chinese concepts of *liuyan* 流言 (flowing words) and *siyu* 私語 (private speech), my definition of gossip here is not so much talk about an absent third party as an intimate discursive mode, a trickle of words that simultaneously confide and publicize, a liminal zone where private and public spheres seep into each other. Especially in the socialist era, in the absence of polyphonous mass media, gossip served as an information network for the quotidian sharing of tips and warnings: "The breakfast stand on Liaoyang Road makes the biggest and crispiest fried dough." "You can't get along with your neighbor? Well, a family in the next alleyway would also like to swap housing." "Don't say that so loudly! My coworker was sent to labor reform for spreading rumors about the Great Leap Forward." But the juiciest gossip taps into still more intimate places, and the subjects are often the domestic dramas of one's closest neighbors: "So I came out of my room to go into the kitchen, and there they were . . . " "Last night, he broke the mirror on the wardrobe . . . " "Her mother-in-law came to stay with them this week. Finally, *someone* can control that woman!"

Alleyway residents enjoy such gossip because in other people's pain and embarrassment they find catharsis or consolation for the unspeakable in their own lives. Descriptions of scenes and moments unravel into complicated and serialized narratives featuring complex relationships playing out over several generations. While telling or listening to these stories, alleyway residents exercise judgment and deal out compassion. Most importantly, from the stories they draw lessons on how to live their own lives. The "best" gossip is "melodramatic" in that it contains "intense emotional and ethical drama" and seeks to establish "moral legibility."[3] But most tales told through gossip remain morally turgid, ambivalent, and deviant from any established moral codes. Thus, gossip teaches, reinforces, and questions the sense and sensibility, pride and prejudice of the alleyway community.

Whereas home is a foothold defined by square meters in the first chapter and a haven defined by the boundaries of privacy in the second chapter, it is a site of private storytelling and unofficial narratives in this chapter. The first section, a cultural genealogy of Shanghai gossip, seeks to theorize and historicize gossip as a social practice, a literary trope, and an alternative history mediated by word of mouth, newspapers, fiction, cinema, and alleyway architecture. As an antithesis to official historiography and the state's memory of itself, gossip has remained a privileged mode of narrative production in this metropolis from the late Qing to the present. The second section, which explores why and how the alleyway space ferments gossip, takes the reader on a trip with me to Alliance Lane. As we navigate the alleyway maze, we will consider how the intersection of people and activities in communal spaces facilitated the spinning of mesmerizing narratives as well as a voyeuristic and exhibitionist theater of everyday life. Weaving together some of these narrative strands, the third section reconstructs the lives or legends of a few women who grew old in this alleyway. By examining their stories and the ways in which they were told, I show the palimpsest of values that governed the community, values that were in turn shaped by the actual lives of its members. The final section, "A Room of Her Own: The Whispers of Aunt Duckweed," is an intimate autobiographical account by a downstairs neighbor in No. 111 Alliance Lane who spent the first twenty-six years of her life with her parents, a sister, and a brother in a single-room home. Her story is about her parents' unhappy marriage, her mother's and brother's mental illness, her father's strident, desolate death, as well as the romantic illusions and sordid realities shared by many Shanghainese alleyway residents of her generation.

A Cultural Genealogy of Shanghai Gossip

What is this thing we call gossip? Does it belong to the study of sociology, literature, or history? Where is gossip? Does it reside in the clouds of celebrity circles or in the gutters of petty urbanites? What does gossip taste like? Is it salty or sour, bland or bitter? Is it the spice of our lives, or is it simply bad taste? Who is the author of gossip? The one gossiping, the one gossiped about, or the one gossiped to? When we gossip, are we actually talking about other people or about ourselves? What is the vehicle of gossip? Is its medium word of mouth, newspaper, fiction, cinema, or space? Is it fact or fiction, public or private, frivolous or serious, a tool of the powerful or of the powerless?

Anthropologists have studied and theorized the social function of gossip since the 1960s. Max Gluckman considers gossip a form of social control that maintains group unity, morals, and values: "The right to gossip about certain people is a privilege which is only extended to a person when he or she is accepted as a member of a group or set. It is a hallmark of membership."[4] By contrast, Robert Paine contends that "it is the individual and not the community that gossips—it is a personal discourse motivated by the self-interests of the gossipers."[5] Reconciling the group-oriented versus individual-oriented analyses, the symbolic-interactionist approach emphasizes the role of gossip in representing and debating cultural reality and social relations: "Gossip provides individuals with a map of their social environment and with current information about happenings, inhabitants and their dispositions. This then provides the resource by which they can devise a program of action."[6] In a Chinese cultural context, Margery Wolf emphasizes the importance of informal gossip networks that rural women in Taiwan formed as a control on men's behavior.[7] In studying youth sex culture in 1990s Shanghai, James Farrer suggests that the humor of gossip dulls its harsh judgments, and "gossipers' wide exposure to different stories makes them more 'realistic' about human nature, even if not overtly tolerant."[8]

Beyond anthropological perspectives, gossip has also attracted the attention of literary critics for its aesthetic and creative qualities. "Gossip, like novels, is a way of turning life into story," according to Rachel Brownstein. "Good gossip approximates art."[9] In a book-length study of gossip in relationship to Anglo-American literature, Patricia Spacks distinguishes between gossip as motivated by pure malice, at one end, and what she calls "serious gossip" that fosters intimacy and a potentially subversive female community, on the other. Although pointing to generic similarities between gossip and the novel, the pastoral, and drama—especially since we act on a voyeuristic desire to know in both gossip and fiction—she also notes gossip's difference from literature in that it is oral rather than written and deals with actual rather than invented characters.[10]

In the Chinese cultural tradition, gossip has occupied a curious place between history and fiction. As a historiographic source, gossip and anecdotal stories have long been considered suspect, for as Confucius says, "To hear it on the roads and to pass it along in the streets is to abandon virtue." Beyond the task of verification, gossip, as Jack Chen observes, is the antithesis of archivist records and animates a tension "between public knowledge, which was articulated along the vertical axes of state hegemonic power, and private knowledge, which circulated along what might be considered the horizontal axes of societal relationships and networks."[11] Yet even early official historians such as Ban Gu 班固 (32–92 CE) did not entirely reject the collection of "street talk and alley gossip, made up by those who engage in conversations along the roads and walkways." He called such gossip *xiaoshuo* 小說, literally "minor talk" or "small talk"—which later became the Chinese term for fiction.[12] Over the dynasties, officials collected miscellaneous anecdotes of the common folk to study popular sentiments and customs, and later on *xiaoshuo* also became a place for literati to chronicle alternative and unofficial histories.[13]

With the rise of modern journalism in Shanghai, the newspaper became a new medium for both fiction and gossip. In his study of Shanghai installment fiction from the 1890s through the 1920s, Alexander Des Forges shows that gossip columns often appeared in close juxtaposition with installments of fictional narratives and that the two genres likely shared some of the same subject matters and pool of readers.[14] As Catherine Yeh suggests in her study of Shanghai's courtesans in the late Qing, men of letters such as Li Boyuan 李伯元 and Han Bangqing 韓邦慶 "collected gossip by and about courtesans" and committed them to the pages of tabloid newspapers and literary works.[15] Both male literati and female courtesans lived and socialized in alleyway spaces, which contributed to the content and the form of the textual production.[16] Written in a richly textured local vernacular and featuring gossiplike psychological speculation and narrative multiplicity, Han Bangqing's 1892 novel *The Sing-song Girls of Shanghai* would later be regarded as a pioneering work of modern Chinese literature and the foundation of what was later called *haipai* 海派, or "Shanghai style."[17]

In Shanghai of the 1930s, however, gossip—both in print and as a social practice—came under vehement attack by progressive intellectuals. In the classic 1934 film *The Goddess* (*Shennü* 神女), directed by Wu Yonggang 吳永剛 and starring the actress Ruan Lingyu 阮玲玉, the malicious gossip of idle housewives made it impossible for a mother who worked as a prostitute to send her only son to school, eventually leading to her incarceration. In her next role in Cai Chusheng's 蔡楚生 *New Women* (*Xin nüxing* 新女性), Ruan Lingyu played a female author, Wei Ming, driven to suicide by the calumnious reporting about her in the tabloid press. In a tragic case of life imitating art, Ruan herself committed suicide in 1935 when besieged with public rumors about her private life. In the wake of her death, renowned writer Lu Xun 鲁迅 wrote a memorial essay highlighting a phrase from a suicide note attributed to Ruan: "'Gossip is a fearful thing' [*renyan kewei* 人言可畏] is what we read in movie star Ruan Lingyu's suicide note, found after her death. After much empty chatter over this sensational event, public attention has gradually cooled. As soon as the drama 'Lingyu's Fragrance Vanishes with the Wind' stops playing, the whole incident will fade away without a trace, just like Ai Xia's suicide a year ago. Their deaths were but a grain of salt dropped into the endless sea of gossip, adding some flavor. But soon, the gossip trade will be the same as before—tasteless and meaningless."[18]

Lu Xun went on to issue a battle cry against the kind of "gossip journalism" that titillated the curiosity and satisfied the schadenfreude of Shanghai's petty urbanites, all of whom participated in the victimization of a famous but powerless woman. However, although condemning gossip's cannibalistic powers in which the entire society was complicit, Lu Xun himself liked to participate in informal evening chats with his alleyway coresidents—often intellectuals like himself—and wrote about some of those discussions in an essay entitled "Outdoor Chatting on Language and Literature." The topics of the chats "included the drought, prayers for rain, the flirt, the [so-called] three-inch dwarf, exposed thighs, as well as ancient Chinese prose, vernacular, the language of the masses."[19] With its concern for more public than private matters, it is questionable whether Lu Xun's outdoor chatting fully qualifies as "gossip," yet here we also see the fluid boundaries between public and private spheres in the alleyway, which consisted of residents from all walks of life and widely different backgrounds. Participation in these outdoor chats helped one gain a savvy understanding of the wider world.

A decade later in wartime Shanghai, the celebrity writer Eileen Chang (Zhang Ailing 張愛玲) would redefine and redeem gossip by using the word *liuyan* for the title of her essay collection, literally "flowing words." As Nicole Huang explicates Chang's use of the term, "She does not expect her writing to endure; instead her work should be thought of as words written on water . . . lingering momentarily and eventually fading. But she also hopes that her writing will be endowed with the spirit of 'rumors' or 'gossip'—a second denotation of the word *liuyan*—flowing freely and swiftly in order to reach the widest possible audience."[20] Comparing the essay genre to "a fluid form of gossip or a series of leisurely chats with her readers," the collection also contains a significant autobiographical essay entitled "Siyu," which can be translated as "Private Talk" or "Whispers," which "mimics the lowered voice and fragmented syntax used in speaking of the most intimate moments of one's private life."[21] Far from fearing gossip, Chang embraced it as an art form as well as a medium for its transmission—a mode of sharing her own personal experience with a community of strangers. Not only do her essays employ the tone of leisure chats and contain scraps of gossip she overheard on the streets, but gossip about "trivial" domestic matters also constitutes a source for her fiction. Living in an age of war and revolution, Eileen Chang chose not to write about extraordinary feats of heroes, but about quotidian episodes involving "equivocal characters," petty urbanites with "unalloyed passion for material life," for they were the resilient "majority who actually bear the weight of the times."[22]

After the Communist takeover of Shanghai, gossip ceased to occupy the printed page as virtually all tabloid newspapers and popular literary magazines closed down in the early years of the People's Republic.[23] As Shanghai literary historian Wang Xiaoming observes, "The increasing monotony of newspaper and radio made alleyway gossip all the more captivating, for how else could petty urbanites without power or influence obtain credible information?"[24] With the establishment of neighborhood committees, however, gossip about alleyway residents also became an instrument of surveillance as professional or recreational busybodies informed the police about their neighbors' private affairs, from how their ancestors made a living to what they had for supper last night. As the revolution's mass campaigns divided and subdivided the housing of once privileged households, as household registration made mobility and anonymity increasingly difficult, each family's privacy depended increasingly on their neighbors' discretion and compassion. Indeed, knowledge of gossip about others could become a weapon to defend one's own privacy, for it was the best way to shut up other people's gossip about oneself. At the same time, the presence of a judgmental community could also embolden many women in domestic conflicts. Some even created scenes before the many eyes and ears of the alleyway to make certain family members would lose face, so that not even those who professed to despise gossip were oblivious to it when it concerned them.

Under state socialism, family secrets and personal histories entered the bureaucratic registers of work units and police files in the form of confessions and denunciations. Whether in personnel files or in public performances, as Geremie Barmé points out, "the individual story was submerged by a collective tale of History writ large," in which "the complex skeins of personal lives were reduced to undifferentiated stereotypes and formulaic accounts."[25] In an oppressive, ideologically saturated atmosphere, however, gossip in the sense of informal chats and private storytelling allowed individuals to articulate and recuperate their diverse experiences of historical turmoil. As a common saying from the late socialist era went, "When there are two people, one tells the truth; when there are three people, one makes jokes; when there are four people, one talks nonsense; when there are five people, one tells lies."[26] Beneath the false, big, and empty talk of loudspeakers and mass rallies, small talk between family members and trusting neighbors provided rare occasions of honesty, solace, and humor. Their murmurs and whispers created multiple alternative histories in the shadows of an officially sanctioned master narrative.

It was perhaps in recognition of these alternative histories that the writer Wang Anyi 王安憶, considered the heir to Eileen Chang's literary legacy,[27] wrote a tribute to alleyway *liuyan*, gossip, as the "dream" and "heart" of Shanghai in her acclaimed 1996 novel *The Song of Everlasting Sorrow*. Although rarely featuring characters engaged in the actual act of gossiping, Wang Anyi's oeuvre is permeated by the kind of "emotional speculation" so central to the construction of gossip.[28] Using a detailed and rambling style not unlike gossip itself, Wang Anyi describes gossip not just as speech, but also as "landscape" and as "atmosphere" that "sneaks out through the rear windows and the back doors." Gossip begins to "brew" at dusk; it has smells and tastes that "cling to the skin." Vulgar and dirty yet occasionally yielding "small treasures," gossip mixes truths and falsehoods, shallow sensations and genuine feelings. Gossip is heteroglossic, has collective authorship, and generates its own communities: "It does not stand in opposition to society—it forms its own society," and it "deviates from traditional moral codes but never claims to be anti-feudal." Gossip erodes privacy at the same time that it is the essence of the alleyway's intimacy.[29] Linking gossip to architecture and to the senses, her poetic meditation resituates it from print media to the alleyway as a social space and as a horizon of experience.

Alleyway Space as a Milieu for Gossip

"If Shanghai's alleyways could speak, they would undoubtedly speak in gossip," wrote Wang Anyi. "If the alleyways could dream, that dream would be gossip."[30] How might the architecture of the alleyway, along with its sights, sounds, and smells, become a medium for the discursive mode and narrative genre that we call gossip? Without the mechanical qualities of the printing press or cinema, how has the alleyway labyrinth produced and reproduced stories, spun out yarns and woven them into a fabric with color, nuance, and variety? Taking the reader with me on a homecoming journey, this section provides a thick description of how the semipublic, semiprivate spaces of Shanghai alleyways served as a unique loom for gossip.

The Big Alleyway

After leaving Shanghai at the age of eleven, I did not return to visit the alleyway home of my grandparents until after six years of living in the United States. Since Alliance Lane in my memory was big and bustling, rife with traffic and danger, I was surprised to discover what now seemed to be its inconspicuous entrance, merely a slit in a row of ever-changing shop fronts (see figs. 1.1G and 1.2). A tourist could whiz through Shanghai streets all day without noticing a single alleyway, but if you stood before one, the city's two-dimensional commercial facade would suddenly open up to a third dimension of mazes, porous for residents who knew their twists and turns while remaining somewhat impenetrable to outsiders. Whereas shops dressed up the city's outer appearance, alleyways contained its pulses, veins, and intestines.

With a room suspended above it (called *guojielou* 過街樓), the main entrance accommodated various small businesses at different times: a cobbler, a bicycle repair stand, a public telephone kiosk, a fruit stand, a porridge-cooking service, and so on. After supper, men and women gathered here to gossip, meanwhile serving as the alleyway's informal security guards. Until private telephones became widespread in the mid-1990s, the person in charge of the public telephone had to go fetch the person being called by walking over to her alleyway branch and shouting out her name, and that person would then run out to take the call. This way, many neighbors would find out when someone received a phone call, just as they knew about the arrival of certified mail and telegrams with the post-man's bicycle bell.

If every phone call or letter was a communal event, the constant stream of wanderers through Shanghai alleyways also created occasions for collective excitement. In Grandma Apricot's childhood in the 1930s and 1940s, itinerant peddlers hawked noodles, wonton, lotus seed porridge, and red bean soup up and down the big alleyway (see fig. 1.3); there were also sing-song girls, *huqin* players, and blind fortune-tellers. Some of those voices faded away in my mother's childhood in the 1950s and 1960s, though she still recalls the candy seller, the popped-rice man, and the picture-book man who set up their businesses at the alleyway entrance in some after-noons. Aunt Duckweed also misses the "hair-combing auntie" with a red bamboo basket who came every morning to comb and coil the long hair of the old women into a horizontal or vertical S-shaped bun, dipping her comb into shaving wood oil to make her client's hair look bright and shiny. Most such peddlers disappeared during the Cultural Revolution, though some reemerged in my own childhood in the 1980s: craftsmen who repaired bowls and pots, sharpened knives and scissors, as well as various junk collectors, whose transactions with residents always attracted a few onlookers.

These itinerant peddlers often hawked their goods with melodious chanting and, in cases such as the pear syrup candy man, storytelling entertainment. Hanchao Lu's book *Beyond the Neon Lights* contains a rich description of the variety of roaming peddlers and craftsmen in early-twentieth-century Shanghai.[31] In addition to enriching the smells and sounds of the alleyway, itinerant men and women were impor-tant carriers and objects of gossip. Chatting with old customers, they brought news from other parts of Shanghai or even other parts of the country, sometimes sharing their own stories of adventure or misery. Moreover, every transaction with the local residents was a semipublic event, so that neighbors readily saw who among them had a sweet tooth, which woman was shrewd at bargaining, which child was a parent's favorite, or which family was in dire financial straits so that they could no longer afford this or that. These peddlers and craftspeople provided a material basis for the neighborhood's gauge of private emotions and family dynamics.

Most residents came out to the big alleyway to dispose of their waste. Indeed, to walk through the big alleyway always required a rite of passage through "two big stinks," as Waipo put it—the garbage dump and the night-soil dump or latrine. Both repositories of communal waste tended to overflow by late morning, before the arrival of the trash and fertilizer trucks, the memory of which quickly dispels any romantic wistfulness one might harbor toward the old alleyway's way of life. Before the 1960s, the night-soil man came before dawn with a big wheelbarrow to collect the night soil with a little bell and a hoarse cry: "Bring down your night stools." At this point, the alleyway women would emerge from every back door with their heavy, mahogany-colored wooden night stools. After emptying their night stools, they would scrub them with bamboo brush and clamshells, sounding the alleyway cantata that nobody could sleep through. It had always been a woman's task to clean the night stools, for if a man did it, he would become the object of gossip and mockery.[32] Some better-off families hired poor women in the same alleyway to perform this filthy task, and in the socialist period the hired night-stool washers in Alliance Lane were often former bourgeois women reduced to such a lowly vocation after their husbands were labeled counter-revolutionaries. And since "gossip delights in a plight,"[33] these women also provided rich material for talk amidst their patrons.

Alleyway Branch

If the big alleyway was still reminiscent of a small street or traffic route that most people walked through only to buy goods and services or to dispose of waste, the alleyway branches hosted more intimate communities where any stranger would feel like an intruder (figs. 1.4 and 3.1). Back in Shanghai for a visit, as we turned into my grandparents' alleyway branch, we could feel the special scrutiny of neighbors hovering out in the alleyway doing chores, wondering whose house *we* were going to. One old woman who recognized my mother told another: "That's the daughter of the Third Floor Auntie of No. 111—she just came back from America. . . . And that's *her* daughter. . . . " My mother nodded at them and said "Auntie," while I mumbled "Grandma" almost out of instinct, even though I didn't know or couldn't remember who they were.

FIGURE 3.1 An alleyway branch in Alliance Lane in 1984. Photograph by my father.

Since the early twentieth century, the system of greetings in the alleyway had been "a combination of what might be called the 'age and sex typing' of a person with the type of room she or he lived in," and neighbors could live in the same compound for years without knowing each other's proper names.[34] So my grandmother was known as "Third Floor Auntie" or "Yaqing's Mother," and she taught me to call our downstairs neighbors "Grandma Front Bedroom," "Grandma Back Bedroom," and "Pavilion Room Uncle." Aside from the casualness of relations, these pseudo-kinship terms also reflected the substantial role neighbors assumed in raising each other's children, who treated the alleyway as their playground— their "gym, casino, and battleground."[35] Neighbors watched out for their safety, mediated their conflicts, and taught them moral lessons whenever the occasion arose. Meanwhile, the children could overhear grown-ups' conversations and learn about adult life and about the outside world, and the neighborhood became an extension of the family.

As in much of rural China, "Have you eaten?" was the most common form of alleyway greeting—an expression of basic concern for a fellow human being from a time when mere subsistence was an achievement. Other conversation openers were more specific: "Have you received this month's retirement pension?" "Is your husband feeling better?" "Did your son hear about college?" Such questions elicited the sharing of news and complaints, boasts and worries. Once I heard an alleyway grandma telling

FIGURE 3.2 Waipo gossips with her alleyway neighbors in 2000. Video stills by the author.

Waipo that her daughter had just had a baby: "They got married in April, and she had the baby in February. Let's see," she counted with her fingers, "that's May, June, July, August, September, October, November, December, January, February—ten months exactly, not a single day less!" "Exactly right," said Waipo, who did not approve of sex out of wedlock either.

Such small talk became much more extensive when neighbors did household chores in close proximity to one another—from washing laundry or night stools to sorting through rice and bean sprouts—or when they cooled themselves out in the alleyway (fig. 3.2). In the 1930s and 1940s, according to Grandma Apricot, servants gossiped over their chores in the back alleyways while looking after children, whereas the masters and mistresses, who cooled themselves in their own sky well or terrace, gossiped only with select neighbors over mahjong games. Overpopulation in later decades obliterated any such spatial hierarchy and created a space where, to borrow Walter Benjamin's description of the streets of Naples, "every private attitude act [became] permeated by streams of communal life. The house is far less the refuge into which people retreat than the inexhaustible reservoir from which they flood out . . . the living room reappears on the street, with chairs, hearth, and altar."[36] This spill-over of private life into a more public realm was less an invasion of privacy than it was a domestication of the alleyway space.

Apart from serving as an extension or substitution of living rooms, kitchens, washrooms, and backyards, the alleyway branch on sunny days also displayed the contents of bedrooms in the form of hanging laundry—linens, pajamas, and other intimate apparel—with each bamboo pole representing the male and female, old and young members of every household. After the rainy season every year, overshadowing the regular display of everyday laundry would be an annual special exhibition of "antique" clothing from the bottom of storage chests as well as the dowry collections of alleyway maidens. From this parade of intimacy, one could read the thrift and dexterity of homemakers, the economics and aesthetics of households, and, above all, the material reality of the present against the past histories and future dreams of one's neighbors.

Lost Faces and Thick Skins

The alleyway was also a site of violent clashes that often splashed out of the kitchen like dirty water into the gutters. Quarrels between neighbors and even members of the same family usually broke out over trifles, yet there was often long-standing antagonism behind such outbursts. When they grew loud, the neighbors stood around or watched the show from their windows and balconies (fig. 3.3), turning the alleyway into a theater and an open court of mutual accusations and communal judgment. In fact, a family row in 1956 was responsible for the permanent removal of the original Wang household from house number 111. It was a fight so historical even my unsociable grandfather recalled it. At the time, Grandma Apricot had moved across the alleyway branch to her husband's house in No. 83, whose front door faced the back door of No. 111. Her mother had died from pneumonia and—according to Apricot—grief because her (Apricot's) father had married a concubine and treated her mother like a servant (see "Foundations and Original Residents" in chapter 1). After her death, Apricot's father lived in the old living room of No. 111 with

FIGURE 3.3 An alleyway quarrel. Drawing by my parents.

the concubine and their children along with Apricot's grandmother and brother. The following was Grandma Apricot's account of the incident.

My brother had a fight with one of the concubine's children, and my father scolded only my brother even though it wasn't his fault. When I heard my brother cry, I went across the alleyway and talked into their back door: "My mother has only just died, and you're already abusing my brother?" I talked so loud all the neighbors could hear, so my father came out and punched my face with his fist. I fell off balance and hit the ground. The concubine came out and snorted: "A married daughter is water out of the door. The Wang family is none of your business." "How is it not my business?" I began crying. "You hounded my mother to death." Everyone in our alleyway knew my mother and was sympathetic to her plight. My father threatened to hit me again, so I ran back to my husband's house, shut the door, and continued to curse my father and the concubine through the mail flap.

The neighbors gathered, and someone fetched my mother-in-law from the park. She came home to back me up: "You're married to the Huo family, and you belong to the Huo family! Let's see who has the nerve to beat up the Huos!" So I opened up the front door, and the concubine got scared. She went back into the house, shut the door, and cursed me through the kitchen window while my mother-in-law dared her to come out (my mother-in-law hated concubines because my father-in-law had so many concubines). When she came out, my mother-in-law grabbed her by the hair, and the two of them started fighting and rolling on the ground. Meanwhile, my father held me by my collar and was about to hit me when my husband came back and hit him. . . . All the neighbors criticized my father and the concubine—they thought of her as a prostitute, and they had seen how she had behaved in the past. These neighbors had lived with us for two decades, and so my father had no more face to stay here and found a way to swap their ground-floor living room for the smaller living room of the Zhangs.

Not every family could find a way to leave the community after making a disgraceful spectacle of themselves, especially after household registration fixed people in their places. Most simply had to grow some new skin over their shame, and since almost every family had its share of public humiliation, the wise did not reveal other people's secrets unless others threatened to reveal theirs. As Zhang Zhen writes of her Shanghai alleyway in the 1960s, because most families "had some 'blemishes' on their class background and had probably enough political drama going on at their workplaces, people seemed to want to keep their home environment a place for rest."[37] Nevertheless, as a target of political persecution at his workplace, my paternal grandfather often vented his workplace frustrations in domestic quarrels with Nainai over the tight household budget. Flustered and inarticulate, Yeye knew only how to turn up the volume of his voice, and as the conflict escalated, both he and Nainai relapsed into their native Subei dialect so despised by the Shanghainese majority from the Jiangnan area.[38] Although they fought mostly in their bedroom upstairs rather than in the alleyway, neighbors gathered downstairs and rubbernecked with concerned and bemused expressions. On those occasions, my father and his siblings often wished they could dig a hole in the ground to hide. For Nainai, who often burst into tears, the alleyway audience was a source of humiliation as well as consolation—she would have liked to think that "the masses" were on her side, even though deep down she knew that her anguish was little more than a farce in their eyes.

The Eyes of Grandma Front Bedroom

Sitting on a small bamboo chair as if it had grown into her flesh, Grandma Front Bedroom of No. 111 was an eternal presence in our alleyway branch. She sat at the threshold of No. 111 the day I left Shanghai and was still sitting at the same spot when I returned to visit six years later. A widow whose children had left home by then, she was having supper by herself: a bowl of rice, a bowl of fish, and a bowl of pig thigh chops. Old, haggard, and enormous, she could barely walk up to her room on the second floor without resting on the way, but her eyes remained as sharp as ever. As soon as we turned into the alleyway branch, she saw us and called out my name. I called her "Grandma," and she said, holding her hand up to her knees: "I've watched you grow up since you were *this* little."

Grandma Front Bedroom could proudly pronounce that every person who lived in this branch of the alleyway since 1953 had grown up under her searching scrutiny. When Little Aunt's then boyfriend and later husband came to visit, he always heard a squeak while passing by the second floor on his way upstairs. The next day Grandma Front Bedroom would tell Grandma Zhou, who lived in the pavilion room two houses down, how many hours Little Aunt had spent with her boyfriend the evening before in exchange for gossip about Grandma Zhou's immediate neighbors. This way Grandma Front Bedroom learned something about everyone within a ten-house radius, from what their great-grandparents did for a living down to the brawl they had the night before. With this knowledge, according to Waipo, she had often informed on her neighbors during the Mao era whenever it was to her advantage to do so.

Shortly after my grandparents moved into No. 111 in 1954, Grandma Front Bedroom befriended Waipo and told her that Apricot's family, their second landlord living downstairs, played mahjong with old neighbors all night long even though the Communists had recently banned it. Waipo said that it was none of their business, but Grandma Front

Bedroom reminded her that they all had to split the same electricity bill and dragged Waipo along as a witness to inform the police. The police came immediately, crashed the players' game, and confiscated their mahjong set. Waipo suffered from pangs of guilt for months afterward and dared not look at her second landlords in the eye, whereas Grandma Front Bedroom continued to schmooze with them as though she had done nothing at all.

Waipo herself was not a big gossip, yet the only neighbor she talked about obsessively was Grandma Front Bedroom, objecting to her on ten counts:

1. She picked fights all the time—with her neighbors, with her husband, even with her children.
2. If she herself did not pick a fight, she would sow discord between her neighbors by telling one nasty things about the other. She was a double-dealer and a backstabber.
3. She was always snooping about other people's private matters.
4. She was full of pride and prejudice and constantly insulted neighbors who seemed less well off.
5. She cared only for money and had little human feeling.
6. She collected every piece of trash she could get her hands on and cluttered the kitchen, staircase, and hallways.
7. She ate too much and in public—showing off the meat and fish in her bowl.
8. She was so stingy that she would hire a servant (in her old age) to clean up her mess for three days, work her to exhaustion, and then fire her on the fourth day.
9. Instead of considering herself lucky to have a job at the factory, she feigned illness and lived off a sick-leave pension. This was too bad because she was actually made out of the stuff of cadres—so quick to learn the official policies and so good at denouncing people, she could have easily become a party member!
10. While taking sick leave, she got free prescriptions for nutritional supplements, which she used as bribes for other advantages. It was precisely because of people like her that the socialist system went bankrupt. She always said she didn't need her children because the work unit would take care of her. Now that the factory has closed down, see who's going to take care of her now?

The Communal Kitchen and Faucet Room

Since the front door was reserved for the family in the guest and ancestral hall, the four other families in the house entered or exited the house via the back door that led into the communal kitchen, the staircase, and the faucet room (see fig. 1.17). Dark and dirty, greasy and wet, the communal kitchen and faucet room were once the most bustling and contentious sites of the whole house. In the morning, everyone would be busy filling and emptying their basins, washing their night stools, lighting and fanning their coal stoves. In the late afternoon, there would be a symphony of kitchen knives drumming against cutting boards, whistling kettles and cackling woks, clothes scrubbing against washboards, water splashing into aluminum buckets, and the occasional crescendo of bickering neighbors. By dusk, the fragrance of various dishes would emanate from the kitchen into the alleyway branch and waft upstairs through the back windows. From the dominant ingredients, you could smell the changing of the seasons; from the fermented sweet rice, the sour pickles, the chili peppers, or the raw garlic, you could smell your neighbors' native place origins and culinary nostalgia; from the aroma of boiling milk and the bitterness of herbal medicine, you could also smell the beginnings and endings of lives.

In the summer, when many families moved their tables and chairs out to the alleyway branch to eat, a passing glance and sniff could help you assess a family's quality of life. If a family had enough money and planned well, their table would have a variety of dishes that looked and smelled good. A shrewd homemaker such as Grandma Front Bedroom knew how to pinch every last drop of flavor from limited resources. If she bought a vegetable such as amaranth, she could cook the leaf and then stir-fry the stem with smoked tofu or green pepper to make two dishes instead of just one. Since the meat seller did not collect ration coupons for bones, she could buy bones and make a meat soup without meat. Less-shrewd homemakers would simply buy pork chops, but since a whole month's meat rations covered only two or three pieces, their tables would look sumptuous for a few days and then dull and pitiful for the rest of the month. Those who ate nothing but rice with soy sauce often resented those "bourgeois parasites" and "blood-sucking vampires" who seemed to "eat meat and fish everyday."

By the mid-1990s, the kitchen once teeming with tension fell into disuse, yet the thick, stale scent of smoke and oil lingered in the air. When I returned to visit in the late 1990s and early 2000s, it was still congested with stoves, cabinets, stools, paper boxes, and empty jars and bottles lined up against the window like trophies for territorial conquests. Four light-bulbs dangled from the ceiling, wired to four electric meters. There were also four gas meters connected to four sets of gas stoves and four faucets with separate water meters. A notebook hanging from the hinge of the doorway kept a chronicle of every family's monthly water, electricity, and gas uses. All of this confirms all too well the most stereotypical feature of the "Shanghai temperament"—that is, "astute calculation of practical advantage."[39] Before the 1980s, electricity used to be divided up by the number of lightbulbs per household, water by the number of persons per household, and everyone used coal stoves. Although neighbors wrangled occasionally over the division of the bills, they tried to maintain some semblance of harmony. After the Cultural Revolution, with the bankruptcy of collective ideologies and the increased use of electrical appliances, each household or family installed its own faucet, lightbulbs, and electricity, gas, and water meters to avoid paying more than its share. Some even locked up their oil and spices in cupboards as well as their faucets—putting a metal can on top, stringing a wire through the can, and locking up the wires—not allowing others to use even a drop of their water. Even so, Grandma Front Bedroom and Grandma Back Bedroom often accused each other of stealing this or that and drew lines with chalk to mark out each other's territory.

Besides contestations, the kitchen and faucet room also enabled alternative communities for those who wished to socialize outside of their families. Grandma Front Bedroom made as many friends here as she made enemies, chatting with other women about their family troubles, exchanging advice and information, and occasionally even lending them a yuan or two. However scrounging Pavilion Room Auntie might be about electricity, whenever she cooked a pot of mung bean soup with lotus seed, she would ladle out a bowl and send her daughter to take it to the grandma in the guest and ancestral hall next door. The kitchen was where children and adolescents overheard the adults' gossip and learned about the ways of the world.

A Dark Staircase with Four Lightbulbs

As we walked past the kitchen and squeezed ourselves into the hallway— also cluttered with cabinets, stoves, and paper boxes—lying before us was the perpetually shut door to the guest and ancestral hall and to our right an upward-spiraling staircase minimally illuminated with the light from a window that opened into the faucet room. Prompted by the ghost of habit, I pulled on one of the four strings by the handle of the stairway to turn on the lightbulb that belonged to my grandparents. I had been trained since childhood to remember which string belonged to us, for to turn on any other light would earn the ire of neighbors who fumbled in the dark to save electricity. My grandparents also taught me to walk on tiptoe for fear of waking up Uncle Pavilion Room, who worked late-night shifts just as Waigong and Waipo had often done in the 1960s and 1970s.

Ascending toward the pavilion room, we could see that one step beneath our feet was in the shape of a large right triangle. This was the corner of clashes and graciousness, for if someone went up and someone else went down this flight of stairs at the same time, one of them would inevitably have to yield momentarily into this corner. If two neighbors were cross with each other, there might be a standstill, and if one happened to be holding a bucket or a basin, she might deliberately spill water on her opponent. In her most voraciously expansionist days, Grandma Front Bedroom left an empty night stool in this corner, rendering it difficult for neighbors to move anything bulky up or down the stairs. But this wasn't the only stumbling block along the way—Uncle Pavilion Room kept his basins and mops on the staircase landing outside of his door; Back Bedroom Auntie dangled her collection of baskets and buckets overhead; even the towels my grandparents and I hung along the stairs toward the third floor might dribble on your head.

Walls and Curtains

As we tiptoed our way upstairs, past the pavilion room, and walked up to the second floor, before us was a short, dark corridor, to the right of which was a door that opened into the back bedroom, and the door at the corridor's end opened into the front bedroom. Each bedroom housed an entire family from the mid-1950s to the mid-1990s, with only a thin wooden wall in between (see fig. 1.17). Aunt Duckweed has vivid memories of this particular wall:

> When I was about nine, my parents' big bed was pushed up against
> this wall. My parents made me sleep in their bed when I was sick, but

when I couldn't sleep, I would poke at this wall. On the other side lived a man, his wife, and her son. We children nicknamed the man "the Troll" because he was nasty and smelly; the woman "the Ghost" because of her uncombed long hair; and her son "the Sin" because his mother and stepfather didn't love him. Their room was only a little more than half the size of our room and contained only a bed, a desk, and a dresser. They had a loft in the upper part of their room, where "the Sin" slept.

A thin wall divided our bed from their bed. When I lay awake, I could hear everything on the other side of the wall. I was still a child and so did not quite understand what went on. All I knew was that they fought a lot and that when they fought, "the Troll" would curse and pinch "the Ghost" in places one could not ordinarily see—yet we all knew because she would go around lifting up her skirt and show her bruises to the neighbors. All the while, "the Sin" would whine and weep. Later, he became ill and grabbed every girl who came his way. Meanwhile, they could hear everything that went on in my family, all my parents' bitter brawls, all my brother's hysterical fits. We could tell apart the sound of each other's footsteps, sneezes, and even urinations. How intimately our families hated each other!

In the absence of soundproof walls, conversations between family members and close friends became hushed into whispers and murmurs, further teasing the desire to eavesdrop. One reason why interior partitions did such a poor job of sound insulation was that greater privacy would come at the expense of light and ventilation. The perforations at the top of this wall allowed not only a bit of breeze to pass through, but also a full view of the front bedroom to anyone in the loft in the back bedroom, so there had been many quarrels over whether to seal those perforations. The final compromise was to leave it open over the summer and seal it for the rest of the year.

Besides such tenuous partitions, there were many other porous thresholds in the house: curtains that covered windows and doorways as well as divided up spaces within single-room homes. Most curtains consisted of collages of fabric; some had so many patches it was hard to figure out which piece was the original. As these curtains opened, closed, or rustled, every change in the lighting, every crisscrossing shadow tantalized the eyes. They suggested a theatricality of everyday life that entertained its dwellers for decades before television soap operas took over their thirst for drama.[40] In the Cultural Revolution, as I showed in chapter 2, actual stages for struggle sessions were set up in the big alleyway, and with home searches "old news" was dug up, private scandals exposed, and domestic objects displayed in public. Revelations from 1966 naturally became the subject of gossip, but even on an everyday basis the alleyway was full of spectacles and spectators. From almost every threshold, terrace, or window, one could see several stages in the form of other people's thresholds, terraces, and windows. The windows of the back bedrooms, pavilion rooms, and staircases of any two adjacent households looked onto one another and the two faucet rooms below. The front bedroom looked into the sky wells of several guest and ancestral halls below, and every terrace looked onto a row of front bedrooms and tiger windows of attics across the alleyway. The next section tells the stories of a few women whose lives were thus watched and overheard by their neighbors.

Several Lifetimes to a Life: Women on the Margins

"My mother-in-law never went to a day of school," Grandma Apricot told me, "but she was something of a philosopher. For instance, she liked to say, 'It takes several lifetimes to live one life' ['yishi rensheng jishi guo' 一世人生幾世過), to describe those who had experienced violent twists of fate, such as the many older residents in our alleyway."[41] This section traces the lives of four women who lived within fifty feet of each other on Alliance Lane for several decades spanning the Republican, socialist, and reform eras: Mother Mao in No. 81 (directly across from No. 111, fig. 1.1C), Mother Yang in No. 109 (adjacent to No. 111, fig. 1.1D); and Mother Huo (Apricot's mother-in-law) and her daughter Peace in No. 83 (diagonally across from No. 111, fig. 1.1B). It was possible to glimpse into these women's rooms from the terrace and staircase of our old house.

Except for Peace, who came to Alliance Lane as a child, all of these women had come to the alleyway by means of marriage or concubinage to well-to-do men who could afford to take over a whole house. Though known by their husbands' surnames, all of them had greater presence in the neighborhood, either because their husbands had women elsewhere or because they were exiled, jailed, or shot after 1949. These women had to share the burden of their husbands' misfortunes and bear punishment for their crimes. They were labeled "counterrevolutionary family members" (*fangeming jiashu* 反革命家屬), even if they were their husbands' greatest victims.

Not allowed to work outside the household after marriage, they were labeled housewives by default after 1949 and had no state-sponsored jobs in work units. Men were their only means of livelihood, but when the men were gone and the women had to provide for themselves and their children, the only livelihood available to them, after pawning away precious belongings, was temporary work such as knitting, laundry, babysitting, and cleaning out other people's night stools in the morning—despised and underpaid jobs without benefits. Their family affiliations often disqualified them from employment in alleyway kindergartens or factories. Alternatively, they could remarry, as Mother Yang eventually did, or rely on their grown children, as Mother Huo did on her daughter, Peace. Without work units, they existed only in terms of their families and their neighbors and were practically invisible to the state. Because their stories did not fit into the official discursive frame of the "bitter past and the sweet present,"[42] they could only "speak bitterness" in private conversations with their children and their close neighbors, who relayed their stories to me.

Of course, oral narratives, especially secondary and tertiary retellings, are not equivalent to or even accurate about the lives they describe, but they do reflect the way these lives are remembered and made meaningful, in this case both by the women themselves and by those who had known them. If we listen, as Natalie Zemon Davis did in her study of three seventeenth-century women's autobiographies, "for the inner contention around which [their lives] swirled, and for [their] account of why things happened to [them] and others as they did,"[43] we might uncover the tacit philosophies, values, and prejudices these women held—palimpsests of several historical epochs rather than a neat, coherent belief system. To their listeners and observers, each of these women's lives stood as an example, "with its own virtues, initiatives, and faults,"[44] and constituted a different and perhaps more powerful kind of education than schools, mass media, and other ideological training grounds. Like grass growing out of stone cracks, these are stories of resilient survival in a world that did not allot these women proper places. These stories without redemptive endings briefly turn these shadowy figures and marginal characters into the protagonists of their own narratives, woven into but not subsumed by larger historical events.

FIGURE 3.4 Grandma and Grandpa Mao as seen from Waipo's terrace around 2000. Drawing by my parents.

Mother Mao (Moth)

From the terrace of my childhood home, we could see the inside of the front bedroom in No. 81. There was a square table by the window, a bed against the back wall, a wardrobe to the left, and a cupboard to the right. An old woman with snow-white hair spent her days sitting by the table, playing a solitaire mahjong game and smoking a cigarette. An old man would sometimes join her at the table to read a newspaper or drink tea (fig. 3.4). Waipo told me that they were Grandpa and Grandma Mao. Grandma Mao was also known by her maiden name, Moth. In an afternoon chat in 2000, Grandma Apricot, their next-door neighbor, told the story of Grandma Moth to Waipo and me. In the writing and translation of this oral narrative, I retain the colloquial tone of voice and the digressive structure. I also include some of Waipo's reactive interjections, for what interests us here is not just the story itself, but also the way it was received as gossip.

> Through no fault of her own, Moth suffered more than anyone else I know. Her father died when she was still very young—he choked to death. His death must have upset his wife's nerves, and she became

crazy. Every afternoon she would wait outside for her husband to come home, and so little Moth had to take care of her mother. At the age of fifteen, Moth married into the Mao family in No. 81, a well-off family that owned a small factory. Let me see . . . this was the early 1940s. Who was the matchmaker? It was her aunt, who lived in No. 103. The son of the family she married—the old man you see from your terrace, let's call him young Mr. Mao—was a little slow in the head. [Waipo, "Wasn't his daughter also a little dim-witted?"] Yes, his mother was a little stupid too, so were his daughter and her son, so I guess it's inherited by the offspring of the opposite sex.

Young Mr. Mao's father, old Mr. Mao, took a courtesan as his concubine, a beautiful and shrewd woman who immediately took charge of the household. Once, when burglars broke into their house and she happened to be on the terrace, she was astute enough to drop her diamond ring inside a vat of pickles. The alleyway children called the concubine "Pretty Mother" and the proper wife "Ugly Mother." "Pretty Mother" was childless—in brothels they made you take a certain drug so you wouldn't get pregnant—so this stupid son was the family's only seedling. He had no job and depended on his father, old Mr. Mao.

After Moth married into this family, she was treated like a servant, especially by Pretty Mother the Concubine. Unlike my family, the Maos could not afford to hire servants—old Mr. Mao only had a small factory of maybe twenty workers. Now, the family has to eat, right? Since they didn't have enough money to feed everyone equally, Pretty Mother, old Mr. Mao, and young Mr. Mao ate white rice while Ugly Mother and Moth ate unhusked grain. Moth was given no spending money—she was so poor she couldn't even buy a sewing needle. [Waipo shakes her head: "That *is* truly pitiful. . . ."] Meanwhile, her stupid husband spent all his money on brothels and only returned home at one or two in the morning. He'd call Moth from the back alley (she slept in the pavilion room) so she had to open up for him before his father (who slept in the front bedroom) could find out that he had been to the prostitutes again. Later [hushed tone], he got syphilis. . . . [Waipo clicks her tongue.] He had been to every kind of brothel there was in town and told us that the Japanese brothels were the cleanest because their prostitutes were sterilized. [Waipo, with livened interest: "Is that so?"] Yes, and the dirtiest were the lower-class Chinese brothels.

After Liberation, the Communists got rid of brothels. And after the collectivization of private enterprises in 1956, old Mr. Mao's workshop merged into a state-owned factory. As a former capitalist, he was allowed one spot in the factory, which he passed on to his son, Moth's husband. It was a job in the packaging department and made seventy yuan a month. Not too bad, eh? But this stupid man got into a fit of stupidity. Believing the factory still to be his family property, he once took a pair of pliers from the factory. The next day they accused him of stealing public property and sent him to a labor reform camp in Gansu Province. [Waipo: "Back in Chairman Mao's time they were truly tough on criminals."]

Unlike jail sentences, labor reform didn't have termination dates; they could keep you there as long as they liked—if you survived, that is. During the three years of natural disasters,[45] we had food shortages in Shanghai, but many people starved to death in the countryside. Moth's husband later told us that he and his fellow prisoners got up in the middle of the night to steal the grain they had planted for civilians before the harvest. That was how some of them managed to stay alive. In the winter he had no blankets—Moth could hardly provide enough blankets for the kids—so he had to cover himself with straw instead, and that was where he got his lung sickness.

When her husband went to labor reform, Moth did not have a job, but she still had to support herself and five kids plus Ugly Mother. (Old Mr. Mao had died in the mid-1950s, after which Pretty Mother went to stay with an adopted daughter.) So Moth did temporary work—taking out people's night soil in the morning, washing clothes, and mopping floors in the evening. She worked herself half to death and still made only about twenty yuan a month, which had to feed and clothe seven people. [Waipo: "That's why the children were picking up leftover vegetables from the market after school! They turned out all right, didn't they?"] Yes, all five children were filial to their parents. After all, their mother ate much bitterness raising them. She had to work day and night, inside and outside the house. You see her hair? It had turned snow white when she was only thirty.

At some point the neighborhood committee found Moth a real job at an alleyway cardboard workshop, and finally she had a bit of security. Then the police told her that her husband could come home if she would sign his release, but she said: "What good would it do if he came back? He'd never share my burden. He'd only make more trouble." In the end she forgave him, and he came back to Shanghai, but he had no job here—his old factory would not take him back. Now, Moth was a really smart woman: she told him to go back to the farm and work there. Now that he was rehabilitated, he got paid, and she promised that she would visit him there at least twice a year. And so that's how they made it through the decades.

When Moth's husband retired, they actually counted him a retiree of his old factory and gave him medical insurance. This was truly fortunate because his body was full of illness from his time in labor reform. In their old age, with a retirement pension and the support of their children, they finally stopped toiling for food and clothing but remained as parsimonious as ever. They never threw out their old cotton shoes and often picked up old cardboard or bottles, wires or twine that others had discarded. [Waipo: "They had eaten too much bitterness and do not know how to taste sweetness anymore."]

Mother Yang

Through the window on the staircase that opened into the faucet room of No. 111, we could see the staircase of the house next door, No. 109. Half a century ago, a beautiful woman made daily trips up and down these stairs to and from her attic with slanting ceilings. The neighbors called her "Mother Yang." I first heard about her from Aunt Duckweed, who was two generations younger than Mother Yang and thus called her "Grandma Yang":

When I was a child, Grandma Yang was already in her late forties, but people said that she was as beautiful as in her youth. She spent her days sitting out in the back alleyway on a small bamboo chair and knitting sweaters for her neighbors. This was the way she eked out a living since she had neither a job nor a husband to support her— people said her husband was a counterrevolutionary. When she had no business, she would have little to eat for days on end, so my mother might ladle a half bowl of rice and vegetables from our pot and tell me to take it up to her attic. Once Grandma Yang gave me a coin to go buy her a piece of candy from a peddler, and she held it in her mouth for many hours to pacify her hunger.

Yet Grandma Yang looked like someone who had known a good life. Though she was emaciated, her skin seemed translucent and well nourished, and her long earlobes had large perforations left by heavy earrings, which she probably pawned long ago. Although she always wore the same few items of old-fashioned clothing, they were clean and unwrinkled, for she pressed her clothes under her pillow every night. I know this because my mother asked Grandma Yang to look after me when she went back to her hometown in Suzhou.

Hot in the summer and cold in the winter, Grandma Yang's attic had sloping ceilings with a single tiger window [dormer; see fig. 1.5E for an example]. When I went to greet Grandma Yang on Chinese New Year, she would make me stand tall wherever my head was to touch the ceiling and mark the spot with a pencil. As I got bigger, Grandma Yang got smaller from malnutrition and constantly bending her back, while her room became sparse and barren. The electric fan and the gramophone disappeared when I was still small, likewise a mahogany dressing table with a folding mirror, lots of little drawers, colorful boxes, and fragrant bottles. Later, the only furniture she had left was a leather suitcase, a bed, and a dresser, and the only decorations were a small mahogany elephant and a framed photograph of her younger self.

One day—this must have been during the Cultural Revolution— when I was staying overnight with Grandma Yang, she asked me to accompany her on a walk. She took out a jade bracelet from her suitcase, wrapped it inside a piece of newspaper, and put it inside her pocket. At the big alleyway entrance, she looked about to make sure nobody was in sight and then hurled the bracelet into the dump. The next night, she did the same thing with the mahogany elephant. That photograph of herself in a splendid *qipao* also disappeared, so the only items with some vitality in her attic were gone.

It was Grandma Apricot who unveiled to me the mystery of Mother Yang's past.

Mother Yang had first come to our alleyway as a mahjong player back in the early 1940s. Her husband, Mr. Yang, owned a small filature factory. She played mahjong with my family and with the Xies next door in No. 109. Mr. Xie, a special agent for the Nationalist police bureau, was a powerful and awe-inspiring man. He always wore a black cape around his shoulders and a bayonet around his waist. His wife, Mother Xie, had two daughters and a son. Their guest and ancestral hall had a huge wardrobe and a large mahogany round table with a bronze top. On an armoire was a pot of flowers made out of emerald and other gifts from people at the mercy of his power. Mother Yang, coquettish and voluptuous, became a frequent guest at the Xies, and while Mother Xie cooked downstairs, Mother Yang and Mr. Xie had an affair. When Mr. Yang heard about his wife's adultery, he swallowed opium mixed with blood and killed himself (after all, opium alone wouldn't do the job). And since Mother Xie was such a passive woman, Mother Yang walked right over her and became Mr. Xie's concubine.

Mr. Xie loved Mother Yang much more than he did Mother Xie, and under Mother Yang's scrutiny he rarely ever went upstairs to Mother Xie, who lived in the front bedroom while Mother Yang lived in the back bedroom of the guest and ancestral hall. Mr. Xie became very mean to Mother Xie, sometimes even grabbing her by the hair. We all felt very sorry for Mother Xie, but nobody could deny how handsome Mr. Xie and Mother Yang looked together. Unable to stand his abuse, Mother Xie left for Taiwan in 1948 with her daughter, who was engaged to a Nationalist officer. In 1949, the Communists took over, and Mr. Xie lost his job and was labeled a counterrevolutionary. He was sent to a labor reform farm, and Mother Yang had to take care of Mr. Xie's remaining son and daughter without any source of income. After pawning her valuables, she sublet the rooms out one by one until she and his children were left with an attic. How far she had fallen! If she had only stayed with Mr. Yang, she would never have come to such an end. [Waipo: "Mother Yang really miscalculated (buhuasuan 不划算), didn't she?"]

Although Mr. Yang was dead, when his silk workshop was collectivized, there was still a job opening under his name at the now state-owned factory. As his official widow, Mother Yang could have taken the slot, but instead she gave the slot to Mr. Xie's second daughter, Golden Precious [see fig. 1.7 on the right]. Neighbors commended Mother Yang's generosity and shook their head at her naïveté—if only she had taken the job that was rightfully hers, she would have had a stable income and a retirement pension.

Golden Precious grew up with me and was one of the prettiest girls in the alleyway. Many men pursued her, but she always said: "I want to marry into the 'upper corner' of the city."[46] Because of her vanity, people really did set her up with a man from the upper corner, in the French Concession. She was already engaged to someone in our alleyway, but after being introduced to this man, she decided to marry *him* instead. At her wedding banquet, there was a little girl, probably a child from a previous marriage, next to her new husband. Then we went to see their future marriage chamber, which turned out to be an attic—that's an "upper corner" all right! There was a nice set of furniture and a large standing radio, but a few months later, when I visited Golden Precious again, the nice furniture and the radio were gone—her husband had borrowed them for the wedding and had to return them. It turned out that he didn't even have a stable job, and even though she was the main wage earner of the family, he dumped his child and housework on her. Just as Golden Precious was going to have her first baby, he committed depraved acts with another woman and was sent away for labor reform. When she visited him in prison, she got pregnant again. With three children depending on her wage, Golden Precious was no longer able to support Mother Yang.

Without the help from Golden Precious, Mother Yang landed in a financial crisis. At this juncture, Mr. Xie came home from the labor reform camp on sick leave, and Mother Yang made him go out to look for a job because there was already no rice in the pot. In those days, however, you couldn't just find a job if you looked, so Mother Yang went to the neighborhood committee to ask if they might give Mr. Xie a job. The neighborhood committee said: "Is that so? If he has recovered, he should go back to labor reform." So, you see, Mother Yang wasn't a very bright woman. Mr. Xie died in the labor reform camp a few years later.

Fortunately, Golden Precious had not forgotten Mother Yang's kindness and so made a match for her, a seventy-year-old widower who had once owned an eyeglass glass shop in the former French Concession. With a son in America and a son in Hong Kong, he had suffered much at the beginning of the Cultural Revolution when they paraded him around and struggled against him. They also evicted him from his house and stuck him in a pavilion room nearby, but he weathered through all this unscathed—the milk powder and nutritious supplements his sons sent him from abroad must have made him tough and healthy. After the initial revolutionary craze was over, they left him alone, and that's when Mother Yang married him. She was fifty-seven years old at the time but still looked lovely. The old man, surnamed Zhang, was also very good-looking.

Aunt Duckweed remembered well Mother Yang's departure:

Grandma Yang told only a few close neighbors about her remarriage. On the day she left, she wore an old-fashioned blue chemise with large sleeves, meticulously washed and pressed overnight under her pillow. She only carried a small black bag, so she must have already carted her luggage off at night, when nobody could see her. As she walked out of our alleyway, my mother nodded to her, and she nodded back. Later, a neighbor took me to visit Grandma Yang at her new home, a pavilion room in another alleyway. Looking a bit chubbier than before, she was very happy to see me: "Amei missed me? Amei really has a conscience." (She called me "Amei," "Little Sister.") She also gave me a giant juicy peach to eat while she played cards with the neighbor.

Grandma Apricot tells the end of the story: "When we visited Mother Yang at her new home, we did not call her 'Mother Yang' anymore because Mr. Zhang wouldn't like it. With help from abroad, they lived well. When the old man died, he told his sons that they must treat her as his proper wife because he had married her after their mother's death, and his sons obeyed. Mother Yang died at the age of eighty-four, and this had been her life."

Three Generations of Women in a Pavilion Room

After several afternoon chats, Grandma Apricot asked me if I might also interview her sister-in-law, Grandma Peace, who was diagnosed with stomach cancer and wished for someone to write down the story of her

life to pass on to her great-grandchil-
dren. Grandma Peace had moved to
Alliance Lane with her mother and
brother (Apricot's husband) at the age
of ten in 1939 and lived there until 1979,
when her daughter's work unit allotted
her family an apartment. So I went to
visit a bedridden Grandma Peace at her
daughter's house, first recording what
they wanted to tell me and then asking questions to flesh out the details.
Quite agitated during the interview,
Grandma Peace often had her daughter, Aunt Ping, finish her half-spoken
sentences. As the hours passed, Aunt
Ping took over the storytelling, and
Grandma Peace simply nodded her

FIGURE 3.5 Aunt Ping and her grandmother at
the Bund in the early 1960s. Photograph courtesy of
Aunt Ping.

confirmation. Our second interview proceeded similarly, so I wrote the
story from Aunt Ping's perspective, structured around the pavilion room
of No. 83, where her grandmother, mother, and she had lived for three
decades (fig. 3.5).

My grandmother was born in 1911 as the seventh child of a peasant
family in the suburbs of Shanghai. Her parents gave her away for
adoption, but her foster mother was a mean woman who smoked,
inhaled white powder, and treated her like a servant girl, forcing
her to work for pay starting at the age of seven. My grandmother
never went to school. This is most regrettable because she was such
a smart woman. Without having learned any math, she was able to
figure out without error how much each of the five families ought to
contribute to the collective water and electricity bills in our house.
She often mocked herself: "I'm too good at calculating. That's why
I'm so poor."

My grandmother did many different types of work in her youth:
stringing beads, filling matchboxes, and making watch parts. When
she worked at the British American Tobacco factory, she even had
a small managerial position, but she had to stop working and stay
home after getting married. After Liberation, she didn't even have a

worker's pension. In our most difficult days, my grandmother often said: "If only I had worked until Liberation, I would have gotten this much retirement pension by now."

My grandmother's marriage to my grandfather came about this way. When she was eighteen, her foster mother sold her to a police officer as a concubine, but she refused to obey and fled to a distant relative's place. It was her manager at the cigarette factory who freed my grandmother from her marriage contract with the policeman by paying him what he had paid for her. This manager, surnamed Huo, later became my grandfather. I do not know whether she had married him out of love or desperation, only that there had been no ceremony to accept her formally into the Huo. Her mother-in-law always claimed that my grandmother was not my grandfather's proper wife, only a piece of property he had bought with two hundred silver dollars.

My grandmother gave birth to six babies, but only my mother and my uncle lived—he later married Apricot. The birth of a boy improved her status in the family, but it did not prevent my grandfather from marrying a second, third, and fourth time. Every time he had a new woman, my grandmother ran away from home and stayed with an old factory sister until my grandfather came to beg her to come home, and she always did. My grandfather took out a lease on House No. 83 in Alliance Lane for his third and favorite wife in 1935. When she got sick, my grandfather sent for his second wife to come cook and take care of the third wife, who lived in the front bedroom with my grandfather while the second wife lived in the smaller and darker back bedroom. Although not initially sick, the second wife died in a few months, probably from suicide. The third wife died soon after that. With nobody to cook for him, my grandfather moved my grandmother to Alliance Lane—that was in 1939. Soon afterward, my grandfather hooked up with a dance hostess and moved to the French Concession. He rarely came back to Alliance Lane, nor did he send my grandmother money to cover basic living expenses, so she had to wait outside the cigarette factory on payday every month to ask for money. Meanwhile, my eleven-year-old mother went to work in a local Japanese cigarette factory to help the family and to make my grandfather lose face—in the eyes of this alleyway, a rich man like my grandfather was supposed to provide for his family.

In 1945, a distant nephew of my grandmother, named Han, came to live in No. 83—he was dodging the Nationalist draft in Manchuria. With a high school degree, he soon found employment at a small company in Shanghai. My grandmother thought it might be a good idea to have such a capable son-in-law, so she asked him if he would marry my mother. He consented but asked my barely literate mother to go to school. She studied her heart out during their three-year engagement. In the winter of 1948, my father said he wanted to get married immediately because, he said, he was going abroad for business and wanted to take my mother along. And so they were hurriedly married, their temporary marriage chamber being the pavilion room of No. 83.

Nobody knew at the time that my father was an underground Communist Party member who used his marriage to my mother to protect himself from Nationalist persecution—my grandfather had connections with the Shanghai gangs and the Nationalist Party. Yet my mother, who did not even read the newspaper, could not have known that my father was marrying her for the sake of the revolution. She only knew that the day of their wedding was filled with unlucky omens: a wedding chopstick fell from the top of the chest, and the heel of her right shoe got caught in the trolley tracks. My mother became pregnant with me in the first month of marriage. In the second month, January 1949, my father said he had to leave for Hong Kong and promised to come back to get my mother once he settled there. Four months later Shanghai was liberated, and the two of them lost touch. I was born in September 1949. Not knowing where my father was, my mother often held me in her arms and cried.

To save expenses, my grandfather moved his fourth wife and their children to our house in Alliance Lane. She held onto all his money, while my grandmother pawned her jewelry, mahogany furniture, porcelain, and even some blankets to take care of daily expenses. In March 1951, my grandfather was accused of having suppressed worker strikes on behalf of the Green Gang boss at his cigarette factory, so the People's Government arrested and sentenced him to death in the Campaign to Suppress the Counterrevolutionaries. They also took my grandmother to the police station for interrogation: "They told me to confess my crimes, asking if I had assisted my husband in his counterrevolutionary activities. I told them to go ask my neighbors and factory sisters about my character and my sufferings. I told them to go search my house and see how bare it was. So they did and, when they found out the truth, let me go." My grandfather's concubine, on the other hand, fashioned herself as a victim and so nobody bothered her at all. The day after my grandfather's arrest, she took all the jewelry he bought for her and moved out of the house with her children. She was remarried within two months.

After my grandfather's execution, my grandmother sublet her back bedroom to another family and moved into the pavilion room with my mother. Fortunately, my mother found a job as a schoolteacher in an elementary school in the suburbs, earning thirty yuan every month, just enough to keep the three of us alive. With the stigma of a counterrevolutionary father, my mother always had her heart in her throat whenever there was a political campaign at her work unit. Trying to pass for one of the masses, she never expressed her opinions or joined any political organizations. As she put it, "I've always stood on the sidelines and kept quiet."

In the mid-1950s, my mother finally got hold of my father. He told her to join him in Hong Kong, but the local police wouldn't let the "daughter of a counterrevolutionary" leave. Then he told her to go join his family in Manchuria, but having heard about the difficult life there, my grandmother would not let her go. So my father proposed a divorce, and since having overseas relations was always suspect, my mother consented but begged the local police and cadres at her work unit to keep her divorce a secret, for she feared the alleyway folks would look down on her and me. She considered remarrying, but my grandmother discouraged her: "You've already had your chance with a good man, but you weren't able to keep him. Now you have a daughter plus a bad class status, what makes you think you'll find another good man? And if you marry a bad man, you'll really suffer, and your child too." My grandmother probably had her own interests in mind as well, for if my mother really did remarry, she would have no one to depend on.

In the Cultural Revolution, I took free train rides with millions of other young people around the country and visited my father in Tianjin, where he lived with his new wife and their two sons in a luxurious three-story Western-style house, with a living room, three bedrooms, a study, and a bathroom with flush toilet and a bathtub. My father took me to dinner and asked me whether my mother and I still lived in the pavilion room. When I told him yes, he fell silent. Then he told me that his colleagues had accused him of being a Nationalist spy (because of his stay in Hong Kong), but he told me not to worry: "Nothing will happen to me. My real dossiers are at the Public Security Bureau—they will protect me." Still, my father was soon exiled to the countryside with his entire family. His investigators found my mother and asked her if she and my father were like "severed lotus roots, with silk threads still attached." My mother was so scared she clipped my father's face out of all of their wedding pictures. She also no longer tried to hide her divorce from the alleyway neighbors.

In the countryside, my father's second wife became ill from hard labor and died. My father, on the other hand, seemed to adapt easily to his environment, using a straw rope as a belt and working harder than the peasants. Everyone said he didn't look like someone who came back from abroad. He smoked and drank heavily, and when he was drunk, he never said a word. He was, as they say, someone who could endure humiliation in order to carry out an important mission. His handwriting was hard and angular, like his personality. When he died of lung cancer in 1977, more than four hundred people came to his funeral, many of them high officials who came in jeeps. The Gang of Four had just been smashed, and his death was perceived as a result of political persecution.

Although sad about my father's tribulations in the Cultural Revolution, my grandmother, mother, and I were also relieved to have escaped such affliction. While political campaigns turned the outside world upside down, the alleyway folks were still occupied with the necessities of daily existence. After historical tempests have calmed, we stand firm on the sediments of our dreams and fears, wishing for nothing more than to live in peace.

A Room of Her Own: The Whispers of Aunt Duckweed

Born in 1958, Aunt Duckweed lived in the front bedroom of No. 111 Alliance Lane until the age of twenty-six. Not only does she remember every corner of this house by heart, but she also knows the stories of many other neighbors and relayed them to me. Yet when I asked her to revisit Alliance Lane with me after her family moved out and before its demolition, she refused: "I don't want to see old neighbors, to answer their questions, or return their looks. To go there would be to hear my mother's curses at the sky and the earth, at the neighbors, at my father, my sister, my brother, and me. I don't want see my father's ghost, stripped of peace." Instead, Aunt Duckweed gave me a key to the empty room and gave me permission to film the "ruins" of her childhood home (fig. 3.6), the footage of which served as prompts for her reminiscences from the alleyway. In assembling the following narrative, I hope I retained the unhurried, intimate quality of her voice as she related quotidian yet poignant episodes from her personal and family life over several summer nights while the green coil of mosquito incense slowly turned into white ashes.

FIGURE 3.6 Aunt Duckweed's empty childhood home in 2000. Video stills by the author.

FIGURE 3.7 The first meeting of Aunt Duckweed's parents in 1951. Photograph courtesy of Aunt Duckweed.

Orphaned at a young age, my father came to Shanghai from the countryside as an adolescent in the 1930s and apprenticed as a silk weaver, specializing in seamlessly joining two bolts of silk into one. Since this skill was in great demand and he had no one to support back home, my father made a good living and could afford a few luxuries. In the bottom of our storage chests, I had seen some of his old Chinese long gowns and Western-style shirts and trousers—all made out of sturdy, high-quality fabric—as well as a pair of white embroidered slippers, an Italian watch, an American shaving razor, even a bottle of cologne. He loved the movies. When the actress Ruan Lingyu died in 1935, he took a day off to join a five-kilometer procession of mourners at her funeral.

FIGURE 3.8 Aunt Duckweed and her elder sister around 1961. Photograph courtesy of Aunt Duckweed.

By the time my father married my mother at the age of thirty-eight, he had saved up quite a bit of money. My maternal grandfather was originally a landowner in the Suzhou countryside. He had four daughters but no sons, so he bought four poor boys to raise them as his future sons-in-law and hired a private tutor to teach the eight children at home—that's why my mother knows how to read and write. When the Japanese occupied his village, my grandfather lost his nerves when drunken soldiers shot at him in jest with empty guns. Every time he heard artillery fire, he would stick his head and upper body under an Eight Immortal Table while leaving his butt exposed. My aunt told me all this. By the end of the war, my grandfather had lost most of his land and instead managed a hot-towel and snacks service for a storytelling teahouse in Suzhou. His two elder daughters married the two elder sons-in-law, but when Communist Liberation came, the remaining two boys fled their engagements to my mother and little aunt, both of whom began working as silk workers.

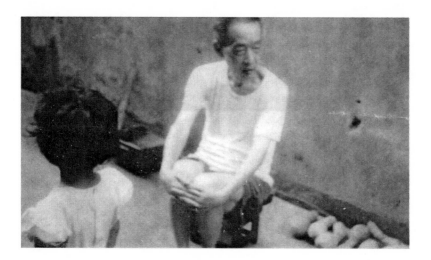

FIGURE 3.9 Aunt Duckweed's father in the alleyway, 1984. Photograph courtesy of Aunt Duckweed.

In 1951, my mother's coworker married my father's coworker, so the couple made a match for my parents. Fifteen years my father's junior, my mother agreed to the marriage after learning that he had no parents or siblings to take care of. My father spent lavishly on the wedding—my mother often bragged about her wedding trousseau and told my sister and me that was what a woman was worth. I don't think there had been any courtship between them, only a meeting in the park in the presence of the matchmaker [fig. 3.7]. He was drawn to her youth and feisty personality, whereas she saw in him a quiet and passive man she could easily dominate.

When they married, my father paid a high takeover fee to Apricot's grandmother for the front bedroom, the best room in the house. He planned on taking over the back bedroom as well, but the asking price was high, and he wanted to think it over, but Apricot's grandmother needed the money in such a hurry, she rented it to another family instead. Soon after that, housing in Shanghai froze, and they had to work with the fourteen square meters they had [see fig. 1.17H]. In this room they raised my sister, me, and my brother, born in 1953, 1958, and 1960.

The layout of this room remained basically the same for all the years I lived there: As you enter through the door, you could see in counterclockwise order from your right a large bed against the wall adjacent to the back bedroom, an armoire, a wardrobe with two trousseau chests on top against the right wall, an Eight Immortal Table with two chairs and four stools against the window, a small bed against the left wall, a small cabinet with twelve drawers at the foot of the bed, and a night stool behind the door. In the corridor right outside of our door stood our bowl cabinet, a basin stand, and a few small basins. The spaces beneath the beds housed a wealth of things, including rice buckets, wine jugs, baskets, shoes, a crib, a rocking horse, an extra night stool, and pots and pans not used everyday. In this one room, all five of us conducted all of life's basic necessities.

My father worked three shifts at the silk factory, and my mother took care of the household. She initially had a job at the same factory but took prolonged sick leave because she believed that a woman's place was in the home. An excellent cook, she always decked our supper table with tasty dishes and juicy alleyway gossip, while my father savored his Shaoxing wine and bantered with us children. My mother dressed us like dolls [fig. 3.8], better than most other children in the alleyway, even if her accusing the tailor of stealing fabric embarrassed us. In winter evenings, my mother washed us children one by one—face, butt, feet—and tugged each of us into bed with a hot-water bottle. When my father returned from night shifts at dawn, he would bring home in his large worker's enamel cup three buns stuffed with pork for us children. Those are a few of my fondest childhood memories.

When I was little, I slept on the small bed with my sister while my parents slept on the big bed with my brother. By the time I was ten, my sister fifteen, and my brother eight, we changed our sleeping arrangement to my father and my brother on the big bed, my mother on the small bed, my sister on the floor, and I on a reclining chair—sleeping on the floor made me dizzy. Such a sleeping arrangement meant that as soon as we were old enough to understand sex, my parents stopped sleeping on the same bed. Since I was sleeping on the reclining chair, home became a camping ground. In the morning, I had to fold up the chair because otherwise we wouldn't be able to open up the wardrobe. The chair was so narrow I could not turn over without falling off. Such precariousness gave me insomnia, but since all my friends experienced similar difficulties, I did not think much of this. Besides, my family seemed much better off than many other families since we never had to worry about food or clothing.

Yet my parents still fought all the time over money. My mother would curse until she was hoarse over my father's lending money to a distant relative or if he refused to give her money for an expense he disapproved. It was always over money, but perhaps money was just a camouflage for less speakable matters. I suppose their fights, along with the fights between other couples in the alleyway that I heard on a daily basis due to these paper-thin walls, made me think that I would rather die of loneliness than be caught in a bad marriage.

It did not occur to me until much later that my mother might have been mentally ill—I realized with retrospective horror that many mentally ill people in our alleyway were never even recognized, not to mention treated. In the late 1970s, my mother would disappear for days at a time and then suddenly send us a telegram to pick her up at the train station. The moment she got home, she would run out again or pour a basin of water on the bed so that nobody could sleep. As though possessed by a ghost, she also seemed to have infected my brother. When she talked, he would shriek, "Shut up!" or "I'll kill you!" and then start chasing her around the house or out into the alleyway. He couldn't swallow anymore, and saliva dribbled from the corners of his lips. We had to dress and wash and spoon-feed both of them their medicine and meals, but they would smash their bowls and spit everything out. Once my brother locked my mother inside the room with him and beat her with his fists, so we had to break down the door. For six months we sent my mother to the mental hospital to separate her from my brother. Both got much better, but since bed space at the hospital was limited, they refused to keep her, and once she returned home, the nightmares started again.

All the while, my father applied for a new apartment from the housing authorities, appealing to them on the basis of three counts: (1) Five adults in fourteen square meters, with less than three square meters each. (2) Unmarried adult men and women cohabiting in the same room. (3) Two mentally ill persons who cannot stand the sight of each other in the same room. And yet the housing authorities never responded.

Their illnesses began winding down after two years, but my family was drained emotionally and financially. My father lost most of his hair and his lifelong savings, and yet they never completely recovered. In fact, my mother became even more insufferable: "You call me crazy?" she often said. "Then I *am* crazy." At this point, my father had already retired from the silk factory and was now the one doing most of the household chores. To share his burden I would rush home from work every afternoon to do the washing and the cooking when my sister was dating.

I was twenty-three, twenty-four, at the time and had exchanged letters with an old classmate, someone with whom I felt conversation was possible. He wrote that he was willing to share the burden of my family, but I knew that he couldn't have possibly meant that and broke it off quickly. What pains me much more than this relationship, however, was the way my family had interfered with my education. The Cultural Revolution began when I was eight, and for the next decade we learned close to nothing in school. After high school I was allocated a job as an assembly-line worker at a factory that put together rocket parts. After the Cultural Revolution, university examinations resumed, and I began studying after work every day, reading by a small light in my reclining chair after everyone had gone to bed. But once my mother and my brother got sick, I had no time, space, or heart to study, and with my father's subsequent death in 1987, my dream of college was dissolved gradually in the dirty laundry of exasperation and grief.

But first, let me go back a few years and explain how I moved out of my childhood home. My sister got married in 1984. Her husband's job was in Suzhou, while hers was in Shanghai, so she commuted to see him once a week. One weekend, he came to Shanghai and planned to stay over at our place, but I said I could not sleep in the same room with my brother-in-law, so I sat up in the kitchen all night and then moved over to a friend's house the following day. Besides assembly-line workers, my work unit hired college graduates from other parts of the country and provided dormitories for them. I had applied for a bed in the dorm many times but was always rejected because my residential registration was in Shanghai. This time I became so desperate I asked a friend to find me an empty bed in a women's suite and to spread my blankets on it. I sneaked into the dorm and spent the first few days with my heart in my throat since the dorm guard checked rooms every evening before the lights went out. Meanwhile, I asked my friends to go persuade the cadres, who continued to be reluctant, but then again they didn't kick me out either. By the third week, they asked me to pay for the utilities, which meant I could stay.

The dorm guard loved to abuse what little power she had and constantly reported to the cadres: "This woman has an unhealthy tendency," meaning that she might have been intimate with her boyfriend, or "That man gambles all night." Many dorm residents wanted to get married but were in a long queue for housing, and so they often made the dorm room their marriage chamber by asking their roommates to move into a different room. As long as the dorm guard didn't denounce them, they might even have a baby there, which really helped them get on the housing priority list. Many people bribed the dorm guard with gifts, which she accepted without qualms. Since I made no attempt to get on her good side, she went around talking about me behind my back: "The girl moves in first. Later she'll bring in her boyfriend and get married here. What a way to usurp housing!" When a friend relayed her words to me, I thought to myself: "If I were married and still living here, it would be truly pathetic."

My father was very sad that I moved to the dormitory. He said it made him lose face in the alleyway. I said, "You would lose more face if I lived at home because there would be fights between everyone, and all you do is wait for me to get married and move out." My father said that's not what he meant. He was sad that he didn't have the means to put a roof over my head. So for his sake I had supper at home every evening and only left for the dormitory at night, when fewer neighbors would see me, because in the eyes of the alleyway a daughter should not leave her father's house until she has found a husband.

Yet despite everything I was ecstatic. Twenty-six years old, and it was the first time I had a bed to myself! I hung a curtain from the upper bunk so I could shield myself from the gazes of passersby. I nailed a wooden board onto the wall—my first bookshelf—and bought a small lamp so I could read after the lights went out. I moved my things into the dorm room in trickles and conquered the space inside in a guerrilla fashion. Initially, there wasn't even place for me to put my basin, but then my roommates found better places to live and departed one by one until I had the room almost entirely to myself. Every time someone moved out, I would bring in something new: a bookshelf, a drawer or two, a folding chair, and, finally, a writing desk.

Still, dorm life was far from ideal. The restroom, our only source of water, was shared between men and women and stank so badly I could smell it with my door closed. The corridors were littered with cigarette butts, and if I hung my clothes out to dry, my underwear would be stolen. About a half-dozen men in their fifties lived in the dormitory for most of their lives, bachelors because they thought highly of themselves but had bad class labels. They smoked in the dark, drank alone, and threw up in the restrooms. One talked about his Cultural Revolution traumas incessantly to anyone who said hello to him. Another guy down my corridor wrote calligraphy day and night, once even filling the walls of the hallway and the staircase with his scrawling handwriting.[47] Watching lives like these made me despair of my own future. I wondered if I would also go crazy if only I lived there long enough.

Everyone asked me why I wouldn't get married, but I never in fact made up my mind *not* to get married. Rather, my ideas about marriage were quite different from those around me, for they came from my reading of Western novels and lyric poetry during the Cultural Revolution—Pushkin and Tolstoy, Goethe and Shelley—all of whom I read as coverless, torn, and hand-copied books secretly circulated among alleyway neighbors [see "Home Searches" in chapter 2]. I conceived of love as a spiritual matter rather than a material one, but in the 1980s the talks about marriage around me were all so grounded in reality. Before dating a man, a girl would usually ask such concrete questions as "Does he have housing?" or "Does he have many siblings?" or "Does he have to work three shifts?" I could never be so pragmatic. So long I remained single, at least I had time to read, time to think.

You ask me what kind of man I would have married. I suppose the answer would be a man like my father. My father was not a very ambitious man and never sought power. Even though he had a very good class background, participated in the trade unions, and even helped Communists before Liberation, he never talked about such things in public and never denounced others at political meetings. It could be because during the Three-Anti Five-Anti Campaign in 1952 someone had falsely accused him, and someone immediately hauled him by the collar onto the stage to stand with the other "counterrevolutionaries."

On his way down, my father tripped on his own long gown and fell to the ground—he was utterly terrified. Fortunately, he was "rehabilitated" the following day. Perhaps it was the memory of this incident that prevented him from actively participating in politics, except to improve the quality of life for his fellow workers by getting them group tickets to the movies.

When the Going Up the Mountains and Down to the Countryside movement came into full effect around 1969 and 1970, at least one child per family, usually the eldest, was supposed to migrate to rural areas. My father told my sister that he could support her at home—those who did not obey the policy certainly would not get any job in the city—and so for three years, despite the neighborhood committee's daily harassment, my father held out for my sister until exhortation turned into threat. It pained him to have any single member missing from our family—it was so with my sister, it was so with me, and despite everything my mother did to him, it never once occurred to my father to divorce her. He loved this home and saw it as his responsibility to protect and sustain it with all the means at his disposal.

Around 1982 or 1983, I awoke suddenly one midnight to discover that everything in the room was shaking. The tremors soon stopped, but my father still headed out to find out what was going on and came back a little while later, telling everyone to go back to bed, while he himself sat down on the lid of the night stool before the door: "I'll wait here. If there is an earthquake, I can wake you up." So he sat there all night to watch out for our family [fig. 3.9].

Yet after taking care of us for thirty some years, my father arrived at a most bleak and bitter end. January 20, 1987, was his seventy-second birthday. He had stomach cancer, and we all knew it was going to be his last birthday, and so we cooked a meal for him. He had no appetite but ate a little to please us. My sister was to cook him some birthday noodles. She cooked his noodles, put it aside, and then made some new noodles for her two-year-old daughter, so by the time she brought the two bowls of noodles to the table, our father's noodles were soggy and cold, whereas her daughter's noodles were steaming and full of vitality. My father shook his head and didn't eat a bite. I felt like slapping the bowl over and cooking a new bowl for him, but that only would have made things worse. A few days later my father said he had a craving for shrimp even though the doctor said he shouldn't eat seafood, but since he didn't have long to live, we complied. When he raised a shrimp to his mouth, my brother yelled at him: "Why are you eating shrimp? The doctor told you not to eat shrimp! We bought such expensive medicine for you, why do you waste our money?" And so my father put down his chopsticks and ate no more.

During my father's illness, my mother turned the house upside down to look for an imaginary bank deposit slip. She believed—and told the whole alleyway—that my father had saved up ten thousand yuan and wouldn't give it to her. Her calculation was based on my father's monthly wages minus the amount he handed over to her for everyday expenses, forgetting or refusing to take into account the thousands we had spent on her and my brother's mental illness. In fact, my father had only two hundred yuan left in his account, which he gave me because I was the only child who gave part of my salary back to the family. (I still have the deposit slips with me because they are a memento from my father, and I would never for the world exchange them for cash.) He said he had failed as a father because he didn't leave us an inheritance, and yet in his final week my mother was still searching for the ten thousand yuan—in his bedspreads, in his pillow, underneath his clothes—she also searched my bags every time I turned my back. She would coax and beg and threaten him, and he never said a word.

My father died on the morning of March 20, 1987. As he drew his last breath, the postman arrived with his monthly retirement check. My mother held the envelope in her hand and cried over his body: "Old man, here is your last retirement check!" I wanted to kill her then more than ever. I wished I could block her face from his sight and her voice from his ears; he must have passed away without a shred of consolation. When he finally died, I had no more tears, while the rest of the family bawled. In subsequent years, on the anniversary of his death, my mother and sister would cook up a big feast for his soul. I could only sneer at this—why couldn't you cook a bowl of noodles right when he was alive?

Before his death, my father said to me at the hospital: "After I'm gone, you don't ever have to come back to visit them if you don't want to." So I hardly ever went back to Alliance Lane. His death must have done something to my brain because I couldn't listen to music for the next three years without all the hair on my body sticking up. My mind was often blank, and tears ran down my cheeks without my knowing it. I kept thinking that I would much rather die the way the writer Eileen Chang did, all alone, than to die the way my father did, amidst the hustle and bustle of a heartless family.

In 1991, my work unit started downsizing and said that any worker would be exempt from work if he or she would accept only 75 percent of the salary. Since I had no more family obligations after my father's death, I took that option and spent my time reading in bed. The only time I ran out of money was on New Year's, when I had to buy postage stamps so I could send letters and greeting cards. But my friends told me that I could not go on as a "spiritual aristocrat" and referred me to a Cantonese furniture company, where I got a job as a saleswoman. Although I had hated business, the contempt my colleagues showed toward me because I was a woman egged me on. Besides, I was well paid. In three years, my boss made me into the manager of the company's Shanghai branch. At this point, I moved out of the dormitory into a rented apartment, where I had my first taste of true, complete privacy after thirty-three years of living under other people's eyelids. Here I could finally collect together my books, which had previously been scattered in the homes of friends, and walk around in pajamas.

At the age of forty, I bought this seventy-square-meter apartment for myself and have since made it home, as much as my father made a home for us half a century ago with merely fourteen square meters. Eleven years after my father's death, I decided to let my mother move in with me. After all, she gave birth to me, raised me, and maybe even loved me when I was a child. I remember one day when I was in first grade, it was snowing heavily outside, and my mother carried me to school in the morning on her back. After my father's death, my sister and brother also moved out of Alliance Lane, so my mother lived alone. After a decade of solitude, I thought she might have had a chance to ruminate over things past and hoped for some sort of reconciliation, but besides growing old, she had not changed much. When I went to work, she sat in the corridor outside the apartment and made up wild tales about me to the neighbors, who barely paid her any heed. Already beyond anger and sadness, I felt only pity for the old woman deprived of her gossip milieu. Two years later I decided to put an end to our cold, stale relationship by sending her to a nursing home, where she found a new society among other retirees, so that I could enjoy my own apartment on the nineteenth floor with a view of the Huangpu River, the river that symbolizes the city of Shanghai. I like to spend my evenings by the balcony, read a book, and look out onto the shimmering waters, knowing that my room is adding another glimmer to the panorama of lights.

4

DEMOLITION

ON A HOT AUGUST AFTERNOON in 2006, my maternal grandparents and I returned to visit Alliance Lane in the midst of demolition. The stone portal entrance still stood intact, but what lay beyond looked as if a major earthquake or air raid had struck, laying to ruins some houses and leaving their neighbors unscathed.[1] A handful of residents continued about their daily routines—emptying night stools, hanging laundry, or simply cooling themselves in the shadowy side of their alleyway branches. As we approached No. 111, my childhood home, we saw that the roof and the entire front part of the house were gone. What remained in the rubble were part of a staircase, the kitchen, the pavilion room, and the terrace where my grandparents had washed and cooked, grown flowers and scallions, raised and killed chickens—where three generations of children had once played and daydreamed.

A demolition worker stood on the terrace and struck at our cement water sink. Something came crashing down on the other side, and then all was quiet again. A migrant worker from the countryside, he made the sledgehammer he wielded look like a hoe. Appearing like a mirage under the sun, this was a farmer turning over the earth, getting it ready for a new season of planting, and this old house was just a hard spot in the soil to break and flatten.

While I picked up a few bricks as souvenirs,[2] Waipo went off to chat with an old neighbor at the other end of the alleyway branch: "You are still holding out? Why make life hard for yourself? Just take what they give you and go. We're content with what we got." "That's because your daughter already bought you a new apartment," said the old man, who stared at my camcorder and asked if I came from the television station, for he would like to lodge a complaint against "those corrupt authorities." On our way out, Waipo shook her head: "These greedy nail households!"

How has a familiar home and neighborhood transformed into an uncanny demolition site, rife with violence and ghosts, and eventually a tabula rasa to be filled with futuristic mirages of skyscrapers? This last chapter chronicles the decay, death, and afterlife of Alliance Lane and its associated neighborhood, giving a glimpse into the messiness and complexity of Shanghai's dazzling urban renewal. Demolition is a paradoxical moment that brings together many opposites: it creates "private property" and home ownership through the very destruction of private homes; it is an amnesiac moment that summons effigylike memories to its own bonfire; it resolves as well as heightens familial and neighborly tensions. Accompanied by material and immaterial gains and losses, the process of demolition and relocation (*chaiqian* 拆遷) has been a gold mine for most people involved, yet one also fraught with dangers and pitfalls.[3] Finally, although the privatization of land and housing eventually has led to larger and more private spaces for almost all residents,[4] such a process has also destroyed patterns of everyday life and obliterated the memories and histories of many families and communities, transforming old Shanghai homes into real estate capital and nostalgic photographs.

This chapter first recapitulates the historical changes in the Yangshupu area beginning in the early 1990s, changes that widened the socioeconomic gaps between its citizens and reclassified diverse alleyway residents into newly segregated communities. Using newspaper articles, blogs, and interviews with former residents and housing officials, I reconstruct the demolition of Alliance Lane and surrounding neighborhoods from the ground level, focusing especially on so-called nail households (*dingzihu* 釘子戶) who refuse to move and are often forcibly evicted (*qiangqian* 強遷). However much they appear like opposites, the nail households who defend their property against state capitalist appropriation have been tempered precisely from the selfless and "rustless" bolts (*luosiding* 螺絲釘) of the collectivist era. In this sense, the demolition process both invokes and revokes the city's and the nation's revolutionary legacy.

Demolition Micropolitics

The late 1980s and 1990s saw a gradual relief of the housing crisis and an emptying out of old alleyways as many work units built and allocated housing to their employees. While my parents and I moved abroad by 1991, many aunts and uncles—my relatives and old neighbors—left the alleyways after marriage for newly constructed apartment complexes allocated through work unit welfare programs. After Shanghai's economic renaissance in the early 1990s, private real estate developers remolded the city's housing landscape by building thousands of high-rises with spacious condominiums for sale to those with new wealth or overseas connections or both, among them my parents, who returned to Shanghai from the United States in 1998.[5] Meanwhile, preexisting urban housing also made the transition from "welfare benefit to capitalized asset,"[6] and as the price of commodity housing made many somersaults over the years, everyone who could pool together the money to buy property also received handsome returns from their investments.

By the 2000s, most remaining residents of alleyways in the Yangshupu area were of an older generation with little social or economic capital, mainly workers retired or laid off from bankrupt state-owned enterprises. Those who left the area often sublet their empty rooms to migrants from other provinces. As the metropolis expanded outward and grew upward, the alleyways of the Yangshupu area became Shanghai's new inner-city slum—stains to be erased from the urban planner's map.[7] The first wave of demolitions paved the way for the construction of highways, subways, and bridges, drawing Yangshupu closer to the downtown area—to the Bund and the brand-new Pudong skyline.

In 2005, the Shanghai municipal government announced plans to "renovate old neighborhoods" (*jiuqu gaizao* 舊區改造) through the demolition of several large patches of land filled with old alleyways.[8] The biggest of these neighborhoods to be renovated was Pingliang West Lots (Pingliang Xikuai 平涼西塊), consisting of 0.33 square kilometers and sixteen thousand households.[9] Alliance Lane belonged to the three lots slated for the first round of demolition. The government was to stash away the empty land and auction it off to developers later on, but the professed purpose of the demolition was to improve the livelihoods of the residents, who would be compensated in cash or relocated to modern apartments in the suburbs. Some residents recalled that as demolition plans were publicized in August 2005, Shanghai's powerful party secretary Chen Liangyu paid a visit, showing the municipal government's investment in this project. In September 2006, however, Chen was removed from power ostensibly for embezzling a huge amount of money from the city's social security fund and investing it into the real estate sector.[10]

More than any high politics or astronomical economics, local residents were concerned mainly with the few square meters they occupied—the precise compensation form and amount as well as methods of calculation: that is, how officials would count the bricks (measure the habitable area of a given home) and count the heads (taking into account the number of people in each household and the number of households). For most people who continued to live in the area, demolition was their one hope to revolutionize their living condition. The city's real estate prices had risen far above what was affordable for ordinary citizens—an ordinary two-bedroom apartment easily cost one hundred times a worker's annual retirement pension. Younger generations needed housing for marriage, while elder generations worried about their access to everyday facilities and balancing the conflicts of interest among their children. Everyone had a private calculus, and the entire demolition process became rife with tension and strife, deception and corruption, both in the relocation company and among the residents themselves.

Under the banner "Sunny Relocation," the government allowed residents to vote for their favorite real estate appraisal company from a list and publicized its basic compensation policies and rules,[11] but as many residents put it, the rules were like elastic bands to be endlessly stretched. Without pulling any tricks or connections, the first batch of households to be persuaded to leave received on average about 400,000 yuan (about U.S.$50,000) *or* an apartment in the distant suburbs built by the relocation company, plus an extra cash "prize" and a big television as rewards for their cooperation.[12] The earliest contract signer turned out to be Grandma Apricot, who added her own savings to the compensation to buy a small apartment nearby. Everyone I spoke to seemed to know how much she received because the relocation company used her as a model for those who still hesitated. "The Earlier You Leave," read the motto, "the More You Benefit." But everyone knew that the opposite was true, and old neighbors spoke of Grandma Apricot as the fool who took a television and lost an apartment. When I asked Grandma Apricot about this in person in 2013, she said: "The day the relocation team moved into our alleyway, I had a heart attack and was hospitalized. My sons, now living in England, worried that the negotiations might exasperate my illness, so they told me to take their first offer and leave. All our neighbors cursed us for our betrayal and thought the relocation team had given us an underhanded bribe."

Despite having moved into a new apartment my parents had bought for them by 1999, Waigong and Waipo kept their household registration in Alliance Lane, as did their son Uncle Strong and daughter Little Aunt. From an acquaintance working in the local government, Little Aunt's husband learned six months before the official announcement about the imminent demolition of this area and the freezing of all household registration. This gave my grandparents enough time to transfer into their old home the household registration of a daughter-in-law, a son-in-law, and two grandchildren, thereby receiving a generous 800,000 yuan without bargaining: "We could have easily gotten more," said Waipo, "but we didn't know how to talk, so they talked us into the offer in no time." By contrast, her next-door neighbor with a smaller home not only moved more people into her household registration but also split one household into two to receive more than one million at the end. Indeed, to maximize compensation in some cases, married couples got fake divorces, and widows and widowers got fake marriages to migrant workers to add heads to the household. With good connections and a bit of bribery, it became possible to add strangers or even dead souls to one's household registration booklet.

After a sufficient number of families had signed contracts, the demolition work on their units created so much noise, dust, vermin, and theft that it took nerves and skills to hold out. Meanwhile, experienced relocation teams worked from dawn to dusk, stalking every member of what they called "nail houses" populated by *diaomin* 刁民 (cunning, unruly people), trying to "harmonize" them with both the carrot and the stick. For example, they might give the hesitating households a bit more compensation by counting attic corners and closet spaces or by adding heads to their household. Simultaneously, however, they might send demolition workers to cut the electricity, gas, and telephone lines or destroy water pipes. If they could connect with the residents' employers, the employers might threaten to fire them, or sometimes the relocation teams promised one thing verbally and made the residents sign a piece of paper that said something else at the last minute.

Under such pressure, families and neighbors could either unite in pursuit of their common interests against the relocation company or fragment into what Yunxiang Yan calls "uncivil individuals,"[13] pursuing private interests at the expense of other family members or neighbors. Temporary alliances, conspiracies, and secret deals ruled the day. Relocation teams played neighbors and family members off of each other, creating various conflicts or civil lawsuits whose proceedings were sometimes published in the Internet.[14] The final results of most negotiations and the division of the compensation were veiled in darkness, secrecy, and rumors. As former proletariats suddenly gained consciousness of their private property, they were unable to achieve true unity, and it was rare for any extended family not to have at least one pariah.

If all its threats and temptations failed to help it reach an agreement with the residents still holding out, the relocation company used forced evictions as the very last resort—as happened to 138 families out of about 5,000 households in the first stage of Pingliang West Lots over a period of two years.[15] In her recent book *Shanghai Gone*, Qin Shao calls such forced evictions followed by the demolition of the houses "domicide": "the murder of the home, against the owners' will . . . perpetrated against residents in the form of physical abuse, imprisonment, murder, and suicide as they resist demolition and relocation on the government's terms."[16] Among those to experience the earliest domicides in Alliance Lane was the family of three living on the ground floor of Waipo and Waigong's old house, No. 111. Having moved out in 1999, my grandparents did not know this family because they had only moved there in 2000 after purchasing occupancy and use rights from sitting tenants. Rather, I found their story by searching for my childhood address on the Internet, which yielded a long petition letter from a Ms. Guan entitled "My Road to Forced Eviction," dated September 2007.[17] According to this letter, she was fifty years old, unemployed, and lived in the old house with her husband and daughter, yet the relocation company insisted on compensating according the household registration booklet, which included only her name. Shortly before the forced eviction, they still offered her 650,000 yuan, but she demanded 730,000, the amount she had to pay for a "second-hand" two-bedroom apartment nearby. Moreover, her next-door neighbors received 810,000 for the same area and only two people in the household. Yet the relocation company told her that, having failed to accept their initial offer, she had also lost further negotiation rights. "I'm like the mother of three children," Ms. Guan quotes a relocation team member saying. "I can give whomever a little more as I please. Your demand is that of a pauper driven to robbery." Two days later Ms. Guan, her daughter, and her husband were allegedly kidnapped separately by three groups of strangers, while their home was demolished:

On July 28 [2006], I went out to buy breakfast at around six and was planning to accompany a friend to the crematorium to pick up an ash box. On the way, about a dozen people surrounded me and pushed me into a white van. Not knowing who they were, I resisted with all my might, but in vain, and only after their violent treatment did I find out that they belonged to the relocation team and were in charge of evicting my family. I asked why they restricted my freedom, but those gangsters didn't pay me any heed. When I reached for my cell phone they grabbed that as well. Meanwhile, my daughter got intercepted on her way to work. Ten people from the relocation team also pushed her into a car and detained her for several hours. She called the police, who came but interrogated her rudely and left without making a record. The same happened to my husband. [18]

I showed my grandparents Ms. Guan's petition letter, which eloquently cites various laws in support of her case. Although they acknowledged that forced evictions were violent and criminal, Waigong and Waipo were not too sympathetic to Ms. Guan's plight. "She bought her occupancy rights only six years earlier for some 70,000 yuan, and now demolition was bringing her nine times her investment—still not satisfied? Why were her husband and daughter not part of her household registration book? Probably because they had housing elsewhere already." For my grandparents, their downstairs neighbor was not a hapless victim, but rather a greedy real estate speculator, only of much smaller scale than the real estate developers who had driven up the housing prices. Nevertheless, as Qin Shao points out, demeaning treatment by officials and the trauma of domicide understandably hardened the residents' resistance to compromise, and the "psychological price mark" that included emotional damages became "what petitioners believed to be a necessary part of a fair settlement." [19]

The demolition work on the first three lots of Pingliang West lasted from the end of 2005 to 2008, well after Ms. Guan's eviction in 2006.

Uncle Prosper, the brother of my mother's childhood friend and class-mate, was among the last ten to leave in 2008, so he was able to give me an overview of the process. My mother recalls that her friend's home in Alli-ance Lane was among the most crowded she had ever seen, with five peo-ple occupying ten square meters—the dark and lower half of a back guest and ancestral hall (somewhat smaller than what is shown in fig. 1.17K and without the loft). In the late 1970s, with the help of a family friend who worked in the housing bureau, they were able to move to a complete guest and ancestral hall on the same block with an entrance facing the street. After his brother and sister left Shanghai for employment elsewhere and after he himself lost his factory job, Uncle Prosper converted half of his flat into a seal-carving shop in the early 1990s. When demolition began in this neighborhood, his elderly parents were registered in the same house-hold, as were his daughter and niece, but he sent everyone away to live elsewhere so that the relocation team couldn't harass them into signing an agreement on its terms. After living alone for two years in the rubble, he finally received two large apartments plus half a million yuan. When I asked for the secrets of his success in July 2011, he happily took a puff of his cigarette and ordered two beers:

> Not everyone could hold out onto the end. The noise and the dust alone were enough to drive you crazy, and when they demolished the second story above me, I had to repair the roof so it wouldn't rain in. They didn't cut my electricity or telephone line, but the junk collectors would come and steal wires in the middle of the night. . . . This kind of life was hard on the body and the nerves, so it was no wonder that many people became suicidal. My next-door neighbor took a big red flag on the roof and threatened to jump while playing "The Internationale" on a loudspeaker. Hundreds of people gathered downstairs to watch him. The vice district chief also came and finally persuaded him to come down the staircase. The day after, they force-evicted him—you can be as tough as you want, but you can't beat the government. At least a hundred people came to each forced eviction—can you get a hundred people to come around and protect you? Even if you did, they'd place a phone call and get a thousand people. With every eviction, they got not only demolition workers and bulldozers, but also police to form a blockade around the house as well as firefighters with ladders and a fire truck to pull the people out of their homes or to extinguish fires if

they started throwing Molotov cocktails or set themselves on fire—so they also prepared ambulances.

Forced evictions were not technically illegal, but they were always a spectacle that cost money and face, so the relocation company didn't want to stage them too often. They certainly didn't want to get anybody killed in the process, which would then create a scandalous media event that made them look bad. You ask me why they wouldn't just give everybody what they wanted to begin with—well, those who left early with little compensation would come back and protest. So the forced evictions were in part a spectacle staged for the other residents, both to appease the ones who had left and to intimidate the ones who remained.

Why they didn't touch me? First of all, I didn't present crazy demands. There would be no way to negotiate further if they offered you 400,000 and you asked for two million, just because. I only asked them to give an apartment to my parents and another to me—and to take care of my livelihood. I talked to them nicely: "Come in, sit down, have a cup of tea." I didn't beg or curse or hit them. I didn't care what others got, but I did my research and knew of the prices of apartments nearby and asked for comparable compensation. Second, they didn't dare evict me, since I had lots of pals in the local gangs. I also let them know that my sister was a doctor in the most important Beijing hospital with central government officials as her patients. Connections were key. They say that those relocation team people would meet up every evening and ask one another: "Does So-and-So have anything up his sleeve? If not, let's evict him!"

An informal survey of all former residents I could find showed that those who persisted usually got their way, and as many as fifty households from Alliance Lane moved to the same new apartment complex in the suburbs as Uncle Prosper, who also found paid employment in his new neighborhood committee. Every evening a few old neighbors from Alliance Lane met in the open space in front of the neighborhood committee to chat. Joining them one July evening in 2011, I learned that even the forced evictees were eventually appeased, including Ms. Guan of No. 111, but not before staging a number of melodramatic protests. "She sure was a tough lady," said an uncle who used to live in No. 123 Alliance Lane. "When the district authorities tried to detain her, she began taking off her clothes and said she wanted to take a bath. *That* scared them off so that she could go off petitioning in Beijing." Another legendary protester was a family forcibly removed from what is today a park in front of the Dalian Road metro station. On the day to celebrate the completion of the park—also named the National Anthem Memorial Square because the song was first recorded here in 1935 for a film—the family took lots of paper wreaths and burned them in the middle of the park, crying and recounting their forced eviction to their dead ancestors and the surrounding onlookers. This broke up the party, and all the bigwigs left. A more tragic case, however, was the family in No. 117, with nine siblings born in the 1940s and 1950s, of whom Hunchback and Little Nine still lived in the house. Dissatisfied with the offer from the relocation company, Hunchback's wife lay in the middle of the street to block the traffic, and Little Nine threatened to stab herself. When they finally received two new apartments as compensation, Little Nine, Hunchback, and another brother died of cancer. Their story became a cautionary tale of greed among former residents such as my grandparents.

According to Ms. Guan's later online postings, she had petitioned in vain for a year at the Yangpu District before going to the municipal and the national levels, only to be intercepted by local officials, who also detained her for the entire duration of the "two meetings" (the National People's Congress and the Chinese People's Political Consultative Conference). The local officials informed her husband's work unit that if she were to continue petitioning at upper levels, they would fire him.[20] Besides acting on her own, she and more than one hundred other forced evictees in Pingliang West joined forces and staged multiple demonstrations in front of the Yangpu District Relocation Headquarters, where they were in turn ignored and harassed.[21] These demonstrations often displayed photographs of violent demolitions along with slogans such as "In Great Sorrow We Mourn Our Homes, Forcefully Demolished by the Yangpu District Government."[22] The demonstrations were in turn photographed, videotaped, and published on the Internet with the hope of attracting more attention and thereby putting more pressure on the government to satisfy their demands. By early 2010, the local government finally appeased all evictee-petitioners, and members of a few former nail houses told me that Ms. Guan received an extra apartment as compensation for her emotional damages—which she sold for more than one million yuan. This closed the file on No. 111 Alliance Lane.

Ruins of the Old Neighborhood

When I revisited my childhood neighborhood in July 2011, the entire square lot (of which Alliance Lane took up about a third) was surrounded by a short white wall and overgrown with weed. Inside, a few cars and trucks were parked next to the makeshift huts of migrant workers amidst piles of bricks, wood, and sand from nearby demolition sites or construction sites. Under this vast, open sky—which in the past had appeared only in small patches to alleyway residents—two men were flying kites, the tips of which seem almost to touch the Pudong skyline in the southeast. To the northeast, one could see the newly minted glass complex of the Siemens Shanghai headquarters, and to the northwest the China Tobacco Museum and the Shanghai Tobacco Corporation.

Walking south and retracing the old path I used to take to primary school, I came across another alleyway in the midst of demolition, a hutment where Waigong and Waipo had first lived when they married and gave birth to my mother. Constituted as "privately owned housing" (*sifang* 私房) that workers constructed for themselves from the 1930s through the 1960s, the homes in Pingle New Village had no indoor running water or plumbing. With no architectural style to speak of, the ground floors had over time sunken by a third into the ground, and second or third stories were added on top. In 2011, two-thirds of the housing had been demolished, but in this mixture of ruins and residences I could still hear the muffled sound of cooking, washing, and television from behind closed doors and windows. A few houses still standing turned the rubble next door into a "backyard" to raise chickens; meanwhile, other animals— rats, roaches, flies, and mosquitoes—overran the place. The walls were full of writing: apart from the totemic 拆 (*chai,* "demolish") with a circle around it, there was also propaganda from the relocation team on banners and on wall posters: "Sunny Relocation, Results Open to the Public," yet almost every paper slogan seemed to have been violently scratched into semi-illegibility. The remaining residents, for their part, posted on their doors a new talisman—the new national laws forbidding forced demolitions. Indeed, housing rights activism from the mid-1990s to the 2000s had led to significant changes in state responses. Whereas in the 1990s local governments had the authority and power to enforce demolition, by the mid-2000s developers had to seek the consent of residents before demolition. Nevertheless, many crucial details, such as the percentage of residents whose consent was needed to tear down a neighborhood, were left unspecified.[23]

In the middle of the lot, a gray four-story "fortress" overlooked an open square full of rubble and weed—an archetypal nail house. At the top, large red national flags, faded and torn at the edges, marked the house's four corners. Several loudspeakers decked the roof terrace, further reminiscent of the flag-raising ceremonies in my elementary school, where we had to sing the national anthem and salute the flag by stating that "the People's interests are above all." Beneath the national flags, horizontal and vertical red banners decked the nail house:

河蟹色賄貪腐無罪: River Crab Sexual Bribery (homonymous with "Harmonious Society"); Corruption Is Not a Crime (reminiscent of the Maoist slogan "Revolution Is Not a Crime")

沒有強拆私房就沒有新中國: Without the Forced Demolition of Private Housing There Would Be No New China (reminiscent of the slogan "Without the Communist Party There Would Be No New China")

楊浦正腐搶劫逼遷私有住宅共欺共鏟: Yangpu Now Corrupt (homonymous with "Government") Robs and Coerces the Relocation of Private Housing—by Collective Deception and Collective Shoveling (homonymous with "Communist")

對抗中央非法拆遷強佔民宅法理不容: Resist Central Government's Illegal Demolition and Coerced Occupation of Commoner Homes, Tolerated by Neither Law nor Reason

In addition to the red banners, the outer wall of the ground floor featured the following handwritten slogans:

捍衛憲法 Protect the Constitution

私有財產神聖不可侵犯 Private Property, Sacred and Inviolable

違法強＊拆＊者＊斬 Those Who Illegally **Demolish** by Force, **Decapitate** (with the characters for "Demolish" and "Decapitate" bearing a graphic resemblance)

私自闖入者　斬　Those Who Enter on Their Own　**Decapitate**

掠奪民財者　斬　Those Who Raid People's Things　**Decapitate**

Just as this four-story house had been constructed in different eras with different materials, the writings on the wall were a palimpsest of different eras. The word *decapitate* evoked the stringent punishments of Qing legal systems. The red banners, loudspeakers, and phrases accusing corrupt officials evoked the Cultural Revolution, when the government bureaucracy came under attack and when smashing the four olds and factional warfare laid to ruins public buildings. Yet by evoking the Constitution and inviolable private property, the content of the slogans stood in diametric opposition to the Mao era's collectivization of property. Rather, they echoed ostentatious real estate billboards that boasted "private gardens" with security guards to bar access to outsiders. Next to these big handwritten mottos on the wall, notices of forced demolition from the relocation company and the district court were pasted on the door, ordering the residents to move to an assigned apartment in the distant suburbs of Pudong. Underneath the notice, the residents replied in bold: "Only 460,000!" (A new apartment in the area cost at least two million, so this amount was indeed quite measly.)

Fleeing from the mosquitoes, I walked farther down the alleyway and spoke to a middle-aged woman from another house, one of thirty households remaining in this neighborhood. When asked of her family's troubles, she explained that her husband had inherited their house from his parents after all his brothers and sisters moved out, but the relocation team tracked down the siblings and moved their household registration back to this house, so they all came for a share of the demolition-and-relocation money. "We argued and fought, and nobody in the family is speaking to anybody else now, but we are not going to leave before being compensated a few apartments. The longer you stay, the more you get— we learned that from them," she pointed in the direction of Alliance Lane and then asked if I also heard the rumor that the son of some Taiwanese official was going to buy that piece of land. Since I wasn't a journalist and had no new information to offer, she didn't want to waste more time and took off in a hurry.

Looking up the address of this fortress of a nail house on the Internet, I learned that the relocation company had tried in vain to demolish it in the early morning of December 29, 2010. As shown through a video taken from nearby ruins, entitled *Shanghai's Coolest Nail House*, more than a hundred men surrounded the house with ladders and sticks, throwing stones and explosives that let off white smoke. The residents resisted by throwing firecrackers and Molotov cocktails from the third and fourth floors, igniting a few fires in the rubble, and burning up a ladder. The battle lasted until dawn, when the demolition fighters finally retreated. Journalistic reports added that the residents were dressed in funeral clothes and prepared to perish with the house.[24]

Later, I spoke to a resident of this nail house about the battle with the demolition team. "So you saw our video online—we are world famous!" He went on to give me some behind-the-scene details: "They sent a thousand strong, but we knew they were coming—we had our own spies—so we were prepared." They set up a video camera in an abandoned old house across from their house, bought firecrackers and gasoline, and gathered plumbing pipes in the rubble to use as weapons. Besides those who attacked the house, hundreds of men surrounded the block, patrolled by the local police, who refused to answer the family's emergency phone calls. A few demolition workers guarded the entrance of every inhabited house on the demolition site with iron sticks to beat back anyone who tried to come to the nail house residents' aid. At one point, the invaders occupied the first and second stories, but the residents managed to repel those who came up to the third floor—one man whose leg was slashed open had to get sixteen stitches later. Another demolition worker climbed up to the terrace on the fourth floor and stepped into an electrical trap set by the owners. The electric shock caused him to fall from the heights into the rubble below, his injuries putting him into a coma from which he never woke. The nail house resident claimed to have warned the attackers: "We told them that we are all poor people and that they better leave, but they wouldn't listen. We only managed to scare them away after pouring gasoline all over and threatening to light up the place."

The man I spoke to used to be a sent-down youth in Jiangxi and did not move his household registration back to Shanghai until 2008. "After forty years in the countryside," he proclaimed, "I'm not about to be sent back to the countryside," by which he meant the Shanghai suburbs. The nail house belonged to his wife's family, who tore down the original two-story shanty to construct this four-story fortress in 2005, just as the larger neighborhood itself was slated for demolition. The construction itself cost merely 20,000 yuan and was clearly motivated by the imminent demolition. Moreover, because most sent-down youths had already returned to Shanghai in the late 1970s, those who did not move back usually lacked housing and employment in Shanghai. It was only in demolition that this man saw his opportunity to make a comeback to the city with his wife and two married children. With now sixteen members in their household registration booklet, they refused to accept the two apartments in the suburbs offered them by the relocation company. After the battle, the demolition team softened and offered them six apartments instead. They wanted seven, so they were close to reaching an agreement.

Nail Houses and Rustless Bolts

"Children who know how to cry will get the milk." Such folk wisdom characterized the nail houses and forced-evictees-turned-petitioners. A more heroic popular imagining of the nail houses emerged with the release of the Hollywood blockbuster *Avatar* in China in 2010, a film widely interpreted as a *Chinese* allegory for the struggle of nail households against relocation companies and real estate developers. The media also helped to cultivate indigenous heroes and martyrs with the use of headlines such as "The Coolest Nail House in History" in 2007.[25] Indeed, the nail house facing off the bulldozer in the midst of demolition rubble against the backdrop of skyscrapers serves as a perfect allegory for the massive construction and destruction of Chinese cities today. Such grotesque spectacles render visible the structural and epistemic violence of state-driven capitalist modernization and of the so-called harmonious society. They have sharpened unprecedented citizen consciousness of private-property rights and, by extension, human rights, yet alongside protecting their rights (*weiquan* 維權) and appealing to the rule of law, protestors have often resorted to revolutionary rhetoric and protest repertoires from the Cultural Revolution. In this sense, it is worth juxtaposing the nail house against the famous figure of the "rustless bolt" from the Maoist era. In contrast to bloggers and scholars who have paired these two types of "nails" as antitheses,[26] I contend that the "individualistic" nail house is tempered precisely from the rustless bolt of the collectivist era, whose memories and legacies have not simply been erased in an era of privatization but rather have returned in a deformed manner.

"To be a rustless bolt" was a slogan popularized in the 1963 national movement to "emulate Comrade Lei Feng," a model soldier and automobile mechanic whose "greatest desire in life was to be nothing more than a revolutionary bolt that never rusts."[27] The metaphor derived from Mao's speech at the Yan'an Forum on Literature and Art, which quotes Lenin for saying that proletarian literature and art are "the cogs and wheels in the whole revolutionary machine."[28] Lei Feng was less of a real person than a hagiographic construct in the service of propaganda,[29] yet his "bolt spirit" connoted a self-sacrificial position vis-à-vis the great revolutionary machine and an unthinking willingness to be attached or detached wherever needed. Embodying such a "bolt spirit," a whole generation of Chinese urban youths were sent to the countryside in the Cultural Revolution with the slogan "I will shine and glitter wherever the Motherland and the Party wants to fasten me." Because every family usually needed to send only one child to the countryside in the Cultural Revolution, the sent-down youths also enacted self-sacrifice in a more private sense for their younger siblings, who became bolts with "iron bowl" jobs in Shanghai's factories.

From the 1990s on, however, many state-owned enterprises went bankrupt, and old industrial zones became China's rustbelts as workers' iron bowls got smashed.[30] The factories that once employed my grandparents, my aunts and uncles, and their neighbors were shut down by the turn of the millennium. The elder generation continued to receive a retirement pension and medical insurance from the government even after their factory's demise, but the middle-aged generation experienced varying success in finding alternative employment in the private sector. Aunt Duckweed opened up and closed down several furniture shops in the span of fifteen years, but the only job Uncle Strong ever had besides "stir-frying" his savings in the stock market was to oversee a demolition team over a period of two years. It is true that, even if only subsisting on their pensions and unwilling to take on more physically demanding jobs, former Shanghai workers such as my uncle were more resourceful and empowered than laid-off workers or "disgruntled proletariats" in China's interior. At the same time, the Maoist era's "iron rice bowls" had cultivated a sense of entitlement to urban social welfare beyond the mechanisms of the market. Hence, beside the market value of their land—a potential realizable only with the demolition of their homes—many nail households cited poverty and privation as the reason why they deserved better compensation. Still thinking of their welfare as the responsibility of the state, many nail households were the same rustless bolts abandoned by the revolutionary machine.

As erstwhile bolts became nail houses, the revolutionary machine also transformed into a capitalist machine through the collusion between the Communist Party and real estate developers—in the case of Pingliang West, the government *is* the developer. At first glance, this process of privatization seems like an ironic reversal of history, where the same Communist Party that expropriated capitalist property half a century ago now expropriated property from ordinary people *for* the capitalist investors. Yet both Communist and capitalist forms of expropriation laid siege to the human habitat of the home as a space of belonging, where personal and familial artifacts, rituals, and memories accumulated over the years. As Shanghai homes are converted into fluid wealth or capital, according to Samuel Liang, a relaxed and slow-paced lifestyle in the old alleyways is "replaced by a stressful, fast-paced lifestyle" where "residents are always busy working, saving, investing, and consuming."[31] Perhaps this is true of modernization more generally, for as Hannah Arendt points out, "instead of inhabiting a stable world of objects made to last, human beings [have] found themselves sucked into an accelerating process of production and consumption."[32] With the rise of both communism *and* capitalism, individuals became cogs and wheels, bolts and nails to be placed and displaced according to the blueprint of a larger economy. In this sense, the privatization of land and housing in Shanghai does not simply reverse but instead inherits the legacies of Communist expropriation.

Rather than heroically resisting the conversion of homes and communities into money, as may be the romanticized view through *Avatar*, nail households were often market-savvy residents who turned their tiny foothold in a crowded city into a gold mine of speculation. A "happy end" for the nail household is to receive multiple big and new apartments rather than being allowed to keep their old homes. A frustrated housing official responsible for the area told me that some nail households in her area now make money by advising other residents how to squeeze more money out of the relocation teams.[33] While partaking in such capitalist logic, the carnivalesque spectacles nail houses generate as well as the tactics they employ are often reminiscent of the Cultural Revolution. Studying demolition protests in a western Shanghai neighborhood, Qin Shao gives an insightful account of the "tactical," "ironic," and "transgressive" uses of the red flag, "the Internationale," the study group, and the big-character posters. Rather than uncritical nostalgia for the Maoist era, she shows that residents often link the housing dispute with the violence and chaos of the Cultural Revolution, a time when many homes were raided and private property confiscated. In this context, she concludes that "waving the red flag [is] no less pointed than burning it would be."[34]

Although I agree with Shao's thesis, the demolition of my childhood neighborhood also shows that some nail houses and rustless bolts share a passive-aggressive ethos of martyrdom that combines self-sacrifice with megalomania. Just as Lei Feng the "selfless bolt" was all too eager to document and flaunt his selflessness, these nail households have been all too eager to document and flaunt their victimhood. When lacking connections to the government or to local gangs, nail houses derive power from the pathos of their injuries, from self-destructive actions such as threatened suicides, a demonstrated willingness to perish with one's house, or even occasionally an invitation of state violence that they eagerly document and spread online—visible and sensational injustice to justify whatever they demand. All of this lends their struggle a grandeur and absurdity reminiscent of the Cultural Revolution, waged in the name of Chairman Mao but oftentimes with real, hidden, and private interests at stake. In contrast to the "selfless bolts," nail houses are much less hypocritical and much more unabashed in the defense of their self-interests, ultimately showcasing the moral bankruptcy of collective values.

At the same time, nail houses have sharpened citizens' awareness of their private interests and rights, ultimately forcing the government to slow its pace of development. In January 2011, the State Council released new rules that outlawed forced evictions and required greater transparency and public involvement in the expropriation of buildings on state-owned land. The new legislation also stipulated that only local governments—rather than developers—could engage in demolition and relocation, which must serve public interests, and that compensation to residents may not be lower than the market price of the existing real property.[35] The new national legislation dovetailed with recent policies in Shanghai that required every neighborhood committee to collect signatures from at least 90 percent of the households agreeing to the demolition and relocation of their alleyway. Next, the district government was to come up with a scheme for compensation that must win the approval of at least two-thirds of the residents, meanwhile giving an appraisal of the market value and freezing the household registration of every home. Only then could a relocation team begin negotiating and signing contracts with individual households.[36] Meanwhile, many Shanghai residents are now petitioning the government *for* demolition, putting out banners that "welcome the sunshine of the relocation team." Yet some cynical government officials I spoke to thought the very same residents would all become nail households if the demolition work actually got started.

In July 2013, I revisited Yeye and Nainai's old alleyway on Pingliang Road and spoke with the current chairman of the neighborhood committee where Nainai used to work more than half a century ago. Wearing a cowboy hat and sunglasses, Mr. D spoke to me in the alleyway's old canteen and meeting hall that had been converted into a service center where elderly men and women could get their blood pressure checked. He explained that Lane 1695 is far enough from downtown to be granted a "demolition-and-return" (*yuanchai yuanhuan* 原拆原還) policy whereby each of the 350 households is entitled to receive in compensation a new apartment built on the very same grounds of the alleyway after its demolition. This new apartment is to have at least fifteen square meters more than what residents had before, plus an independent bathroom and kitchen. Depending on the number of persons in the household register, the family may also receive additional cash. If a family with several married siblings wants more than one apartment, they may be able to exchange their old apartment for two or three new apartments in the suburbs as long as the prices are commensurate. Given such reasonable-sounding conditions, I asked him, "Are there still nail houses?" "Of course there are always nail houses," he explained, commenting that they tend to be disharmonious families: current residents have siblings elsewhere who also demand an equal share of the compensation for relocation, so that current residents feel that they would be worse off after demolition. His everyday job was to mediate not only between the community and the government, but also between family members.

True to his role, Mr. D began advising my father concerning his parents' old house. Yeye and Nainai passed away in the spring and autumn of 2011. In the last ten years of their lives, they had hoped for demolition and relocation to convert their six-decade-long tenancy of public housing (*gongfang* 公房) into the private ownership of commodity housing (*shangpinfang* 商品房), which they could then sell and/or bequeath to their children as a "family estate." Their deaths before demolition, however, meant that the municipal government could take their old house without compensation unless other family members remained on their household registry. Nainai and Yeye's two sons, my father and Uncle Lucky, had American citizenship. Of their three daughters, Aunt Pearl had died of leukemia in the 1980s, and Aunt Treasure had moved to Shenzhen. Ironically, only Aunt Bean, the daughter Yeye and Nainai had sued in 1998 for trying to "rob their house" (see "A New Generation Comes of Age" in chapter 1), was eligible to move her household registration back into the old house, thereby becoming its sole heir. Uniting briefly over shared interests, the four children of Yeye and Nainai agreed to let Aunt Bean move her family's household registration back into the old house in 2012—by pulling some connections, of course—provided that each sibling would have an equal share in the demolition compensations. Still, given Aunt Bean's unfilial history, exclusive household registration, and professed "need" of housing for her adult son to get married,[37] the just division of this family inheritance remains so contentious as to have Yeye and Nainai turning over in their graves.

CODA

IN THEIR OLD HOUSE, in boxes and plastic bags and cloth bundles, Yeye and Nainai kept yellowed newspapers, rusty tools, a bicycle wheel, and fragments of wood bored through by worms. Under the bed, they kept Ovaltine cans and kerosene cans, medicine bottles and rat poison bottles. They kept straw-mat repair kits and sock-fixing threads and milk-delivering carts. They kept leftover cloth from the tailor for clothes that had already been donated to flood relief. They kept dust-covered documents and confessions of impure thought to the authorities. They kept foresights that turned into afterthoughts. They kept overdue hopes that soured into regrets. They kept out of habit, helplessness, and superstition. They kept out of oblivion for the sake of memory. They kept a world of ghosts that cramped their living space into narrow twisted pathways.

At the beginning, they kept things in preparation for war or earthquakes or any other disaster that made goods scarce, although they learned early that real disasters meant discarding things rather than keeping them. From those early days of their lives, they learned to sort their possessions by the values they held on the spur of the moment. They learned to keep things close to their bodies: keys and jewels, heirlooms and babies. They learned about love the hard and crude way—through loss—and knowing that some things were inevitably lost, they learned to remember.

Standing amid the rubble of their dreams after a century of war and revolution, Yeye and Nainai retained the conviction that at the end of your life you were supposed to leave something for posterity. The conviction sprang from their aborted hopes to be of some use to this family, this country, this world and seemed to grow more insistent and desperate with age. Yet after a lifetime of hard work and thrifty living, they found that they had accumulated little worth passing on. The money they saved from their youth depreciated sharply over the decades, and all they had was a ghost of a house that leaked in the rain and shook in the wind.

In this house they raised five children, and with the children they also reared hopes and fears, pride and misgivings. They watched each of them grow up or grow old, grow considerate or grow ungrateful, and wondered about what they did right or wrong. On the insomniac nights that came with old age, they counted their possessions like misers, settling accounts with memory, conscience, and each other. They tallied their children and grandchildren one by one, first counting the dead, then the sick, then the well. They went over their regrets, ruminated the "if's" at the crucial joints of their lives, and also thanked heaven for all their blessings. They drank out of separate cups the same bitter tea that left muddy stains over time, impossible to wash away. There were corresponding lumps of bitterness accumulated in the deep places of their minds. With age, their senses dulled with the paint on the thermos, while their nerves multiplied along with the precarious homespun wiring on the ceiling. And their hearts, rusty like the locks on the doors, made painful squeaks with every waking hour.

In the spring and autumn of 2011, Yeye and Nainai passed away when I began revising the manuscript of this book. Returning to their old house in Shanghai, I helped sort through their dusty hoardings, bringing over to my parents' new house enlargements of their photographs on an altar, a bamboo bookshelf with a selection of Yeye's old books, as well as his confessions and autobiographies, his abacus and accounting books, and a collection of Nainai's handmade clothing and basins that were awarded her by the neighborhood committee. Apart from these sentimental souvenirs, the pending demolition of their old house may yet provide their children with handsome monetary compensation, a legacy that is already causing much contestation between my father and his siblings.

As for the remainder of their things, we called a recycling man, someone who rides a tricycle with a little bell around Shanghai alleyways. A new immigrant to the city, this man with a heavy Subei accent like that of Yeye offered us 30 yuan for the several piles of books and cardboard boxes, mildewed clothing and blankets, an old wok and several basins, tangled wires and plastic bottles, Yeye's shopping cart and Nainai's "refugee basket," a small black-and-white television, a cassette player from the 1980s, and a large broken radio from the 1970s with a slogan that read "Be Vigilant and Protect the Motherland." He then sorted all this neatly into paper, metal, plastic, and cloth and finally loaded everything onto his tricycle: "Everything is worth something, except cement, bamboo, and vegetables." He also told me that he was one of two thousand recyclers in Yangpu District, but since he didn't have a license, he had to play "guerrilla" with the police or pay 5 yuan a day in fines. Thanks to the demolitions, he made a very good living, with a monthly income greater than Yeye's retirement pension.

I followed his tricycle all the way to the recycling stations, and as we crisscrossed the unruly traffic through narrow alleyways, I kept picking up bits and pieces of rubbish that fell from the tricycle, until we reached a bleak corner of the city next to the now closed Yangshupu Power Plant with its enormous chimneys. Beside it were giant, almost monumental collection stations for cloth, paper, plastic, and metal, and everyone was busy weighing and sorting. Before selling Yeye's clothes at 0.8 yuan per kilo, my recycler checked through every single pocket of Yeye's many "Mao suits" because old people tend to forget or sew money inside, sometimes even a fortune: "If I find money," he said in all earnestness, "then let's split it fifty–fifty." Then he looked through Yeye's books and deemed everything worthless except as old paper: 1.5 yuan per kilo. "What kind of books might be worth something?" I asked. "Cultural Revolution books," he replied, "because researchers buy them." He did keep for himself, however, a book of ghost stories, a wok, a brush, a pair of cloth shoes, and a small television—all of which he told his wife to come and pick up with her bicycle. When he told her that he had made some 150 yuan in profit that day, she was all smiles and went home into a back alleyway to make his lunch. And this was how I saw off some of Yeye and Nainai's things as they took on a "new life" at the recycling station, where the artifacts of everyday life were turned into raw materials for a new generation.

NOTES

Introduction

1. Throughout the book, I refer to my grandparents as "Yeye" ("Grandpa" on my father's side), "Nainai" ("Grandma" on my father's side), "Waigong" ("Grandpa" on my mother's side), and "Waipo" ("Grandma" on my mother's side) rather than using their names.

2. On the history of St. John's University in the Republican era, see Wen-hsin Yeh, *Alienated Academy: Culture and Politics in Republican China, 1919–1937* (Cambridge, Mass.: Council on East Asian Studies, Harvard University, 1990), 49–88.

3. For one example of how a new regime refashions a public space, see Wu Hung, *Remaking Beijing: Tiananmen Square and the Creation of a Political Space* (Chicago: University of Chicago Press, 2005), and Chang-tai Hung, *Mao's New World: Political Culture in the Early People's Republic* (Ithaca, N.Y.: Cornell University Press, 2011).

4. This formulation borrows from a paraphrase of Jean-François Lyotard by June Yip in *Envisioning Taiwan: Fiction, Cinema, and the Nation in the Cultural Imaginary* (Durham, N.C.: Duke University Press, 2004), 92.

5. Qin Shao, *Shanghai Gone: Domicide and Defiance in a Chinese Megacity* (Lanham, Md.: Rowman & Littlefield, 2012); Yomi Braester, "Tracing the City's Scars: Demolition and the Limits of the Documentary Impulse in the New Urban Cinema," in *The Urban Generation: Chinese Cinema and Society at the Turn of the 21st Century*, ed. Zhang Zhen (Durham, N.C.: Duke University Press, 2007), 161–80; Robin Visser, *Cities Surround the Countryside: Urban Aesthetics in Post-socialist China* (Durham, N.C.: Duke University Press, 2007), 35–52. For an excellent recent photo collection of Shanghai's disappearing alleyways, see Howard French and Qiu Xiaolong,

Disappearing Shanghai: Photographs and Poems of an Intimate Way of Life (Paramus, N.J.: Homa & Sekey Books, 2012).

6. Wang Anyi 王安憶, *Chang hen ge* 長恨歌 (Beijing: Beijing chubanshe, 1996), translated by Michael Berry and Susan Egan as *The Song of Everlasting Sorrow: A Novel of Shanghai* (New York : Columbia University Press, 2008), 3. In giving the titles of written Chinese works or films in the text, I give an English translation first, followed by the pinyin and Chinese versions in parentheses. In the notes and bibliography, I give the pinyin and Chinese titles first, followed by an English translation in parentheses.

7. Nancy Shatzman Steinhardt, "The House: An Introduction," in *House, Home, Family: Living and Being Chinese*, ed. Ronald G. Knapp and Kai-Yin Lo (Honolulu: University of Hawai'i Press, 2005), 13–35; Nancy Berliner, *Yin Yu Tang: The Architecture and Daily Life of a Chinese House* (Boston: Tuttle, 2003), 29.

8. Francesca Bray, *Technology and Gender: Fabrics of Power in Late Imperial China* (Berkeley: University of California Press, 1997), 4.

9. Samuel Y. Liang, "Where the Courtyard Meets the Street: Spatial Culture of the *Li* Neighborhoods, Shanghai, 1870–1900," *Journal of the Society of Architectural Historians* 67.4 (2008): 482–503.

10. Tess Johnson and Deke Ehr, *A Last Look: Western Architecture in Old Shanghai* (Hong Kong: Old China Hand Press, 1993). Also see a book series on Shanghai's "foreign cultural maps" (Shanghai de waiguo wenhua ditu 上海的外國文化地圖) published by Shanghai jinxiu wenzhang chubanshe in 2010–11, which seeks to map the cultural (mainly architectural) heritage of the Americans, the British, the French, the Germans, the Japanese, the Jews, the Koreans, and the Russians in Shanghai prior to 1949.

11. Hanchao Lu, *Beyond the Neon Lights: Everyday Shanghai in the Early 20th Century* (Berkeley: University of California Press, 1999), 139–142.

12. Chunlan Zhao, "From *Shikumen* to New-Style: A Rereading of *Lilong* Housing in Modern Shanghai," *Journal of Architecture* 9.1 (2004): 49–76; Liang, "Where the Courtyard Meets the Street," 482–85.

13. Lu, *Beyond the Neon Lights*, 163, 197; see also Ma Changlin 馬長林, *Lao Shanghai chengji: Longtang li de da lishi* 老上海城記：弄堂里的大歷史 (The story of Old Shanghai: Big histories in alleyways) (Shanghai: Shanghai jinxiu wenzhang, 2010).

14. Leo Ou-fan Lee, *Shanghai Modern: The Flowering of a New Urban Culture in China* (Cambridge, Mass.: Harvard University Press, 1999), 34. Renowned Republican era writers including Bao Tianxiao, Lu Xun, Eileen Chang, and Xia Yan have offered lively glimpses into the curious, savvy, quarrelsome, and ultimately pragmatic residents of Shanghai's alleyways. See Bao Tianxiao 包天笑, *Shanghai chunqiu* 上海春秋 (Shanghai annals) (Guilin, China: Guangxi lijiang chubanshe, 1987) and *Chuan ying lou hui yi lu* 釧影樓回憶錄 (Memoirs of a bracelet shadow chamber) (Hong Kong: Dahua chubanshe, 1971); Eileen Chang [Zhang Ailing 張愛玲], *Ban sheng yuan* 半生緣 (Half a lifetime) (Guangzhou, China: Huacheng chubanshe, 1988); Lu Xun, "Ah Jin," trans. David Pollard, in *The Chinese Essay*, ed. David Pollard

(New York: Columbia University Press, 2000), 116–121; Xia Yan, *Under Shanghai Eaves* (*Shanghai wuyanxia* 上海屋簷下, 1937), trans. George Hayden, in *Columbia Anthology of Modern Chinese Drama*, ed. Xiaomei Chen (New York: Columbia University Press, 2010), 397–447.

15. Alexander Des Forges "Shanghai Alleys, Theatrical Practice, and Cinematic Spectatorship: From *Street Angel* (1937) to Fifth Generation Film," *Journal of Current Chinese Affairs* 39.4 (2010): 32, 38. See also Yuan Muzhi 袁牧之, dir., *Malu tianshi* 馬路天使 (Street angel) (Shanghai: Mingxing, 1937), and Zheng Junli 鄭君里, dir., *Wuya yu maque* 烏鴉與麻雀 (Crows and sparrows) (Shanghai: Kunlun, 1949).

16. For an overview of the recent scholarly trend to focus on Republican era Shanghai, see Joshua Fogel's review "The Recent Boom in Shanghai Studies," *Journal of the History of Ideas* 71.2 (2010): 313–333.

In the epilogue of *Shanghai Splendor: Economic Sentiments and the Making of Modern China, 1843–1949* (Berkeley: University of California Press, 2007), Wen-hsin Yeh reflects on the way that Chinese historians in the 1990s turned away from a socialist historiography of colonialism and capitalism, of workers and martyrs, to a new historiography of cultural and material modernity, of women, merchants, entertainers, and petty urbanites who "supplied indigenous grounding to the post-Mao policies of openness toward the outside world" (211–212).

On old Shanghai nostalgia, see Xudong Zhang, "Shanghai Nostalgia: Postrevolutionary Allegories in Wang Anyi's Literary Production in the 1990s," *positions: east asia cultures critique* 8.2 (2000): 349–387; and Hanchao Lu, "Nostalgia for the Future: The Resurgence of an Alienated Culture in China," *Pacific Affairs* 75.2 (2002): 169–186. Among the best-selling "old Shanghai nostalgia" books is Chen Danyan 陳丹燕, *Shanghai de fenghua xueyue* 上海的风花雪月 (Shanghai memorabilia) (Beijing: Zuojia chubanshe, 2000).

17. Only recently have a few works of literary fiction depicted Shanghai alleyways of the socialist period, among them Wang Anyi's *Qimeng shidai* 啟蒙時代 (The age of enlightenment) (Beijing: Renmin wenxue, 2007) and Jin Yucheng's 金宇澄 *Fanhua* 繁花 (Blossoms) (Shanghai: Shanghai wenyi, 2013). In English, Qiu Xiaolong wrote a book of vignettes concerning the residents of a Shanghai alleyway from the 1940s to the 2000s: *Years of Red Dust: Stories of Shanghai* (New York: Macmillan, 2010).

18. Marie-Claire Bergère, *Shanghai: China's Gateway to Modernity*, trans. Janet Lloyd (Stanford, Calif.: Stanford University Press, 2009), 375–382.

19. Geremie Barmé, "Introduction," in *China Candid: The People on the People's Republic* by Sang Ye (Berkeley: University of California Press, 2006), ix.

20. For an extensive study of demolition in Shanghai, see Shao, *Shanghai Gone*.

21. Dai Jinhua, "Imagined Nostalgia," *boundary 2* 24.3 (1997): 158.

22. Zhang, "Shanghai Nostalgia," 383.

23. Samuel Liang, "Amnesiac Monument, Nostalgic Fashion: Shanghai's New Heaven and Earth," *Wasafiri* 23.3 (2008): 52–53; Shao, *Shanghai Gone*, chap. 2, 91–144.

24. Walter Benjamin, "A Berlin Chronicle," in *Reflections: Essays, Aphorisms, Autobiographical Writings*, trans. Edmund Jephcott (New York: Schocken Books, 1986), 26.

25. The volume *House, Home, Family: Living and Being Chinese*, edited by Ronald G. Knapp and Kai-Yin Lo, includes contributions from architectural scholars, historians, and anthropologists. The family saga occupies a prominent place in the Chinese literary canon from Cao Xueqin's *Dream of the Red Chamber* (eighteenth century) to Ba Jin's *Family* (1933), Mo Yan's *Red Sorghum* (1986), and Yu Hua's *To Live* (1992).

26. Walter Benjamin, "Paris, the Capital of the Nineteenth Century," in *Reflections*, 155.

27. Ronald G. Knapp, "China's Houses, Homes, and Families," in *House, Home, Family*, ed. Knapp and Lo, 2–3.

28. Bray, *Technology and Gender*, 51.

29. Gail Hershatter, *The Gender of Memory: Rural Women and China's Collective Past* (Berkeley: University of California Press, 2011), 23.

30. Chapter 3, "Gossip," further elaborates on this polyphony of voices in Shanghai alleyways, which might also be understood in terms of what literary theorist Michel Bakhtin calls "heteroglossia," or the coexistence of a variety of tongues in the novel, an inclusive genre characterized by diversity and multiplicity of style, speech genres, and voices. In contrast to the unitary, homogenizing, and monologic language of the state, common people speak "heteroglossia" that subverts official ideologies (see M. M. Bakhtin, *The Dialogic Imagination* [Austin: University of Texas Press, 1981]).

31. Hou Hsiao-hsien 侯孝賢, dir., *Beiqing chengshi* 悲情城市 (City of sadness) (Taipei, Taiwan: 3-H Films/ERA International, 1989).

32. Abé Mark Nornes and Yeh Yueh-yu, *Narrating National Sadness: Cinematic Mapping and Hypertextual Dispersion* (1994), formerly published at http://cinemaspace.berkeley.edu/Papers/CityOfSadness/srep.html (no longer active, accessed October 1, 2007), e-publication forthcoming. Also see Yip, *Envisioning Taiwan*, chaps. 3–4.

33. Examples of popular narratives of victimization include Jung Chang, *Wild Swans: Three Daughters of China* (New York: Simon and Schuster, 2003), and Nien Cheng, *Life and Death in Shanghai* (New York: Penguin, 1988).

34. For this approach, see James Brooks, Christopher DeCorse, and John Walton, *Small Worlds: Method, Meaning, and Narrative in Microhistory* (Santa Fe: School of Advanced Research Press, 2008). Some examples of microhistories of China are Jonathan Spence, *The Death of Woman Wang* (New York: Viking Press, 1978); Joseph Esherick, *Ancestral Leaves: A Family Journey Through Chinese History* (Berkeley: University of California Press, 2011); Sherman Cochran and Andrew Hsieh, *The Lius of Shanghai* (Cambridge, Mass.: Harvard University Press, 2013); and Henrietta Harrison, *The Missionary's Curse and Other Tales from a Chinese Village* (Berkeley: University of California Press, 2013).

35. Jill Lepore, "Historians Who Love Too Much: Reflections on Microhistory and Biography," *Journal of American History* 88.1 (2001): 129–144.

36. István Szijártó, "Four Arguments for Microhistory," *Rethinking History* 6.2 (2002): 211.

37. For example, some Chinese bloggers deny that tens of millions perished during the Great Leap Famine based on the claim that nobody in the blogger's extended family starved to death. An example can be found at http://bbs.tianya.cn/post-noo5-167039-1.shtml, accessed July 25, 2013.

38. Harrison, *The Missionary's Curse*, 8.

39. Orlando Figes, *The Whisperers: Private Life in Stalin's Russia* (New York: Metropolitan Books, 2007), 12.

40. Yunxiang Yan, *Private Life Under Socialism: Love, Intimacy, and Family Change in a Chinese Village* (Stanford, Calif.: Stanford University Press, 2003), 11.

41. Hershatter, *The Gender of Memory*, 24.

42. As Lisa Rofel points out in her ethnography of women workers under Chinese socialism, their stories are "not transparent descriptions" but rather "evince the culturally specific means by which people represent and therefore experience the worlds in which they live" (*Other Modernities: Gendered Yearnings in China After Socialism* [Berkeley: University of California Press, 1999], 14).

43. Spence, *Death of Woman Wang*, xiv–xv.

44. Hershatter, *The Gender of Memory*, 3.

45. Walter Benjamin, "Moscow," in *Reflections*, 108.

46. Peter Zarrow, "The Origins of Modern Chinese Concepts of Privacy: Notes on Social Structure and Moral Discourse," in *Chinese Concepts of Privacy*, ed. Bonnie McDougall and Anders Hansson (Leiden: Brill, 2002), 129.

47. Yan, *Private Life Under Socialism*, especially the introduction and conclusion.

48. Jeff Weintraub, "The Theory and Politics of the Public/Private Distinction," in *Public and Private in Thought and Practice: Perspectives on a Grand Dichotomy*, ed. Jeff Weintraub and Krishan Kumar (Chicago: University of Chicago Press, 1997), 1–42.

49. Yan, *Private Life Under Socialism*, 9. This definition derives in part from Philippe Ariès and Georges Duby's *A History of Private Life* (Cambridge, Mass.: Harvard University Press, 1987).

50. Dorothy Ko, *Teachers of the Inner Chambers: Women and Culture in Seventeenth Century China* (Stanford, Calif.: Stanford University Press, 1994), 151–152; Eugenia Lean, *Public Passions: The Trial of Shi Jianqiao and the Rise of Popular Sympathy in Republican China* (Berkeley: University of California Press, 2007), 229 n.

51. See, for example, Bonnie McDougall, "Particulars and Universals: Studies on Chinese Privacy," in *Chinese Concepts of Privacy*, ed. McDougall and Hansson, 8–10.

52. See, for example, William Rowe, "The Public Sphere in Modern China," *Modern China* 16.3 (1990): 309–329.

53. McDougall, "Particulars and Universals," 6.

54. Zarrow, "The Origins of Modern Chinese Concepts of Privacy."

55. Ko, *Teachers of the Inner Chambers*.

56. Bray, *Technology and Gender*, 53.

57. Bonnie McDougall, "Privacy in Modern China," *History Compass* 2.1 (2004): 1–8.

58. Harriet Evans, *The Subject of Gender: Daughters and Mothers in Urban China* (Lanham, Md.: Rowman & Littlefield, 2008), 102–103.

59. Paradoxically, individual privacy in such closely monitored circumstances could sometimes be sought only in the most public of spaces: when the housing crisis in Shanghai was at its worst in the late 1970s and early 1980s, the Bund and public parks were packed with lovers with no place to be intimate at home.

60. Yan, *Private Life Under Socialism*, 135–136.

61. Svetlana Boym, *Common Places: Mythologies of Everyday Life in Russia* (Cambridge, Mass.: Harvard University Press, 1994), 47.

62. For instance, in Toni Morrison's novel *Beloved* (New York: Knopf, 1987) the former slave Paul D.'s tobacco tin holds more private memories than a king's palace: "It was some time before he could put Alfred, Georgia, Sixo, schoolteacher, Halle, his brothers, Sethe, Mister, the taste of iron, the sight of butter, the smell of hickory, notebook paper, one by one, into the tobacco tin lodged in his chest. By the time he got to 124, nothing in this world could pry it open" (113).

63. Hannah Arendt, *The Human Condition* (Chicago: University of Chicago Press, 1958), 38.

64. For more on *qiong'er hou gong*, see Stephen Owen, "Singularity and Possession," in *The End of the Chinese "Middle Ages": Essays in Mid-Tang Literary Culture* (Stanford, Calif.: Stanford University Press, 1996), 13–14.

65. Arendt, *The Human Condition*, 72.

1. Foothold

1. For a historical overview of Yangshupu, see Shanghai shi yangpuqu dang'anju 上海市楊浦區檔案局 (Shanghai Yangpu District Archive Office), *Yangpu bainian shihua* 楊浦百年史話 (A hundred years of Yangshupu history) (Shanghai: Shanghai yangpu wenhuaju, 2006), and Emily Honig, *Sisters and Strangers: Women in the Shanghai Cotton Mills, 1919–1949* (Stanford, Calif.: Stanford University Press, 1986), 9–40.

2. Lu, *Beyond the Neon Lights*, 113; Christian Henriot, "Slums, Squats, or Hutments? Constructing and Deconstructing an In-Between Space in Modern Shanghai (1926–1965)," *Frontiers of History* 7.2 (2012): 499–528.

3. For explanations of the local meanings of "upper corner" and "lower corner," see Tianshu Pan, "Historical Memory, Community-Building, and Place-Making in Neighborhood Shanghai," in *Restructuring the Chinese City: Changing Society, Economy, and Space* edited by Laurence J. C. Ma and Fulong Wu (New York: Routledge, 2005), 122–137.

4. Ward Road was named after the American sailor Frederic Townsend Ward (1931–1862), the first commander of the mercenary Ever Victorious Army that defended Shanghai against the Taiping Rebellion. In 1949, the name "Ward Road" was changed to "Changyang Road."

5. Shanghai Yangpuqu renmin zhengfu 上海楊浦區人民政府 (People's Government of Shanghai's Yangpu District), *Shanghai shi Yangpuqu dimingzhi* 上海市楊浦區地名志 (Gazetteer of place-names of the Shanghai Yangpu District) (Shanghai: Xuelin, 1989), 148.

6. Zhao, "From *Shikumen* to New-Style," 2, 15–17; see also Non Arkaraprasertkul, "Towards Modern Urban Housing: Redefining Shanghai's *Lilong*," *Journal of Urbanism: International Research on Placemaking and Urban Sustainability* 2.1 (2009): 11–29.

7. Lu, *Beyond the Neon Lights*, 140.

8. Zhao, "From *Shikumen* to New-Style," 59.

9. For a historical overview of the tobacco industry in Shanghai with British American Tobacco as a case study, see Elizabeth Perry, *Shanghai on Strike: The Politics of Chinese Labor* (Stanford, Calif.: Stanford University Press, 1993), 135–166.

10. In the summer of 2000, I conducted more than one hundred hours of interviews with various residents of the two alleyway homes in this study, about half of which are on video. Transcripts from these interviews formed the basis of many extended first-person narratives, but, as explained in the introduction, the quotations I give are not verbatim. I revisited old interviewees and spoke to additional neighbors in subsequent summers from 2001 to 2013, so I was able to make adjustments and add nuances in later manuscript revisions. Much as I have edited these narrative collages for coherence and readability, I have tried my best to be faithful to the speakers' voices and vocabularies.

11. For an explanation of the takeover fee (*dingfei*) practice in renting *shikumen* homes, see Lu, *Beyond the Neon Lights*, 163.

12. Sun Yumin 孫玉敏, "Yingxiong wangshi" "英雄" 往事" (Hero's past), *Shanghai guozi* 上海國資 (Capital Shanghai) 3 (2012), http://gov.finance.sina.com.cn/chanquan/2012-07-04/123258.html.

13. Ma, *Lao Shanghai chengji*, 123–138.

14. Council of the Foreign Settlements of Shanghai, "Report of the Housing Committee, 1936–1937," in *Municipal Gazette of the Council for the Foreign Settlement of Shanghai*, vol. 30, no. 1653 (Shanghai: Municipal Council, 1937), 98. For an extensive study of Shanghai's housing shortage in the Republican era, see Zhang Sheng 張生, *Shanghai ju, dabuyi: Jindai Shanghai fanghuanng yanjiu* 上海居：大不易：近代上海房荒研究 (Residing in Shanghai is not easy: Shanghai's housing shortage in modern times) (Shanghai: Shanghai cishu, 2009).

15. "Black Man Toothpaste" (Heiren Yagao 黑人牙膏, actually "Darkie Toothpaste" in English) was first manufactured in Shanghai in 1933 by the Hawley and Hazel Chemical Company. The English name changed from "Darkie" to "Darlie" in 1985, but the toothpaste continues to be marketed in China today featuring the logo of "a minstrel singer in a top hat, flashing a white smile." See "China's Controversial Toothpaste," *Daily Beast*, November 30, 2010, http://www.thedailybeast.com/newsweek/2010/11/30/china-s-controversial-toothpaste.html.

16. On the lives of Jewish refugees to Shanghai in World War II, see Irene Eber, *Voices from Shanghai: Jewish Exiles in Wartime China* (Chicago: University of Chicago Press, 2009).

17. Peter Duus, "Zaikabo: Japanese Cotton Mills in China, 1895–1937," in *The Japanese Informal Empire in China, 1895–1937* (Princeton, N.J.: Princeton University Press, 1989), 65–100.

18. Sherman Cochran, *Encountering Chinese Networks: Western, Japanese, and Chinese Corporations in China, 1880–1937* (Berkeley: University of California Press, 2000), 96–100.

19. The cotton mill compound's official and somewhat bulky original name was "Shanghai Textile Shanghai Factory Pingliang Road Company Housing" 上海紡織上海工場平凉路社宅. See Osato Hiroaki and Tomii Masanori, "Zaikabō no kyōjū kankyō ni tsui te—Shanhai no jirei" "「在華紡の居住環境について-上海の事例」" (On Japanese cotton mill housing conditions in China: The case of Shanghai), paper presented at the Kanegawa University 21st Century COE Program Research Conference, Kanegawa-Ku, Japan, December 2007, http://www.himoji.jp/jp/publication/pdf/seika/302s/017-031.pdf.

20. Ibid., 27. A *tatami* mat is equivalent to about 1.65 square meters.

21. This map has been reprinted as *Shanghai 1932: Chengshi jiyi lao ditu* 上海1932:城市記憶老地圖 (Shanghai 1932: Urban memory old map) (Beijing: Xueyuan, 2005).

22. Chen Zu'en 陳祖恩, *Shanghai riqiao shehui shenghuo shi* 上海日僑社會生活史 (A social history of the Japanese diaspora in Shanghai) (Shanghai: Shanghai cishu, 2009), 105, 490.

23. Joshua Fogel, "'Shanghai–Japan': The Japanese Residents' Association of Shanghai," *Journal of Asian Studies* 59.4 (2000): 930–931.

24. Chen, *Shanghai riqiao shehui shenghuo shi*, 98–107.

25. Fogel, "'Shanghai–Japan,'" 931–941.

26. These images can be viewed through gettyimages.co.uk. Search for "George Lacks" and then specify "Shanghai" as the location under "refine searches."

27. Chen Zu'en 陳祖恩, "Shanghai ribenren juliumin zhanhou qiansong zhengce de shixiang" "上海日本人居留民戰後遣送政策的實相" (The repatriation of Shanghai's Japanese residents after the war), *Shehui kexue* 社會科學 (Social sciences) 12 (2004): 101.

28. "Zhongguo fangzhi jianshe gongsi Shanghai shachang fuli ke zhensuo sushi gongfang youzhiyuan shengcai qiju jieshou qingdan" "中國紡織建設公司上海紗廠福利科診所宿舍工房幼稚園生財器具接收清單" (Inventory of items taken over by the China Textile Construction Company from the Shanghai Cotton Mill Welfare Department's clinic, dormitory, and kindergarten), Shanghai Municipal Archives, File no. Q192-9-393. Translations of Chinese-language material are mine throughout unless otherwise noted.

29. From 1998 to 2005, I often asked Yeye, Nainai, Waigong, and Waipo about their past, so each eventually wrote a short "memoir" in answer to my questions.

30. Bergère, *Shanghai*, 367–382.

31. Visser, *Cities Surround the Countryside*, 15–16. See also Xu Gang 徐剛, *Xiangxiang chengshi de fangfa: Dalu 'shiqinian wenxue de chengshi biaoshu* 想像城市的方法：大陸"十七年文學"的城市表述 (Ways of imagining the city: Urban expressions in the literature of the Seventeen-Year Period) (Taipei: Xinrui wenchuang, 2013), 29–35.

32. Soon after taking over cities such as Shanghai, the Communist authorities instituted household registers, with one page per household member including name, birth date, occupation, place of work, family background, and other identifying information. These household registers initially applied only to the urban population but later applied to rural areas to prevent migration to urban areas. See Frederic Wakeman Jr., " 'Cleanup': The New Order in Shanghai," in *Dilemmas of Victory: The Early Years of the People's Republic of China*, ed. Jeremy Brown and Paul Pickowicz (Cambridge, Mass.: Harvard University Press, 2007), 43; Tiejun Cheng and Mark Selden, "The Origins and Social Consequences of China's Hukou System," *China Quarterly* 139 (1994): 644–668.

33. Xu Jilin 許紀霖 and Luo Gang 罗岗, *Chengshi de jiyi: Shanghai wenhua de duoyuan lishi chuantong* 城市的記憶：上海文化的多元歷史傳統 (Metropolitan memories: Shanghai culture's plural historical heritage) (Shanghai: Shanghai shudian, 2011), 194–229.

34. There were 365 silk-weaving factories in Shanghai in 1949, most of them private alleyway factories, which merged into 26 state-owned factories by 1958. See *Shanghai sichou zhi* 上海絲綢志 (Shanghai silk gazetteer) (Shanghai: Shanghai shehui kexueyuan, 1998), 235–240. For an overview of Shanghai workers' experiences of Communist liberation, see Elizabeth Perry, "Masters of the Country? Shanghai Workers in the Early People's Republic," in *Dilemmas of Victory*, ed. Brown and Pickowicz, 59–79.

35. See Frederic Wakeman Jr. and Wen-hsin Yeh, "Introduction," in *Shanghai Sojourners*, ed. Frederic Wakeman Jr. and Wen-hsin Yeh (Berkeley, Calif.: Institute of East Asian Studies, 1992), 1–14.

36. Shanghai Municipal Archives, File no. C21-1-263-10.

37. Ibid.

38. On this point, see Yuan Jin 袁進, *Shenfen jiangou yu wuzhi shenghuo: 20 shiji 50 niandai Shanghai gongren de shehui wenhua shenghuo* 身份建構與物質生活：20世紀50年代上海工人的社會文化生活 (Identity construction and material life: Shanghai worker social and cultural lives in the 1950s) (Shanghai: Shanghai shudian, 2008).

39. Bergère, *Shanghai*, 379.

40. Cui Guanglu 崔廣錄, *Shanghai zhuzhai jianshe zhi* 上海住宅建設志 (Shanghai housing construction gazetteer) (Shanghai: Shanghai shehui kexueyuan, 1998), 27–28.

41. Deborah Pellow, "No Place to Live, No Place to Love," in *Urban Anthropology in China*, ed. Greg Guldin and Aidan Southall (Leiden: Brill, 1993), 396–424.

42. When Michelangelo Antonioni visited China to make a documentary film in 1972, he was shown such workers' new villages as a major socialist achievement in contrast to an exhibition of straw huts from the Old Society. See Antonioni's

documentary film *Chung Kuo—Cina* (Rome: Radiotelevisione Italiana, 1972). Although far from meeting Shanghai workers' actual housing needs, these workers' new villages held great symbolic significance. On their fictional representation, see Xu, *Xiangxiang chengshi de fangfa*, 115–127.

43. See Zheng Wang, "Gender and Maoist Urban Reorganization," in *Gender in Motion: Divisions of Labor and Cultural Change in Late Imperial and Modern China*, ed. Bryna Goodman and Wendy Larson (Lanham, Md.: Rowman & Littlefield, 2004), 189–209.

44. From the Qing dynasty to 1949, the Chinese state tried to extend political control to Shanghai's neighborhoods through the *baojia* system of neighborhood watch and mutual responsibility, but in practice this was no more than a formality. It was only during the Japanese occupation (1938–1945) that people felt that the *baojia* system was part of their lives, used to prevent anti-Japanese activities, levy taxes, assign community services, and impose rationing. See Lu, *Beyond the Neon Lights*, 218–222.

45. Zhang Jishun 张济顺, "Shanghai lilong: Jiceng zhengzhi dongyuan yu guojia shehui yitihua zouxiang, 1950–1955" "上海里弄：基層政治動員與國家社會一體化走向" (Neighborhood committees: Grassroots political mobilization and the trend of state–society integration in Shanghai, 1950–1955), *Zhongguo shehui kexue* 中國社會科學 (Chinese social sciences) 2 (2004): 178–189.

46. Wang, "Gender and Maoist Urban Reorganization," 189–191.

47. "Provisional Act of the PRC for the Organization of Security Defense Committees (1952)," in chapter 2, "Informal Adjustment and Sanctioning," of *The Criminal Process in the People's Republic of China, 1949–1963: An Introduction*, ed. Jerome Cohen (Cambridge, Mass.: Harvard University Press, 1968), 115.

48. For a study of how marriage and divorce were shaped by political considerations from the mid-1950s to the mid-1960s, see Neil Diamant, *Revolutionizing the Family: Politics, Love, and Divorce in Urban and Rural China, 1949–1968* (Berkeley: University of California Press, 2000), esp. chap. 5, "The Politics and Culture of Divorce and Marriage in Urban China, 1954–1966," 177–225.

49. According to Lynn White, street committees often took advantage of political campaigns to garner compliance from families with more than average living space to give part of their housing to the Housing Management Bureau (*Policies of Chaos: The Organizational Causes of Violence in China's Cultural Revolution* [Princeton, N.J.: Princeton University Press, 1989], 99).

50. D. E. T. Luard, "The Urban Communes," *China Quarterly*, no. 3 (July–September 1960): 74–79.

51. Joseph Brodsky, *Less Than One: Selected Essays* (New York: Farrar Straus Giroux, 1986), 11–12.

52. Dudley Andrew, "Interview with Jia Zhangke," *Film Quarterly* 62.4 (2009): 80.

53. Like many other products of the Great Leap Forward, most alleyway workshops closed within two years, though some reopened in the mid-1960s when factories outsourced some of their most menial labor. See *Shanghai laodong zhi* 上海勞動志 (Shanghai labor gazetteer) (Shanghai: Shanghai shehui kexue yuan, 1998),

177–178. Qiu Guosheng 邱國盛, "Ershi shiji wushi niandai Shanghai de funü jiefang yu canjia jiti shengchan" "20世紀50年代上海的婦女解放與參加集體生產" (Shanghai women's emancipation and participation in collective production in the 1950s), in *Dangdai Zhongguo shi yanjiu* 当代中国史研究 (Studies in contemporary Chinese history) 2 (2009): 70–77.

54. Shen Fu沈浮, dir., *Wanzi qianhong zongshi chun* 萬紫千紅總是春 (Women of the Great Leap Forward) (Shanghai: Haiyan, 1959).

55. For a broader overview of the bunker digging in Shanghai starting in 1969, see Jin Dalu 金大陸, *Feichang yu zhengchang: Shanghai wenge shiqi de shehui shenghuo* 非常與正常：上海文革時期的社會生活 (Abnormality and normality: Social life during the Cultural Revolution in Shanghai) (Shanghai: Shanghai cishu, 2011), 357–397.

56. See Yihong Pan, *Tempered in the Revolutionary Furnace: China's Youth in the Rustication Movement* (Lanham, Md.: Lexington Books, 2002).

57. For an overview of the sent-down youth movement in Shanghai, see "Zhuanji er: 'wenhua dageming' zhong de shangshan xiaxiang yundong" "專輯二：'文化大革命' 中的上山下鄉運動" (Appendix II: The Shanghai 'sent-down youth' movement in the Great Cultural Revolution), in Shanghai Youth Gazetteer Editorial Board, *Shanghai qingnian zhi* 上海青年志 (Shanghai youth gazetteer) (Shanghai: Shanghai shehui kexueyuan, 2002), 552–558.

58. Barry Naughton, "The Third Front: Defense Industrialization in the Chinese Interior," *China Quarterly* 115 (1988): 351–386.

59. On Shanghai's eclectic and cosmopolitan architecture, see Edward Denison and Guang Yu Ren, *Building Shanghai: The Story of China's Gateway* (Hoboken, N.J.: Wiley-Academy, 2006).

60. In other words, the construction of the shanty depended on the exchange of gifts and favors and the cultivation of private relationships as essential tactics of survival under the Mao era's state distributive economy with its intricate bureaucratic networks. See Mayfair Yang, *Gifts, Favors, and Banquets: The Art of Social Relationships in China* (Ithaca, N.Y.: Cornell University Press, 1994).

61. Thomas Gold, "Back to the City: The Return of Shanghai's Educated Youth," *China Quarterly* 84 (1980): 755–770.

62. On the replacement policy, see Joe Leung, "Dismantling the 'Iron Rice Bowl': Welfare Reforms in the People's Republic of China," *Journal of Social Policy* 23.3 (1994): 341–361.

63. In the early and mid-1980s, the housing shortage in Shanghai was at its worst, with half of the households in the city having an average of less than four square meters of living space per person. See Shao, *Shanghai Gone*, 7.

64. Boym, *Common Places*, 143.

65. For an overview of the privatization and commodification of formerly "public housing" (*gongfang* 公房), see Deborah Davis, "From Welfare Benefit to Capitalized Asset: The Re-commodification of Residential Space in Urban China," in *Housing and Social Change: East–West Perspectives*, ed. Ray Forrest and James Lee (London: Routledge, 2003), 183–196.

66. Most housing in the socialist era was *gongfang*, "public housing," that belonged to a work unit or the city's housing bureau, but there was also *sifang*, "private housing," that belonged to individual families. After the 1990s, *shangpinfang* 商品房, "commercial housing," came to be bought and sold on the market. See Deborah Davis and Hanlong Lu, "Property in Transition: Conflicts Over Ownership in Post-socialist Shanghai," *European Journal of Sociology* 44.1 (2003): 77–99.

67. Frequently two years elapsed between the time a house was marked for demolition and the day the family moved to a new apartment, which was assigned on the basis of the number of residents in the household registration booklet. To guarantee that no family would use this time to obtain more than their share, housing authorities immobilized household membership by "freezing" every member's household registration as soon as the family was promised space in a new building. See Deborah S. Davis, "My Mother's House," in *Unofficial China: Popular Culture and Thought in the People's Republic* (Boulder, Colo.: Westview Press, 1989), 97.

68. Before market reforms truly took off, as anthropologist David Wank points out, "citizens acquired premium cigarettes not for personal enjoyment but for their exchange value in influencing others, usually officials who had discretionary control over the allocation of centrally redistributed goods, services, and opportunities" ("Cigarettes and Domination in Chinese Business Networks: Institutional Change During the Market Transition," in *The Consumer Revolution in Urban China*, ed. Deborah Davis [Berkeley: University of California Press, 2000], 269).

69. Mayfair Yang, "The Gift Economy and State Power in China," *Comparative Studies in Society and History* 31.1 (1989): 25–54.

70. The idea of replicating a piece of life in a house on stage or onscreen with minimal narrative intervention is inspired by a number of well-known plays and films, such as Xia Yan's *Under Shanghai Eaves*, Zheng Junli's *Crows and Sparrows*, as well as Lao She 老舍's plays set in Beijing's vernacular architecture—*Dragon Whisker Creek* (*Longxugou*龍鬚溝, premiered by Beijing People's Art Theatre in 1951) and *Teahouse* (*Chaguan* 茶館, premiered by Beijing People's Art Theatre in 1957). Yomi Braester analyzes a number of "courtyard plays" set in Beijing siheyuan homes in *Painting the City Red: Chinese Cinema and the Urban Contract* (Durham, N.C.: Duke University Press, 2010), chaps. 1 and 3.

2. Haven

1. Eileen Chang, "Writing of One's Own," in *Written on Water*, trans. Andrew F. Jones (New York: Columbia University Press, 2005), 16–17.

2. Antoine Prost, "Public and Private Spheres in France," in *A History of Private Life*, vol. 5: *Riddles of Identity in Modern Times*, ed. Antoine Prost and Gérard Vincent (Cambridge, Mass.: Harvard University Press, 1994), 64.

3. Susan Stewart, *On Longing: Narratives of the Miniature, the Gigantic, the Souvenir, the Collection* (Baltimore: Johns Hopkins University Press, 1984), 136, 137, 138.

4. Analyzing the statute law of China's last imperial dynasty, John McCreery shows that although women were not guaranteed shareholders of the family property, they could own personal property in the form of dowries distinct from family property ("Women's Property Rights and Dowry in China and South Asia," *Ethnology* 15.2 [1976]: 163–174).

5. For a guide on how to write such autobiographies for party authorities, see Sha Lin 沙霖, *Zenyang xie zizhuan* 怎樣寫自傳 (How to write an autobiography) (Shanghai: Puwen, 1951). On the use of personnel files in work units, see David Bray, *Social Space and Governance in Urban China: The Danwei System from Origins to Reform* (Stanford, Calif.: Stanford University Press, 2005), 115–122.

6. On the arrest and incarceration of former Nationalist officials in the People's Republic of China, see Klaus Mühlhahn, *Criminal Justice in China: A History* (Cambridge, Mass.: Harvard University Press, 2009), 238–248.

7. Mao Zedong, "Talks at the Yan'an Forum of Literature and Art," May 2, 1942, http://www.marxists.org/reference/archive/mao/selected-works/volume-3/mswv3_08.htm, accessed January 31, 2014.

8. Juanjuan Wu, *Chinese Fashion: From Mao to Now* (New York: Berg, 2009), 4.

9. Hershatter, *The Gender of Memory*, 183.

10. "Zhaoxiangye yao wei laodong renmin fuwu: zhuiji zhaoxiangye tianjin huiyi" "照相也要為勞動人民服務：追記照相業天津會議" (Social photography must serve the laboring people: Report on the Tianjin Conference), *Dazhong Sheying* 大眾攝影 (Popular photography), July (1958): 8–9.

11. Ronald G. Knapp, *China's Vernacular Architecture: House Form and Culture* (Honolulu: University of Hawai'i Press, 1989), 167.

12. The song Waigong recalls is probably a later variation of the storytelling *tanci* genre, which became very popular on Shanghai's commercial radio in the 1930s. As Carlton Benson's work shows, it was not unusual for songs broadcast on radio to entertain listeners with gentle social critique and even political satire. See Carlten Benson, "From Teahouse to Radio: Storytelling and the Commercialization of Culture in 1930s Shanghai," Ph.D. diss., University of California, Berkeley, 1996, and "Back to Business as Usual: The Resurgence of Commercial Radio Broadcasting in Gudao Shanghai," in *In the Shadow of the Rising Sun: Shanghai Under Japanese Occupation*, ed. Christian Henriot and Wen-Hsin Yeh (New York: Cambridge University Press, 2004), 279–301.

13. Yeh, *Shanghai Splendor*, 69.

14. Ma, *Lao Shanghai chengji*, 126; Wang Ping, dir., *Yongbu xiaoshi de dianbo* 永不消逝的電波 (The everlasting radio waves) (Beijing: August Eighth Film, 1958).

15. Xu and Luo, *Chengshi de jiyi*, 159–166.

16. Waipo still referred to her illness as "neurasthenia" (*shenjing shuairuo* 神經衰弱), though, as Arthur Kleinman has pointed out, most Chinese diagnosed with this term would be considered depressed in the West. See Arthur Kleinman, *Social Origins of Distress and Disease: Depression, Neurasthenia, and Pain in Modern China* (New Haven, Conn.: Yale University Press, 1986).

17. Feng Jun 馮軍, "Guocao liushi nian" "國操六十年" (Sixty years of national exercise), *Dongfang zaobao* 東方早報 (Eastern daily), August 20, 2011, http://www.dfdaily.com/html/8755/2011/8/20/650657_s.shtml.

18. Elaine Scarry, *The Body in Pain: The Making and Unmaking of the World* (New York: Oxford University Press, 1985), 291.

19. Joseph R. Levenson, *Revolution and Cosmopolitanism: The Western Stage and the Chinese Stages* (Berkeley: University of California Press, 1971), 53.

20. Zhonggong Shanghai Shiwei Dangshi Yanjiushi 中共上海市委黨史研究室 (Chinese Communist Party Shanghai Party History Office), *Zhonggong Shanghai lishi shilu* 中共上海歷史實錄 (Historical records of Chinese Communist Party history in Shanghai) (Shanghai: Shanghai jiaoyu, 2004), 431.

21. Jin Dalu 金大陸, "Beijing hongweibing zai Shanghai" "北京紅衛兵在上海" (Beijing Red Guards in Shanghai), part I, *Shilin* (Historical review) 3 (2008): 97–136; part II, *Shilin* 1 (2009): 107–122.

22. For a history of Shanghai's worker rebels, see Elizabeth J. Perry and Li Xun, *Proletarian Power: Shanghai in the Cultural Revolution* (Boulder, Colo.: Westview Press, 1997).

23. Often written with a brush on a large piece of paper and posted to a wall, big-character posters were used widely throughout the Cultural Revolution to spread revolutionary ideas and to denounce enemies of the people.

24. Daniel Leese, *Mao Cult: Rhetoric and Ritual in China's Cultural Revolution* (New York: Cambridge University Press, 2011).

25. Vaclav Havel, *The Power of the Powerless: Citizens Against the State in Central-Eastern Europe* (Armonk, N.Y.: M. E. Sharpe, 1985), 27–28.

26. For a nuanced analysis of Lei Feng's diary, see Xiaofei Tian, "The Making of a Hero: Lei Feng and Some Issues of Historiography," in *The People's Republic of China at 60: An International Assessment*, ed. William C. Kirby (Cambridge, Mass.: Harvard University Press, 2011), 293–305.

27. Ban Wang, *The Sublime Figure of History: Aesthetics and Politics in Twentieth Century China* (Stanford, Calif.: Stanford University Press, 1997), 209.

28. Nien Cheng's *Life and Death in Shanghai* gives a classic victim's narrative of a Shanghai home being ransacked by Red Guards in the Cultural Revolution.

29. On the transformation of Shanghai fashion during the Cultural Revolution, see Zhu Dake 朱大可, "Ling yu xiu de hongse fengqing" "領與袖的紅色風情" (Collars and sleeves, Red style), in *Jiyi de hongpi shu* 記憶的紅皮書 (Red memory book) (Guangzhou, China: Huacheng, 2008), 118–124.

30. For a fictional yet realistic description of how workers conducted home searches in Shanghai, see Jin Yucheng's novel *Fanhua*, 116–120, 144–147. According to his characters, members of the "working class" ransacked homes for mahogany furniture and jewelry; treating capitalist homes like a farmer's field, they believed in digging deep into the ground for treasures. Students preferred to bring magnifying glasses and comb through documents, photographs, diaries, and letters. They also liked to steal books to read among themselves.

31. "Yangpu qu shimin jiaoyu he sishu linianlai fazhan de qingkuang" "楊浦區市民教育和私塾歷年來發展的情況" (Recent development of civil education and private schools in Yangpu District), November 1955, Shanghai Municipal Archives, File No. B-105-5-168.

32. Xu and Luo, *Chengshi de jiyi*, 208; Andrew Field, *Shanghai's Dancing World: Cabaret Culture and Urban Politics, 1919–1954* (Hong Kong: Chinese University Press, 2010), 263–284.

33. Xu and Luo, *Chengshi de jiyi*, 222, 228–229.

34. For fictional thick descriptions of what one might find in Shanghai's second-hand shops during the Cultural Revolution, see Jin, *Fanhua*, 164–168, and Wang, *Qimeng shidai*, 203.

35. On the clandestine reading done by Red Guards, see Paul Clark, *The Chinese Cultural Revolution: A History* (Cambridge: Cambridge University Press, 2008), 226–231; Yu Hua, *China in Ten Words*, trans. Allan Barr (New York: Pantheon Books, 2011), chap. 4; Barbara Mittler, *A Continuous Revolution: Making Sense of Cultural Revolution Culture* (Cambridge, Mass.: Harvard University Press, 2013), chaps. 3–4; and Barbara Mittler, "Enjoying the Four Olds! Oral Histories from a 'Cultural Desert,'" *Transcultural Studies* 1 (2013): 177–214.

36. On Mao badges, see Melissa Schrift, *Biography of a Chairman Mao Badge: The Creation and Mass Consumption of a Personality Cult* (New Brunswick, N.J.: Rutgers University Press, 2001). Schrift shows in the second part of her book how consumers of Mao badges often maintained traditional forms of social reproduction through revolutionary forms of worship.

37. Yomi Braester, "Photography at Tiananmen: Pictorial Frames, Spatial Borders, and Ideological Matrixes," *positions: east asia cultures critique* 18.3 (2010): 633–670; Nicole Huang, "Locating Family Portraits: Everyday Images from 1970s China," *positions: east asia cultures critique* 18.3 (2010): 671–693.

38. Ann Anagnost, *National Past-Times: Narrative, Representation, and Power in Modern China* (Durham, N.C.: Duke University Press, 1997), 126.

39. Lu, *Beyond the Neon Lights*, 61–63. In *Cities Surround the Countryside*, Robin Visser also discusses the derogatory meaning of the term *xiao shimin* as "connoting a contempt on the part of the speaker for the 'lower' taste the majority of city dwellers display in their everyday practices" (11).

40. Wen-hsin Yeh, "Progressive Journalism and Shanghai's Petty Urbanites: Zou Taofen and the *Shenghuo Weekly*, 1926–1945," in *Shanghai Sojourners*, ed. Wakeman and Yeh, 189.

41. Yeh, *Shanghai Splendor*, chaps. 3 and 6.

42. For a study of Shanghai *shimin* (city-dweller) literature in the post–Cultural Revolution era, see Xueping Zhong, "Shanghai 'Shimin' Literature and the Ambivalence of (Urban) Home," *Modern Chinese Literature* 9.1 (1995): 79–99.

43. Zhang Yuanchen 張苑琛, *Xinmin wanbao fukan yanjiu* 新民晚報副刊研究 (Study of cultural supplements in the *Xinmin Evening News*) (Shanghai: Shanghai jiaotong daxue, 2011), 37–54.

44. Shaoguang Wang, "The Politics of Private Time: Changing Leisure Patterns in Urban China," in *Urban Spaces in Contemporary China: The Potential for Autonomy and Community in Post-Mao China*, edited by Deborah S. Davis, Richard Kraus, Barry Naughton, and Elizabeth J. Perry (New York: Cambridge University Press, 1995), 165.

45. Davis, "My Mother's House," 89, 95.

46. Ibid., 92.

47. On the intensification of private space, see Choon-Piew Pow, "Constructing a New Private Order: Gated Communities and the Privatization of Urban Life in Post-reform Shanghai," *Social & Cultural Geography* 8.6 (2007): 813–833.

48. Whereas in 1970 the average living space per person in Shanghai was 4.4 square meters (up from 3.9 square meters in 1949), it rose to 6.3 square meters in 1989. See Pellow, "No Place to Live," 399.

49. Chiara Saraceno, "The Italian Family: Paradoxes of Privacy," trans. Raymond Rosenthal, in *History of Private Life*, ed. Prost and Vincent, 5:452–453.

50. Wang, "The Politics of Private Time," 157–158.

51. The relationship between my grandparents and their married children was symptomatic of larger trends throughout China, for, as Yunxiang Yan has shown in his extensive study *Private Life Under Socialism*, both the socialist revolution and postsocialist reforms contributed to the crisis of filial piety and the rise of the "uncivil individual."

52. Di Miao, "A Brief History of Chinese Situation Comedies," in *TV Drama in China*, ed. Ying Zhu, Michael Keane, and Ruoyun Bai (Hong Kong: Hong Kong University Press, 2009), 117–128.

53. Xiaobing Tang, "Decorating Culture: Notes on Interior Design, Interiority, and Interiorization," *Public Culture* 10.3 (1998): 542.

54. Zhao, "From *Shikumen* to New-Style," 72–73.

55. Mark Swislocki, *Culinary Nostalgia: Regional Food Culture and the Urban Experience in Shanghai* (Stanford, Calif.: Stanford University Press, 2009), 202–204.

56. Scarry, *The Body in Pain*, 291.

57. Arendt, *The Human Condition*, 124–125.

3. Gossip

1. Lu Xun 鲁迅, "Lun renyan kewei" "人言可畏" (Gossip is a fearful thing), in *Lu Xun quanji* 鲁迅全集 (Complete works of Lu Xun), 16 vols. (Beijing: Beijing renmin, 1981), 6:261–264.

2. Wang, *Chang hen ge*, 9, my translation.

3. Peter Brooks, *The Melodramatic Imagination: Balzac, Henry James, Melodrama, and the Mode of Excess* (New Haven, Conn.: Yale University Press, 1976), 12.

4. Max Gluckman, "Gossip and Scandal," *Current Anthropology* 4.3 (1963): 313.

5. Robert Paine, "What Is Gossip About? An Alternative Hypothesis," *Man* (new series) 2.2 (1967): 280–281.

6. Nigel Rapport and Joanna Overing, *Social and Cultural Anthropology: The Key Concepts* (New York: Routledge, 2013), 153–154.

7. Margery Wolf, *Women and the Family in Rural Taiwan* (Stanford, Calif.: Stanford University Press, 1972), 39–40.

8. James Farrer, *Opening Up: Youth Culture and Market Reform in Shanghai* (Chicago: University of Chicago Press, 2002), 75.

9. Quoted in Patricia Spacks, *Gossip* (Chicago: University of Chicago Press, 1986), 13.

10. Ibid., chap. 1.

11. Jack Chen, "Blank Spaces and Secret Histories: Questions of Historiographic Epistemology in Medieval China," *Journal of Asian Studies* 69.4 (2010): 1072.

12. For an extensive discussion of the term *xiaoshuo*, see Ming Dong Gu, *Chinese Theories of Fiction: A Non-Western Narrative System* (Albany: State University of New York Press, 2006), 17–42.

13. For a glimpse of the different roles gossip played in traditional Chinese literature and historiography, see abstracts for the 2008 University of California, Los Angeles, conference "Anecdote, Gossip, and Occasion in Traditional China," http:// www.international.ucla.edu/china/anecdote/, accessed July 16, 2013.

14. Alexander Des Forges, *Mediasphere Shanghai: The Aesthetics of Cultural Production* (Honolulu: University of Hawai'i Press, 2007), 85, 138.

15. Catherine Yeh, *Shanghai Love: Courtesans, Intellectuals, and Entertainment Culture, 1850–1910* (Seattle: University of Washington Press, 2006), 178–219.

16. Samuel Liang, *Mapping Modernity in Shanghai: Space, Gender, and Visual Culture in the Sojourners' City, 1853–98* (New York: Routledge, 2010), chaps. 2 and 3.

17. Han Bangqing, *The Sing-Song Girls of Shanghai*, trans. Eileen Chang, rev. and ed. Eva Hung (New York: Columbia University Press, 2005). For a genealogy of Shanghai-style (*haipai*) literature, see Yang Yang 楊楊, Chen Shuping 陳樹萍, and Wang Pengfei 王鵬飛, *Haipai wenxue* 海派文學 (Shanghai-style literature) (Shanghai: Wenhui chubanshe, 2008).

18. Lu Xun, "Lun renyan kewei," 262. See Wu Yonggan 吳永剛, dir., *Shennü* 神女 (The goddess) (Shanghai: Lianhua, 1934), and Cai Chusheng 蔡楚生, dir., *Xin nüxing* 新女性 (New women) (Shanghai: Lianhua, 1935).

19. Lu Xun, "Menwai wentan" 門外文壇 (Outdoor chatting on language and literature, 1936), in *Lu Xun quanji*, 6:87; the translation is from Lu, *Beyond the Neon Lights*, 231.

20. Nicole Huang, "Introduction," in *Written on Water* by Zhang Ailing, trans. Andrew F. Jones (New York: Columbia University Press, 2005), xi.

21. Ibid., xv.

22. Chang, "Writing of One's Own," 15–22.

23. Xu and Luo, *Chengshi de jiyi*, 156–193.

24. Wang Xiaoming 王曉明, "Cong jianzhu dao guanggao: Zuijin shiwunian Shanghai chengshi kongjian de bianhua" "從建築到廣告: 最近十五年上海城市空間的變化" (From architecture to advertisements: Transformations of Shanghai's urban spaces in the past fifteen years), in *Dangdai dongya chengshi* 當代東亞城市: 新的文化和意識形態 (Contemporary East Asian cities: New cultures and ideologies), edited by Wang Xiaoming and Chen Qingqiao 陳清僑 (Shanghai: Shanghai shudian, 2008), 90.

25. Barmé, *China Candid*, ix.

26. Yang, *Gifts, Favors, and Banquets*, 18.

27. Wang Dewei 王德威 [David Der-wei Wang], "Haipai wenxue, youjian chuan-ren: Wang Anyi lun" "海派文学:又见传人" (Emergent successors of Shanghai-style literature: On Wang Anyi), in *Dangdai xiaoshuo ershi jia* 当代小说二十家 (Twenty masters of contemporary novels) (Beijing: Sanlian shudian 2006), 16–32.

28. The phrase "emotional speculation" comes from Patricia Spacks, "In Praise of Gossip," *Hudson Review* 35.1 (1982): 19–38.

29. Wang, *The Song of Everlasting Sorrow*, 8–13.

30. Ibid., 9.

31. Lu, *Beyond the Neon Lights*, 198–217.

32. Ibid., 189–198.

33. Blakey Vermeule, "Gossip and Literary Narrative," *Philosophy and Literature* 30.1 (2006): 110.

34. Lu, *Beyond the Neon Lights*, 225.

35. Mu Xin 木心, "Shanghai fu" "上海赋" (Ode to Shanghai), in *Gelunbiya de daoying* 哥倫比亞的倒影 (Reflections of Columbia) (Guilin: Guangshi shifan daxue, 2009), 126.

36. Walter Benjamin, "Naples," in *Reflections*, 171.

37. Zhen Zhang, "The Production of the Senses in and out of the 'Everlasting Auspicious Lane,' Shanghai, 1966–1976," in *Some of Us: Chinese Women Growing Up in the Mao Era*, ed. Zhong Xueping, Wang Zheng, and Bai Di (New Brunswick, N.J.: Rutgers University Press, 2001), 163.

38. Emily Honig, *Creating Chinese Ethnicity: Subei People in Shanghai, 1850–1980* (New Haven, Conn.: Yale University Press, 1992).

39. Yu Qiuyu, "Shanghai People," in *The Chinese Essay: An Anthology*, ed. David Pollard (New York: Columbia University Press, 2002), 356.

40. In "Shanghai Alleys, Theatrical Practice, and Cinematic Spectatorship," Alexander Des Forges also discusses the theatricality of Shanghai alleyway spaces through visual and cinematic representations in the late Qing and Republican eras.

41. For the title of this section, I borrow the phrase "women on the margins" from the title of Natalie Zemon Davis's study of "three seventeenth-century women's lives," *Women on the Margins: Three Seventeenth-Century Lives* (Cambridge, Mass.: Harvard University Press, 1995).

42. Anagnost, *National Past-Times*, 38; see also Hershatter, *The Gender of Memory*, 34–37.

43. Davis, *Women on the Margins*, 7.

44. Ibid., 212.

45. "Three years of natural disasters" was the official euphemism for the post–Great Leap famine from 1959 to 1961.

46. For a discussion of the "upper corner" versus the "lower corner," see chapter 1.

47. For a filmic representation of the type of work-unit dormitories described here, see the film *Linju* 邻居 (Neighbors) (Beijing: Youth Film Studio, 1981), directed by Zheng Dongtian 鄭洞天 and Xu Guming 徐谷明. Yomi Braester provides an insightful description and analysis of the film as well as of the social context that it dramatizes in *Painting the City Red*, 229–233.

4. Demolition

1. Every time the relocation team persuaded all residents in one house to leave, they demolished that particular house to make the environment more uninhabitable for neighbors who were still negotiating.

2. Focusing on demolition sites as "architectural open wounds," I share the "documentary impulse" of Chinese filmmakers since the 1990s, who—as Yomi Braester points out—are "tinged with a fear for the future of memory, an anxiety for the loss of identity, and an urge to preserve images of the city" (*Painting the City Red*, 22, 225).

3. Given the high real estate values in Shanghai, the phrase "demolition and relocation is gold" was used in a 2002 financial magazine article and has since become "common sense" for many Shanghai residents. See Shao, *Shanghai Gone*, 151, 207.

4. The average living space per person in Shanghai increased from four square meters in 1979 to seventeen square meters in 2012; see Wenhui bao, "Ju zhe you qi wu, ju zhe you qi wu" "居者有其屋 居者优其屋" (Residents own their homes; residents improve their homes), May 29, 2012, http://sh.people.com.cn/n/2012/0529/c338988-17090241.html.

5. My parents returned from the United States to live in Shanghai in 1998 and quickly put their savings into the city's skyrocketing housing market. Making a handsome profit with every transaction, they have moved four times in the past twelve years, bought and sold two apartments for investment, and provided the funds for my grandparents and an uncle to purchase their current apartments.

6. Davis, "From Welfare Benefit to Capitalized Asset."

7. At the Shanghai City Planning Exhibition Center, a monumental miniature model of the city's future does not contain any alleyway housing except for a few historical preservation sites. Also see Shiloh R. Krupar, "Shanghaiing the Future: A De-tour of the Shanghai Urban Planning Exhibition Hall," *Public Culture* 20.2 (2008): 307–320.

8. As Qin Shao points out, *jiuqu gaizao* in the 1980s and 1990s was understood as "a government-sponsored, not-for-profit project to bring down entire neighborhoods

and build better, high-rise apartments for the residents, as opposed to for-profit, commercial, real estate development (*shangye kaifa*)." Since the late 1990s, however, "the end of welfare housing and the deepening of market reform essentially changed the meaning of urban renewal to commercial development and gentrification" (*Shanghai Gone*, 8, 148).

9. Xinhua Net, "Shanghai Yangpuqu pingliang xikuai jiuqu gaizao" 上海楊浦區平涼西塊舊區改造" (Renovating old neighborhoods in Shanghai's Yangpu District Pingliang West Lots), December 8, 2005, http://www.sh.xinhuanet.com/2005-12/09/content_5779340.htm.

10. "Shanghaied: Hu Jintao Sticks Out His Elbows and Fires Shanghai's Party Chief," *The Economist*, September 26, 2006, http://www.economist.com/node/7971021.

11. Xinhua Net, "Shanghai yangguang dongqian zhengce quebao jiuqu gaizao guocheng geng touming" "上海陽光動遷政策確保舊區改造過程更透明" (Shanghai's Sunny Relocation policy ensures transparency for the renovation of old neighborhoods), December 8, 2005, http://news.xinhuanet.com/society/2005-12/08/content_3895298.htm.

12. Wang Xiaodong 汪曉東, "Yangguang dadongqian: Shanghai Yangpuqu pingliang xikuai dongqian zhong de gushi" "陽光大動遷：上海楊浦區平涼西塊動遷中的故事" (Sunny Relocation: Stories from the relocation of Shanghai Yangpu District Pingliang West lot), *Renmin wang* 人民網 (People.cn), December 9, 2005, http://www.people.com.cn/GB/paper40/16359/1443886.html.

13. Yan, *Private Life Under Socialism*, 216–236.

14. For an example, see a blogpost entitled "Qing guanzhu yige lieshi zinü zai Pingliang xikuai 12 jiefang dongqian zhong de zaoyu" "请关注一个烈士子女在平凉西块12街坊动迁中的遭遇" (Please pay attention to a martyr's child's plight in the demolition of Pingliang West Lots), June 12, 2011, http://bbs.eastday.com/viewthread.php?tid=1194352.

15. According to government documentation, 120 households were evicted forcibly, but according to petitioner posts the number was 138. See "Shequ jiedao jieshou quewei xuncha gongzuo de qingkuang huibao" "社区街道接受区委巡查工作的情况汇报" (Neighborhood work report responding to district investigation). This text is available as a "sample essay" for cadres at http://www.diyifanwen.com/fanwen/gongzuohuibao/20101061522229318801283.htm, accessed August 15, 2013.

16. Shao, *Shanghai Gone*, 2.

17. Ms. Guan has posted her article on a number of websites, but her own Sina microblog from 2007 has the most complete overview: http://blog.sina.com.cn/changyanglu640111, accessed July 16, 2013.

18. Ibid.

19. Shao, *Shanghai Gone*, 68 and in general 54–69.

20. Guan Shifeng's microblog, http://blog.sina.com.cn/changyanglu640111, accessed July 16, 2013.

21. District Chief Online is a monthly program in which the head of the Yangpu District supposedly answers questions and complaints from the public online. The forced evictees of Pingliang West Lots posted their petition on this website in May 2009, the transcript of which is available at http://xcweb.ypwspy.com/OutPutHtml/Chat20090510.html, accessed July 17, 2013.

22. Photographs of their protests can be found at http://www.dianping.com/group/chaiqian/topic/1026981, accessed July 16, 2013.

23. Xinfei Ran, *Building Globalization: Transnational Architecture Production in Urban China* (Chicago: University of Chicago Press, 2011), 124–132.

24. The video can be viewed at http://v.ku6.com/show/QJIrPjEZE9sM2iPL.html, accessed July 17, 2013. For an extensive description and comment, see "Zhengfu buyao zigan duoluo wei shangren" "政府不要自甘墮落為商人" (Government should not degenerate into businesses), http://blog.sina.com.cn/s/blog_498a18b50100rep2.html, accessed August 15, 2013.

25. Kent Ewing, "The Coolest Nail House in History," *Asia Times Online*, March 31, 2007, http://www.atimes.com/atimes/China_Business/IC31Cb01.html.

26. For example, see Andrew Mertha, "From 'Rustless Screws' to 'Nail Houses': The Evolution of Property Rights in China," *Orbis* 53.2 (2009): 233–249.

27. See Stefan Landsberger, "Chinese Propaganda Poster Pages—Lei Feng," http://chineseposters.net/themes/leifeng.php, accessed January 31, 2014.

28. Mao, "Talks at the Yan'an Forum."

29. For insightful analyses of the Lei Feng myth, see Wendy Larson, *From Ah Q to Lei Feng: Freud and Revolutionary Spirit in 20th Century China* (Stanford, Calif.: Stanford University Press, 2009), esp. 110–113; and Tian, "The Making of a Hero."

30. For a cinematic panorama of such socialist industry in ruins, see Wang Bing's 王兵 nine-hour documentary film *Tie Xi Qu* 鐵西區 (West of the Tracks) (Watertown, Mass.: Documentary Educational Resources, 2003).

31. Samuel Liang, "Property-Driven Urban Change in Post-socialist Shanghai: Reading the Television Series *Woju*," *Journal of Current Chinese Affairs* 3 (2010): 25.

32. Arendt, *The Human Condition*, 12.

33. Shao's *Shanghai Gone* includes a case study of such a "barrack-room lawyer" who "represents the underrepresented with his apparently encyclopedic knowledge of the law and regulations concerning housing reform and his ability to twist them to suit his ends" (190).

34. Qin Shao, "Waving the Red Flag: Cultural Memory and Grassroots Protest in Housing Disputes in China," *Modern Chinese Literature and Culture* 22.1 (2010): 224.

35. For a succinct explanation of the new legislation, see Junhe Law Office Legal Update from January 30, 2011, http://www.junhe.com/uploadpic/news/201129162540804.pdf.

36. Li Haoxiang 李浩翔, "Shu rentou dao shu zhuantou fangwu gujia cheng dongqian buchang jichu" "數人頭到數磚頭房屋估價成動遷補償基礎" (Counting heads and bricks with market estimations becomes the basis for relocation

compensation), *Dongfang wang* 東方網 (East day), March 13, 2009, http://finance. eastday.com/m/20090318/u1a4252204.html.

37. In studying disputes over inherited housing in Shanghai, Deborah Davis and Hanlong Lu found that ordinary people considered multiple factors as they debated the justice of dividing inherited property among different siblings, such as the different levels of filiality, the type of housing, household registration and coresidency, need for shelter, and legal ownership ("Property in Transition").

SELECTED BIBLIOGRAPHY

Anagnost, Ann. *National Past-Times: Narrative, Representation, and Power in Modern China*. Durham, N.C.: Duke University Press, 1997.

Andrew, Dudley. "Interview with Jia Zhangke." *Film Quarterly* 62.4 (2009): 80–83.

Arendt, Hannah. *The Human Condition*. Chicago: University of Chicago Press, 1958.

Ariès, Philippe and Georges Duby. *A History of Private Life*. Cambridge, Mass.: Harvard University Press, 1987.

Arkaraprasertkul, Non. "Towards Modern Urban Housing: Redefining Shanghai's Lilong." *Journal of Urbanism: International Research on Placemaking and Urban Sustainability* 2.1 (2009): 11–29.

Bakhtin, M. M. *The Dialogic Imagination*. Austin: University of Texas Press, 1981.

Bao Tianxiao 包天笑. *Chuan ying lou hui yi lu* 釧影樓回憶錄 (Memoirs of a bracelet shadow chamber). Hong Kong: Dahua chubanshe, 1971.

——. *Shanghai chunqiu* 上海春秋 (Shanghai annals). Guilin, China: Guangxi lijiang chubanshe, 1987.

Barmé, Geremie. "Introduction." In *China Candid: The People on the People's Republic* by Sang Ye, ix–xxiv. Berkeley: University of California Press, 2006.

Benjamin, Walter. *Reflections: Essays, Aphorisms, Autobiographical Writings*. Translated by Edmund Jephcott. New York: Schocken Books, 1986.

Benson, Carlten. "Back to Business as Usual: The Resurgence of Commercial Radio Broadcasting in Gudao Shanghai." In *In the Shadow of the Rising Sun: Shanghai Under Japanese Occupation*, edited by Christian Henriot and Wen-Hsin Yeh, 279–301. New York: Cambridge University Press, 2004.

——. "From Teahouse to Radio: Storytelling and the Commercialization of Culture in 1930s Shanghai." Ph.D. diss., University of California, Berkeley, 1996.

Bergère, Marie-Claire. *Shanghai: China's Gateway to Modernity*. Translated by Janet Lloyd. Stanford, Calif.: Stanford University Press, 2009.

Berliner, Nancy. *Yin Yu Tang: The Architecture and Daily Life of a Chinese House*. Boston: Tuttle, 2003.

Boym, Svetlana. *Common Places: Mythologies of Everyday Life in Russia*. Cambridge, Mass.: Harvard University Press, 1994.

Braester, Yomi. *Painting the City Red: Chinese Cinema and the Urban Contract*. Durham, N.C.: Duke University Press, 2010.

——. "Photography at Tiananmen: Pictorial Frames, Spatial Borders, and Ideological Matrixes." *positions: east asia cultures critique* 18.3 (2010): 633–670.

——. "Tracing the City's Scars: Demolition and the Limits of the Documentary Impulse in the New Urban Cinema." In *The Urban Generation: Chinese Cinema and Society at the Turn of the 21st Century*, edited by Zhang Zhen, 161–180. Durham, N.C.: Duke University Press, 2007.

Bray, David. *Social Space and Governance in Urban China: The Danwei System from Origins to Reform*. Stanford, Calif.: Stanford University Press, 2005.

Bray, Francesca. *Technology and Gender: Fabrics of Power in Late Imperial China*. Berkeley: University of California Press, 1997.

Brodsky, Joseph. *Less Than One: Selected Essays*. New York: Farrar Straus Giroux, 1986.

Brooks, James, Christopher DeCorse, and John Walton. *Small Worlds: Method, Meaning, and Narrative in Microhistory*. Santa Fe: School of Advanced Research Press, 2008.

Brooks, Peter. *The Melodramatic Imagination: Balzac, Henry James, Melodrama, and the Mode of Excess*. New Haven, Conn.: Yale University Press, 1976.

Cai Chusheng 蔡楚生, dir. *Xin nüxing* 新女性 (New women). Shanghai: Lianhua, 1935.

Chang, Eileen [Zhang Ailing 張愛玲]. *Ban sheng yuan* 半生緣 (Half a lifetime). Guangzhou, China: Huacheng, 1988.

——. *Written on Water*. Translated by Andrew F. Jones. New York: Columbia University Press, 2005.

Chang, Jung. *Wild Swans: Three Daughters of China*. New York: Simon and Schuster, 2003.

Chen Danyan 陳丹燕. *Shanghai de fenghua xueyue* 上海的风花雪月 (Shanghai memorabilia). Beijing: Zuojia chubanshe, 2000.

Chen, Jack. "Blank Spaces and Secret Histories: Questions of Historiographic Epistemology in Medieval China." *Journal of Asian Studies* 69.4 (2010): 1071–1091.

Chen Zu'en 陳祖恩. "Shanghai ribenren juliumin zhanhou qiansong zhengce de shixiang" "上海日本人居留民戰後遣送政策的實相" (The repatriation of Shanghai's Japanese residents after the war). *Shehui kexue* 社會科學 (Social sciences) 12 (2004): 91–101.

——. *Shanghai riqiao shehui shenghuo shi* 上海日僑社會生活史 (A social history of the Japanese diaspora in Shanghai). Shanghai: Shanghai cishu, 2009.

Cheng, Nien. *Life and Death in Shanghai*. New York: Penguin, 1988.

Cheng, Tiejun and Mark Selden. "The Origins and Social Consequences of China's Hukou System." *China Quarterly* 139 (1994): 644–668.

Choon-Piew Pow. "Constructing a New Private Order: Gated Communities and the Privatization of Urban Life in Post-reform Shanghai." *Social & Cultural Geography* 8.6 (2007): 813–833.

Clark, Paul. *The Chinese Cultural Revolution: A History*. Cambridge: Cambridge University Press, 2008.

Cochran, Sherman. *Encountering Chinese Networks: Western, Japanese, and Chinese Corporations in China, 1880–1937*. Berkeley: University of California Press, 2000.

Cochran, Sherman and Andrew Hsieh. *The Lius of Shanghai*. Cambridge, Mass.: Harvard University Press, 2013.

Council of the Foreign Settlements of Shanghai. "Report of the Housing Committee, 1936–1937." In *Municipal Gazette of the Council for the Foreign Settlement of Shanghai*, vol. 30, no. 1653. Shanghai: Municipal Council, 1937.

Cui Guanglu 崔廣錄. *Shanghai zhuzhai jianshe zhi* 上海住宅建設志 (Shanghai housing construction gazetteer). Shanghai: Shanghai shehui kexueyuan, 1998.

Dai Jinhua. "Imagined Nostalgia." *boundary 2* 24.3 (1997): 143–161.

Davis, Deborah S. "From Welfare Benefit to Capitalized Asset: The Re-commodification of Residential Space in Urban China." In *Housing and Social Change: East–West Perspectives*, edited by Ray Forrest and James Lee, 183–196. London: Routledge, 2003.

——. "My Mother's House." In *Unofficial China: Popular Culture and Thought in the People's Republic*, 88–100. Boulder, Colo.: Westview Press, 1989.

Davis, Deborah and Hanlong Lu. "Property in Transition: Conflicts Over Ownership in Post-socialist Shanghai." *European Journal of Sociology* 44.1 (2003): 77–99.

Davis, Natalie Zemon. *Women on the Margins: Three Seventeenth-Century Lives*. Cambridge, Mass.: Harvard University Press, 1995.

Denison, Edward and Guang Yu Ren. *Building Shanghai: The Story of China's Gateway*. Hoboken, N.J.: Wiley-Academy, 2006.

Des Forges, Alexander. *Mediasphere Shanghai: The Aesthetics of Cultural Production*. Honolulu: University of Hawai'i Press, 2007.

——. "Shanghai Alleys, Theatrical Practice, and Cinematic Spectatorship: From *Street Angel* (1937) to Fifth Generation Film." *Journal of Current Chinese Affairs* 39.4 (2010): 29–51.

Di Miao. "A Brief History of Chinese Situation Comedies." In *TV Drama in China*, edited by Ying Zhu, Michael Keane, and Ruoyun Bai, 117–128. Hong Kong: Hong Kong University Press, 2009.

Diamant, Neil. *Revolutionizing the Family: Politics, Love, and Divorce in Urban and Rural China, 1949–1968*. Berkeley: University of California Press, 2000.

Duus, Peter. "Zaikabo: Japanese Cotton Mills in China, 1895–1937." In *The Japanese Informal Empire in China, 1895–1937*, 65–100. Princeton, N.J.: Princeton University Press, 1989.

Eber, Irene. *Voices from Shanghai: Jewish Exiles in Wartime China*. Chicago: University of Chicago Press, 2009.

Esherick, Joseph. *Ancestral Leaves: A Family Journey Through Chinese History*. Berkeley: University of California Press, 2011.

Evans, Harriet. *The Subject of Gender: Daughters and Mothers in Urban China*. Lanham, Md.: Rowman & Littlefield, 2008.

Farrer, James. *Opening Up: Youth Culture and Market Reform in Shanghai*. Chicago: University of Chicago Press, 2002.

Feng Jun 馮軍. "Guocao liushi nian" "國操六十年" (Sixty years of national exercise). *Dongfang zaobao* 東方早報 (Eastern daily), August 20, 2011. http://www.dfdaily.com/html/8755/2011/8/20/650657_s.shtml.

Field, Andrew. *Shanghai's Dancing World: Cabaret Culture and Urban Politics, 1919–1954*. Hong Kong: Chinese University Press, 2010.

Figes, Orlando. *The Whisperers: Private Life in Stalin's Russia*. New York: Metropolitan Books, 2007.

Fogel, Joshua. "The Recent Boom in Shanghai Studies." *Journal of the History of Ideas* 71.2 (2010): 313–333.

——. "'Shanghai-Japan': The Japanese Residents' Association of Shanghai." *Journal of Asian Studies* 59.4 (2000): 927–950.

French, Howard and Qiu Xiaolong. *Disappearing Shanghai: Photographs and Poems of an Intimate Way of Life*. Paramus, N.J.: Homa & Sekey Books, 2012.

Gluckman, Max. "Gossip and Scandal." *Current Anthropology* 4.3 (1963): 307–316.

Gold, Thomas. "Back to the City: The Return of Shanghai's Educated Youth." *China Quarterly* 84 (1980): 755–770.

Gu, Ming Dong. *Chinese Theories of Fiction: A Non-Western Narrative System*. Albany: State University of New York Press, 2006.

Han Bangqing. *The Sing-Song Girls of Shanghai*. Translated by Eileen Chang. Revised and edited by Eva Hung. New York: Columbia University Press, 2005.

Harrison, Henrietta. *The Missionary's Curse and Other Tales from a Chinese Village*. Berkeley: University of California Press, 2013.

Havel, Vaclav. *The Power of the Powerless: Citizens Against the State in Central–Eastern Europe*. Armonk, N.Y.: M. E. Sharpe, 1985.

Henriot, Christian. "Slums, Squats, or Hutments? Constructing and Deconstructing an In-Between Space in Modern Shanghai (1926–1965)." *Frontiers of History* 7.2 (2012): 499–528.

Hershatter, Gail. *The Gender of Memory: Rural Women and China's Collective Past*. Berkeley: University of California Press, 2011.

Honig, Emily. *Creating Chinese Ethnicity: Subei People in Shanghai, 1850–1980*. New Haven, Conn.: Yale University Press, 1992.

——. *Sisters and Strangers: Women in the Shanghai Cotton Mills, 1919–1949*. Stanford, Calif.: Stanford University Press, 1986.

Hou Hsiao-hsien 侯孝賢, dir. *Beiqing chengshi* 悲情城市 (City of sadness). Taipei, Taiwan: 3-H Films/ERA International, 1989.

Huang, Nicole. "Introduction." In *Written on Water* by Zhang Ailing, translated by Andrew F. Jones, ix–xxviii. New York: Columbia University Press, 2005.

——. "Locating Family Portraits: Everyday Images from 1970s China." *positions: east asia cultures critique* 18.3 (2010): 671–693.

Hung, Chang-tai. *Mao's New World: Political Culture in the Early People's Republic.* Ithaca, N.Y.: Cornell University Press, 2011.

Jin Dalu 金大陸. "Beijing hongweibing zai Shanghai" "北京紅衞兵在上海" (Beijing Red Guards in Shanghai), part I. *Shilin* (Forest of history) 3 (2008): 97–136. Part II. *Shilin* 1 (2009): 107–122.

——. *Feichang yu zhengchang: Shanghai wenge shiqi de shehui shenghuo* 非常與正常：上海文革時期的社會生活 (Abnormality and normality: Social life during the Cultural Revolution in Shanghai). Shanghai: Shanghai cishu, 2011.

Jin Yucheng 金宇澄. *Fanhua* 繁花 (Blossoms). Shanghai: Shanghai wenyi, 2013.

Johnson, Tess and Deke Erh. *A Last Look: Western Architecture in Old Shanghai.* Hong Kong: Old China Hand Press, 1993.

Kleinman, Arthur. *Social Origins of Distress and Disease: Depression, Neurasthenia, and Pain in Modern China.* New Haven, Conn.: Yale University Press, 1986.

Knapp, Ronald. "China's Houses, Homes, and Families." In *House, Home, Family: Living and Being Chinese*, edited by Ronald G. Knapp and Kai-Yin Lo, 1–9. Honolulu: University of Hawai'i Press, 2005.

——. *China's Vernacular Architecture: House Form and Culture.* Honolulu: University of Hawai'i Press, 1989.

Knapp, Ronald and Kai-Yin Lo, eds. *House, Home, Family: Living and Being Chinese.* Honolulu: University of Hawai'i Press, 2005.

Ko, Dorothy. *Teachers of the Inner Chambers: Women and Culture in Seventeenth Century China.* Stanford, Calif.: Stanford University Press, 1994.

Krupar, Shiloh. "Shanghaiing the Future: A De-tour of the Shanghai Urban Planning Exhibition Hall." *Public Culture* 20.2 (2008): 307–320.

Lao She 老舍. *Chaguan* 茶館 (Teahouse). Stage play premiered by Beijing People's Art Theatre in 1957.

——. *Longxugou* 龍鬚溝 (Dragon Whisker Creek). Stage play premiered by Beijing People's Art Theatre in 1951.

Larson, Wendy. *From Ah Q to Lei Feng: Freud and Revolutionary Spirit in 20th Century China.* Stanford, Calif.: Stanford University Press, 2009.

Lean, Eugenia. *Public Passions: The Trial of Shi Jianqiao and the Rise of Popular Sympathy in Republican China.* Berkeley: University of California Press, 2007.

Lee, Leo Ou-fan. *Shanghai Modern: The Flowering of a New Urban Culture in China.* Cambridge, Mass.: Harvard University Press, 1999.

Leese, Daniel. *Mao Cult: Rhetoric and Ritual in China's Cultural Revolution.* New York: Cambridge University Press, 2011.

Lepore, Jill. "Historians Who Love Too Much: Reflections on Microhistory and Biography." *Journal of American History* 88.1 (2001): 129–144.

Leung, Joe. "Dismantling the 'Iron Rice Bowl': Welfare Reforms in the People's Republic of China." *Journal of Social Policy* 23.3 (1994): 341–361.

Levenson, Joseph. *Revolution and Cosmopolitanism: The Western Stage and the Chinese Stages.* Berkeley: University of California Press, 1971.

Liang, Samuel. "Amnesiac Monument, Nostalgic Fashion: Shanghai's New Heaven and Earth." *Wasafiri* 23.3 (2008): 47–55.

——. *Mapping Modernity in Shanghai: Space, Gender, and Visual Culture in the Sojourners' City, 1853–98.* New York: Routledge, 2010.

——. "Property-Driven Urban Change in Post-socialist Shanghai: Reading the Television Series *Woju.*" *Journal of Current Chinese Affairs* 3 (2010): 3–28.

——. "Where the Courtyard Meets the Street: Spatial Culture of the *Li* Neighborhoods, Shanghai, 1870–1900." *Journal of the Society of Architectural Historians* 67.4 (2008): 482–503.

Lu, Hanchao. *Beyond the Neon Lights: Everyday Shanghai in the Early 20th Century.* Berkeley: University of California Press, 1999.

——. "Nostalgia for the Future: The Resurgence of an Alienated Culture in China." *Pacific Affairs* 75.2 (2002): 169–186.

Lu Xun 魯迅. "Ah Jin." Translated by David Pollard. In *The Chinese Essay*, edited by David Pollard, 116–121. New York: Columbia University Press, 2000.

——. *Lu Xun quanji* 魯迅全集 (Complete works of Lu Xun). 16 vols. Beijing: Beijing renmin, 1981.

Luard, D. E. T. "The Urban Communes." *China Quarterly* 3 (1960): 74–79.

Ma Changlin 馬長林. *Lao Shanghai chengji: Longtang li de da lishi* 老上海城記：弄堂里的大歷史 (The story of Old Shanghai: Big histories in alleyways). Shanghai: Shanghai jinxiu wenzhang, 2010.

Mao Zedong. "Talks at the Yan'an Forum of Literature and Art." May 2, 1942. http://www.marxists.org/reference/archive/mao/selected-works/volume-3/mswv3_08.htm. Accessed January 31, 2014.

McCreery, John. "Women's Property Rights and Dowry in China and South Asia." *Ethnology* 15.2 (1976): 163–174.

McDougall, Bonnie. "Particulars and Universals: Studies on Chinese Privacy," in *Chinese Concepts of Privacy*, edited by Bonnie McDougall and Anders Hansson, 3–24. Leiden: Brill, 2002.

——. "Privacy in Modern China." *History Compass* 2.1 (2004): 1–8.

Mertha, Andrew. "From 'Rustless Screws' to 'Nail Houses': The Evolution of Property Rights in China." *Orbis* 53.2 (2009): 233–249.

Mittler, Barbara. *A Continuous Revolution: Making Sense of Cultural Revolution Culture.* Cambridge, Mass.: Harvard University Press, 2013.

——. "Enjoying the Four Olds! Oral Histories from a 'Cultural Desert.'" *Transcultural Studies* 1 (2013): 177–214.

Morrison, Toni. *Beloved.* New York: Knopf, 1987.

Mu Xin 木心. "Shanghai fu" "上海賦" (Ode to Shanghai). In *Gelunbiya de daoying* 哥倫比亞的倒影 (Reflection of Columbia), 113–165. Guilin, China: Guangshi shifan daxue, 2009.

Mühlhahn, Klaus. *Criminal Justice in China: A History*. Cambridge, Mass.: Harvard University Press, 2009.

Naughton, Barry. "The Third Front: Defense Industrialization in the Chinese Interior." *China Quarterly* 115 (1988): 351–386.

Nornes, Abé Mark Nornes and Yeh Yueh-yu. *Narrating National Sadness: Cinematic Mapping and Hypertextual Dispersion*. 1994. Formerly published at http://cinemaspace.berkeley.edu/Papers/CityOfSadness/srep.html (no longer active). Accessed October 1, 2007. E-publication forthcoming.

Osato Hiroaki and Tomii Masanori. "Zaikabō no kyōjū kankyō ni tsui te—Shanhai no jirei" "「在華紡の居住環境について - 上海の事例」" (On Japanese cotton mill housing conditions in China: The case of Shanghai). Paper presented at the Kanegawa University 21st Century COE Program Research Conference, December 2007, Kanegawa-ku, Japan. http://www.himoji.jp/jp/publication/pdf/seika/302s/017-031.pdf.

Owen, Stephen. "Singularity and Possession." In *The End of the Chinese "Middle Ages": Essays in Mid-Tang Literary Culture*, 12–33. Stanford, Calif.: Stanford University Press, 1996.

Paine, Robert. "What Is Gossip About? An Alternative Hypothesis." *Man* (new series) 2.2 (1967): 278–285.

Pan, Tianshu. "Historical Memory, Community-Building, and Place-Making in Neighborhood Shanghai." In *Restructuring the Chinese City: Changing Society, Economy, and Space*, edited by Laurence J. C. Ma and Fulong Wu, 122–137. New York: Routledge, 2005.

Pellow, Deborah. "No Place to Live, No Place to Love." In *Urban Anthropology in China*, edited by Greg Guldin and Aidan Southall, 396–424. Leiden: Brill, 1993.

Perry, Elizabeth J. "Masters of the Country? Shanghai Workers in the Early People's Republic." In *Dilemmas of Victory: The Early Years of the People's Republic of China*, edited by Jeremy Brown and Paul Pickowicz, 59–79. Cambridge, Mass.: Harvard University Press, 2007.

——. *Shanghai on Strike: The Politics of Chinese Labor*. Stanford, Calif.: Stanford University Press, 1993.

Perry, Elizabeth J. and Li Xun. *Proletarian Power: Shanghai in the Cultural Revolution*. Boulder, Colo.: Westview Press, 1997.

Prost, Antoine. "Public and Private Spheres in France." In *A History of Private Life*, vol. 5: *Riddles of Identity in Modern Times*, edited by Antoine Prost and Gérard Vincent, 1–144. Cambridge, Mass.: Harvard University Press, 1994.

"Provisional Act of the PRC for the Organization of Security Defense Committees (1952)." In chapter 2, "Informal Adjustment and Sanctioning," of *The Criminal*

Process in the People's Republic of China, 1949–1963: An Introduction, edited by Jerome Cohen, 97–199. Cambridge, Mass.: Harvard University Press, 1968.

Qiu Guosheng 邱國盛. "Ershi shiji wushi niandai Shanghai de funü jiefang yu canjia jiti shengchan" "20 世紀 50 年代上海的婦女解放與參加集體生產" (Shanghai women's emancipation and participation in collective production in the 1950s). In *Dangdai Zhongguo shi yanjiu* 当代中国史研究 (Studies in contemporary Chinese history) 2 (2009): 70–77.

Qiu, Xiaolong. *Years of Red Dust: Stories of Shanghai.* New York: Macmillan, 2010.

Ran, Xinfei, *Building Globalization: Transnational Architecture Production in Urban China.* Chicago: University of Chicago Press, 2011.

Rapport, Nigel and Joanna Overing. *Social and Cultural Anthropology: The Key Concepts.* New York: Routledge, 2013.

Rofel, Lisa. *Other Modernities: Gendered Yearnings in China After Socialism.* Berkeley: University of California Press, 1999.

Rowe, William. "The Public Sphere in Modern China." *Modern China* 16.3 (1990): 309–329.

Saraceno, Chiara. "The Italian Family: Paradoxes of Privacy." Translated by Raymond Rosenthal. In *A History of Private Life*, vol. 5: *Riddles of Identity in Modern Times*, edited by Antoine Prost and Gérard Vincent, 451–501. Cambridge, Mass.: Harvard University Press, 1994.

Scarry, Elaine. *The Body in Pain: The Making and Unmaking of the World.* New York: Oxford University Press, 1985.

Schrift, Melissa. *Biography of a Chairman Mao Badge: The Creation and Mass Consumption of a Personality Cult.* New Brunswick, N.J.: Rutgers University Press, 2001.

Sha Lin 沙霖. *Zenyang xie zizhuan* 怎樣寫自傳 (How to write an autobiography). Shanghai: Puwen, 1951.

Shanghai 1932: Chengshi jiyi lao ditu 上海1932:城市記憶老地圖 (Shanghai 1932: Urban memory old map). Beijing: Xueyuan, 2005.

Shanghai laodong zhi 上海勞動志 (Shanghai labor gazetteer). Shanghai: Shanghai shehui kexue yuan, 1998.

Shanghai shi yangpuqu dang'anju 上海市楊浦區檔案局 (Shanghai Yangpu District Archive Office). *Yangpu bainian shihua* 楊浦百年史話 (A hundred years of Yangshupu history). Shanghai: Shanghai yangpu wenhuaju, 2006.

Shanghai sichou zhi 上海絲綢志 (Shanghai silk gazetteer). Shanghai: Shanghai shehui kexueyuan, 1998.

Shanghai Yangpuqu renmin zhengfu 上海楊浦區人民政府 (People's Government of Shanghai's Yangpu District). *Shanghai shi Yangpuqu dimingzhi* 上海市楊浦區地名志 (Gazetteer of place-names of the Shanghai Yangpu District). Shanghai: Xuelin, 1989.

Shanghai Youth Gazetteer Editorial Board. *Shanghai qingnian zhi* 上海青年志 (Shanghai youth gazetteer). Shanghai: Shanghai shehui kexueyuan, 2002.

Shao, Qin. *Shanghai Gone: Domicide and Defiance in a Chinese Megacity.* Lanham, Md.: Rowman & Littlefield, 2012.

——. "Waving the Red Flag: Cultural Memory and Grassroots Protest in Housing Disputes in China." *Modern Chinese Literature and Culture* 22.1 (2010): 197–231.

Shen Fu 沈浮, dir. *Wanzi qianhong zongshi chun* 萬紫千紅總是春 (Women of the Great Leap Forward). Shanghai: Haiyan, 1959.

Spacks, Patricia. *Gossip.* Chicago: University of Chicago Press, 1986.

——. "In Praise of Gossip." *Hudson Review* 35.1 (1982): 19–38.

Spence, Jonathan. *The Death of Woman Wang.* New York: Viking Press, 1978.

Steinhardt, Nancy Shatzman. "The House: An Introduction." In *House, Home, Family: Living and Being Chinese,* edited by Ronald G. Knapp and Kai-Yin Lo, 13–35. Honolulu: University of Hawai'i Press, 2005.

Stewart, Susan. *On Longing: Narratives of the Miniature, the Gigantic, the Souvenir, the Collection.* Baltimore: Johns Hopkins University Press, 1984.

Sun Yumin 孫玉敏. "Yingxiong wangshi" "英雄" 往事 (Hero's past). *Shanghai guozi* 上海國資 (Capital Shanghai) 3 (2012). http://gov.finance.sina.com.cn/chanquan/2012-07-04/123258.html.

Swislocki, Mark. *Culinary Nostalgia: Regional Food Culture and the Urban Experience in Shanghai.* Stanford, Calif.: Stanford University Press, 2009.

Szijártó, István. "Four Arguments for Microhistory." *Rethinking History* 6.2 (2002): 209–215.

Tang, Xiaobing. "Decorating Culture: Notes on Interior Design, Interiority, and Interiorization." *Public Culture* 10.3 (1998): 530–548.

Tian, Xiaofei. "The Making of a Hero: Lei Feng and Some Issues of Historiography." In *The People's Republic of China at 60: An International Assessment,* edited by William C. Kirby, 293–305. Cambridge, Mass.: Harvard University Press, 2011.

Vermeule, Blakey. "Gossip and Literary Narrative." *Philosophy and Literature* 30.1 (2006): 102–117.

Visser, Robin. *Cities Surround the Countryside: Urban Aesthetics in Post-socialist China.* Durham, N.C.: Duke University Press, 2007.

Wakeman, Frederic, Jr. "'Cleanup': The New Order in Shanghai." In *Dilemmas of Victory: The Early Years of the People's Republic of China,* edited by Jeremy Brown and Paul Pickowicz, 21–58. Cambridge, Mass.: Harvard University Press, 2007.

Wakeman, Frederic, Jr., and Wen-hsin Yeh. "Introduction." In *Shanghai Sojourners,* edited by Frederic Wakeman Jr. and Wen-hsin Yeh, 1–14. Berkeley, Calif.: Institute of East Asian Studies, 1992.

Wang Anyi 王安憶. *Chang hen ge* 長恨歌 (The song of everlasting sorrow). Beijing: Beijing chubanshe, 1996.

——. *Qimeng shidai* 啟蒙時代 (The age of enlightenment). Beijing: Renmin wenxue, 2007.

——. *The Song of Everlasting Sorrow: A Novel of Shanghai.* Translated by Michael Berry and Susan Egan. New York: Columbia University Press, 2008.

Wang, Ban. *The Sublime Figure of History: Aesthetics and Politics in Twentieth Century China.* Stanford, Calif.: Stanford University Press, 1997.

Wang Dewei 王德威 [David Der-wei Wang]. "Haipai wenxue, youjian chuanren: Wang Anyi lun" "海派文学，又见传人：王安憶論" (Emergent successors of Shanghai-style literature: On Wang Anyi). In *Dangdai xiaoshuo ershi jia* 当代小说二十家 (Twenty masters of contemporary novels), 16–32. Beijing: Sanlian shudian, 2006.

Wang Ping, dir. *Yongbu xiaoshi de dianbo* 永不消逝的電波 (The everlasting radio waves). Beijing: August Eighth Film, 1958.

Wang, Shaoguang. "The Politics of Private Time: Changing Leisure Patterns in Urban China." In *Urban Spaces in Contemporary China: The Potential for Autonomy and Community in Post-Mao China*, edited by Deborah S. Davis, Richard Kraus, Barry Naughton, and Elizabeth J. Perry, 149–172. New York: Cambridge University Press, 1995.

Wang Xiaoming 王曉明. "Cong jianzhu dao guanggao: Zuijin shiwunian Shanghai chengshi kongjian de bianhua" "從建築到廣告：最近十五年上海城市空間的變化" (From architecture to advertisements: Transformations of Shanghai's urban spaces in the past fifteen years). In *Dangdai dongya chengshi* 當代東亞城市：新的文化和意識形態 (Contemporary East Asian cities: New cultures and ideologies), edited by Wang Xiaoming and Chen Qingqiao 陳清僑, 86–118. Shanghai: Shanghai shudian, 2008.

Wang, Zheng. "Gender and Maoist Urban Reorganization." In *Gender in Motion: Divisions of Labor and Cultural Change in Late Imperial and Modern China*, edited by Bryna Goodman and Wendy Larson, 189–209. Lanham, Md.: Rowman & Littlefield, 2004.

Wank, David L. "Cigarettes and Domination in Chinese Business Networks: Institutional Change During the Market Transition." In *The Consumer Revolution in Urban China*, edited by Deborah Davis, 268–86. Berkeley: University of California Press, 2000.

Wasserstrom, Jeffrey N. *Global Shanghai, 1850–2010: A History in Fragments.* New York: Routledge, 2008.

Weintraub, Jeff. "The Theory and Politics of the Public/Private Distinction." In *Public and Private in Thought and Practice: Perspectives on a Grand Dichotomy*, edited by Jeff Weintraub and Krishan Kumar, 1–42. Chicago: University of Chicago Press, 1997.

White, Lynn T. *Policies of Chaos: The Organizational Causes of Violence in China's Cultural Revolution.* Princeton, N.J.: Princeton University Press, 1989.

Wolf, Margery. *Women and the Family in Rural Taiwan.* Stanford, Calif.: Stanford University Press, 1972.

Wu, Hung. *Remaking Beijing: Tiananmen Square and the Creation of a Political Space.* Chicago: University of Chicago Press, 2005.

Wu, Juanjuan. *Chinese Fashion: From Mao to Now.* New York: Berg, 2009.

Wu Yonggan 吳永剛, dir. *Shennü* 神女 (The goddess). Shanghai: Lianhua, 1934.

Xia Yan 夏衍. *Under Shanghai Eaves* (*Shanghai wuyanxia* 上海屋簷下) (1937). Translated by George Hayden. In *Columbia Anthology of Modern Chinese*

Drama, edited by Xiaomei Chen, 397–447. New York: Columbia University Press, 2010.

Xu Gang 徐剛. *Xiangxiang chengshi de fangfa: Dalu 'shiqinian wenxue de chengshi biaoshu* 想像城市的方法：大陸"十七年文學"的城市表述 (Ways of imagining the city: Urban expressions in the literature of the Seventeen-Year Period). Taipei: Xinrui wenchuang, 2013.

Xu Jilin 許紀霖 and Luo Gang 罗岗. *Chengshi de jiyi: Shanghai wenhua de duoyuan lishi chuantong* 城市的記憶：上海文化的多元歷史傳統 (Metropolitan memories: Shanghai culture's plural historical heritage). Shanghai: Shanghai shudian, 2011.

Yan, Yunxiang. *Private Life Under Socialism: Love, Intimacy, and Family Change in a Chinese Village*. Stanford, Calif.: Stanford University Press, 2003.

Yang, Mayfair. "The Gift Economy and State Power in China." *Comparative Studies in Society and History* 31.1 (1989): 25–54.

——. *Gifts, Favors, and Banquets: The Art of Social Relationships in China*. Ithaca, N.Y.: Cornell University Press, 1994.

Yang Yang 楊楊, Chen Shuping 陳樹萍, and Wang Pengfei 王鵬飛. *Haipai wenxue* 海派文學 (Shanghai-style literature). Shanghai: Wenhui chubanshe, 2008.

Yeh, Catherine. *Shanghai Love: Courtesans, Intellectuals, and Entertainment Culture, 1850–1910*. Seattle: University of Washington Press, 2006.

Yeh, Wen-hsin. *Alienated Academy: Culture and Politics in Republican China, 1919–1937*. Cambridge, Mass.: Council on East Asian Studies, Harvard University, 1990.

——. "Progressive Journalism and Shanghai's Petty Urbanites: Zou Taofen and the *Shenghuo Weekly*, 1926–1945." In *Shanghai Sojourners*, edited by Frederick Wakeman Jr. and Wen-hsin Yeh, 186–238. Berkeley: Institute of East Asian Studies, 1992.

——. *Shanghai Splendor: Economic Sentiments and the Making of Modern China, 1843–1949*. Berkeley: University of California Press, 2007.

Yihong Pan. *Tempered in the Revolutionary Furnace: China's Youth in the Rustication Movement*. Lanham, Md.: Lexington Books, 2002.

Yip, June. *Envisioning Taiwan: Fiction, Cinema, and the Nation in the Cultural Imaginary*. Durham, N.C.: Duke University Press, 2004.

Yu Hua. *China in Ten Words*. Translated by Allan Barr. New York: Pantheon Books, 2011.

Yu Qiuyu. "Shanghai People." In *The Chinese Essay: An Anthology*, edited by David Pollard, 350–361. New York: Columbia University Press, 2002.

Yuan Jin 袁進. *Shenfen jiangou yu wuzhi shenghuo: 20 shiji 50 niandai Shanghai gongren de shehui wenhua shenghuo* 身份建構與物質生活：20世紀50年代上海工人的社會文化生活 (Identity construction and material life: Shanghai worker social and cultural lives in the 1950s). Shanghai: Shanghai shudian, 2008.

Yuan Muzhi 袁牧之, dir. *Malu tianshi* 馬路天使 (Street angel). Shanghai: Mingxing, 1937.

Zarrow, Peter. "The Origins of Modern Chinese Concepts of Privacy: Notes on Social Structure and Moral Discourse." In *Chinese Concepts of Privacy*, edited by Bonnie McDougall and Anders Hansson, 121–146. Leiden: Brill, 2002.

Zhang Jishun 张济顺. "Shanghai lilong: Jiceng zhengzhi dongyuan yu guojia shehui yitihua zouxiang, 1950–1955" "上海里弄：基層政治動員與國家社會一體化走向" (Neighborhood committees: Grassroots political mobilization and the trend of state–society integration in Shanghai, 1950–1955). *Zhongguo shehui kexue* 中國社會科學 (Chinese social sciences) 2 (2004): 178–189.

Zhang Sheng 張生. *Shanghai ju, dabuyi: Jindai Shanghai fanghuanng yanjiu* 上海居：大不易：近代上海房荒研究 (Residing in Shanghai is not easy: Shanghai's housing shortage in modern times). Shanghai: Shanghai cishu, 2009.

Zhang, Xudong. "Shanghai Nostalgia: Postrevolutionary Allegories in Wang Anyi's Literary Production in the 1990s." *positions: east asia cultures critique* 8.2 (2000): 349–387.

Zhang Yuanchen 張苑琛. *Xinmin wanbao fukan yanjiu* 新民晚報副刊研究 (Study of cultural supplements in the *Xinmin Evening News*). Shanghai: Shanghai jiaotong daxue, 2011.

Zhang, Zhen. "The Production of the Senses in and out of the 'Everlasting Auspicious Lane,' Shanghai, 1966–1976." In *Some of Us: Chinese Women Growing Up in the Mao Era*, edited by Zhong Xueping, Wang Zheng, and Bai Di, 155–178. New Brunswick, N.J.: Rutgers University Press, 2001.

Zhao, Chunlan. "From *Shikumen* to New-Style: A Rereading of *Lilong* Housing in Modern Shanghai." *Journal of Architecture* 9.1 (2004): 49–76.

Zheng Dongtian 鄭洞天 and Xu Guming 徐谷明, dirs. *Linju* 邻居 (Neighbors). Beijing: Youth Film Studio, 1981.

Zheng Junli 鄭君里, dir. *Wuya yu maque* 烏鴉與麻雀 (Crows and sparrows). Shanghai: Kunlun, 1949.

Zhong, Xueping. "Shanghai 'Shimin' Literature and the Ambivalence of (Urban) Home." *Modern Chinese Literature* 9.1 (1995): 79–99.

Zhonggong Shanghai shiwei dangshi yanjiushi 中共上海市委黨史研究室 (Chinese Communist Party Shanghai Party History Office). *Zhonggong Shanghai lishi shilu* 中共上海歷史實錄 (Historical records of Chinese Communist Party history in Shanghai). Shanghai: Shanghai jiaoyu, 2004.

Zhu Dake 朱大可. *Jiyi de hongpi shu* 記憶的紅皮書 (Red memory book). Guangzhou, China: Huacheng, 2008.

INDEX

Italic page numbers refer to illustrations.

Communist Liberation, 15, 60, 87, 96, 121, 174, 181

Communists: alleyway house as site of founding of Communist Party, 10; bureaucracies of, 49, 66, 90; dichotomy between state and family, 19; dismantling of kinship system, 18, 93–94; Grandma Yang Lingying as party member, 59–60; and household registration system, 9, 49, 56, 63–64, 81, 83–84, 85, 96, 147, 156, 195, 196, 197, 198, 203, 208, 209, 210, 223n32, 226n67; and mass campaigns, 90, 147; and private realm, 21; in Republican era, 38; takeover commissioners, 62–63; underground Communists of Alliance Lane, 36, 107; and Waigong, 93; and Yeye's cousin, 96–97

Communist Youth League, 67

confessions, 16, 65–66, 68, 87, 90, 98, 112–113, 117, 125, 148, 211–212

Confucian hierarchies, and traditional family, 8, 36, 87

Confucius, 145

consumerism: conspicuous consumption turning into clandestine consumption, 121; and declining worth of things, 136, 139–140; and fast-paced lifestyle, 207; and private realm, 17, 21, 22, 121, 132–135, 136

Council of the Foreign Settlements of Shanghai, 37

counterrevolutionaries: family members of, 75, 115, 163–164, 166–167, 168, 170; and home searches, 111, 115, 119, 120; labeling of, 60, 75, 96, 115, 120, 151, 164, 168, 170, 176; and labor reform camps, 116, 170; as one of four elements, 64, 125; and redistribution of housing, 61; and struggle sessions, 117; suppression of, 50, 87, 93, 176

Cultural Revolution (1966–1976): and attack on the "four olds," 111, 112, 114–115, 116, 126, 129, 203; and big-character posters, 111, 228n23; clandestine reading during, 126–129; confessions during, 97–98; ending of, 76–77; exhibitions during, 120–121; home searches of, 1, 9, 22, 50, 90, 110–129, 228nn28, 30; and little red book, 99, 129; localized perspectives on, 14, 113–129; nostalgia for, 129; and photography, 99, 100; and radios, 109; rebel groups of, 69, 98, 112, 116; Red Guards of, 1, 111, 113–117, 119, 124, 228n28; struggle sessions in, 1–2, 28, 54, 62, 66, 111, 113, 116, 117–119, 124, 164, 172; and theatricality, 113–114, 117

Dagongbao (Impartial Daily), 38

Davis, Deborah, 131–132, 236n37

Davis, Natalie Zemon, 164

demolition: of Alliance Lane, 30, 191, 192, 193, 196, 199, 200; and forced evictions, 192, 196, 198–199, 200, 201, 203, 208, 234n15, 235n21; and household registration system, 85, 195, 196, 197, 198, 203, 208, 209, 210, 226n67; micropolitics of, 193–200; and nail households, 24, 192, 202–208, 209; and real estate market, 192, 194, 205, 206, 233n3; and recyclers, 212–213; and relocation teams, 23, 85, 194–197, 198, 199, 203, 205, 207, 208–209, 233n1; and ruins, 201–205; of Shanghai alleyways, 10–11, 192, 193; and Sunny Relocation, 194–195, 201

denunciations, 10, 66, 90, 148

deprivation, and private life, 21, 23, 136

Des Forges, Alexander, 8, 145, 232n40

domestic objects: and bricolage, 139–140; and coal stoves, 137–138, 139; and cookie tins, 137; as historical

Jia Zhangke, 72
Jin Yuchen, 217*n*17, 228*n*30

Kleinman, Arthur, 227*n*16
Ko, Dorothy, 18

labor reform, 68, 75, 97, 101, 116, 142,
  166–168, 170–171
Lacks, George, 43, *43*
land reform, 17, 93–94
Lane 1695. *See* Pingliang Road Lane 1695
  compound
Lao She, 226*n*70
Lee, Leo Ou-fan, 8
Lei Feng, 113, 205–206, 208, 228*n*26,
  235*n*29
Lenin, Vladimir, 72, 205–206
Levenson, Joseph, 111
Li Bin (father): on Cultural Revolution,
  98–99, 114–115; diary of, 113; and
  Going Up the Mountain and Down
  to the Countryside movement, 76,
  99; on Great Leap Forward, 73; and
  No. 183 Pingliang Road, 209–210;
  photographs of, *63, 99*; and Shanghai
  real estate market, 193, 233*n*5; and
  Yeye's written confessions, 98
Li Boyuan, 145
Liang, Samuel, 7, 207
Life magazine, 43, *43*
lilong. See alleyway homes
Little Aunt, 134, 157, 195
Little Sister (of Zhang family), 122, *123*,
  124–126
Little Uncle (of Waigong), 92–93
longtang. See alleyway homes
loudspeakers, 73, 88, 129, 148, 198, 202, 203
"lower corner," 27, 220*n*3
Lu, Hanchao, 6, 150
Lu Xun, 141, 146, 216*n*14

Mao badges, 99, 128–129, 229*n*36
Mao cult, 112–114, 129

Mao era (1950s–1970s): alleyway
  homes of, 9, 217*n*17; changes in
  usage of housing, 25, 49, 57, 61, 89;
  collective spaces in, 70–74, 203;
  destruction of private realm, 17–20,
  21, 22, 23, 90, 113; and gossip, 142,
  148, 157; graphomania of, 100;
  political campaigns of, 60, 90, 96;
  propaganda of, 73, 114, 129; and
  radios, 107–109; rationing system
  of, 136–138, 159; and rustless
  bolts, 192, 205–210; and sent-
  down movements, 68, 74–77; and
  work-unit-based socialist housing
  compounds, 9, 49, 56, 57, 61, 111,
  223–224*n*42, 226*n*66
Mao Zedong: and Chiang Kai-shek,
  38; on cleanliness of peasants, 101;
  portraits of, 112–113; *Selected Works*
  of, 96, 129; speech at Yan'an Forum,
  205–206; and Third Front, 76;
  thought-propaganda troupes, 114;
  works of, 125
market economy: and market reform,
  91, 134, 135, 226*n*68, 234*n*8; and
  private realm, 18, 22
Marxism, 131, 139
Master Chen (Aunt Duckweed's
  father), 55–56, 109, 178–179
memory: alleyway homes as repository
  of, 3, 5, 12–15, 21–23, 26, 207; and
  demolition, 24, 192, 207; of radio,
  109; reliability of, 16, 97; of socialism,
  49, 72, 103, 109, 129, 136, 138, 205
Metropolitan Ltd., 27
microhistory: alleyway homes as
  microhistorical stage, 86–88,
  226*n*70; diversity of contexts within
  investigation, 14; local perspective
  of, 12, 14–15; sources of, 15
model workers, 49, 57, 59–61, 64, 76.
  See also Grandma Yang Lingying
Morrison, Toni, 220*n*62

subletting, 8, 36, 52, 53, 55, 56, 87, 170, 176
Suppression of Counterrevolutionaries, 50, 119, 175

Taiping Rebellion, 220n4
takeover fees (*dingfei*), 31, 52, 55, 87, 181, 221n11
Tang, Xiaobing, 134–135
television, 132, 133, 134, 140, 194
Third Front, 76
Three-Anti Five-Anti Campaign (1952), 65, 97, 186
Three-Five Brand clocks, 108, *108*
thrift, 102–103, 106, 119, 120, 135–140, 154, 212
Tiananmen Square, 109–110, 113, 129
Tolstoy, Leo, 126
24 City (film), 72
"20,000 Households" housing project, 61

Uncle Little Brother, 117
Uncle Lucky: family photographs, *63*, *99*; marriage chamber of, 130; and No. 183 Pingliang Road, 80, 81, 82, 83, 88; Westernized furniture of, 81, 88, 130, 132, 133
Uncle Morning Sun, 48
Uncle Pavilion Room, 57, 161
Uncle Prosper, 118, 198–199
Uncle Strong, 58, 84–86, 195, 206
Uncle Zhao, 80, 81, 83, 84
"upper corner," 27, 36, 170–171, 220n3

Visser, Robin, 229–230n39
Voice of America, 109

Waigong (maternal grandfather): collective wedding of, 54, 55; with coworkers from silk factory, *54*; and demolition, 195, 197; family photograph of, *58*; first impressions of Shanghai, 36–37, 38–39; and

grain bed in attic, 23, 53, 90, 91–94; grandparents and uncles of, 91–94; on home searches in the Cultural Revolution, 116; and housing for Uncle Strong, 84–86, 88; as migrant from countryside, 26, 37, 39, 52, 54, 75, 87, 94, 107; and moving to Alliance Lane, 55–56; nostalgia for revolutionary songs, 73; on petty urbanites, 131; photographs of, *37*, *104*; and photographs on Eight Immortal Table, 104–105; and radios, 23, 105–110, 108, 136; as silk worker, 36, 37–38, 54, 93, 94, 104, 105, 108, 136, 161; on third floor of No. 111, Alliance Lane, 53, 57, 86, 87, 107
Waipo (maternal grandmother): on big alleyway, 151; collective wedding of, 54, 55; with coworkers from silk factory, *54*; and demolition, 191–192, 195, 197; family photograph of, *58*; and gossip, 141–142, 153, *153*, 157–158; and grain bed in attic, 23, 53, 90, 91–94; and housing for Uncle Strong, 84–86, 88; on housing for workers, 61; on Mao era, 167; as migrant from countryside, 26, 36, 37, 39, 52, 54, 75, 87, 94, 107; on Mother Mao, 165, 166, 167, 168; mother of, 94, *94*; on Mother Yang, 170; on moving into No. 111, Alliance Lane, 52, 54, 55–56; neurasthenia of, 108, 227n16; photographs of, *37*, *104*; and radios, 23, 105–110, 108; as silk worker, 36, 37, 72, 104, 105, 108, 116, 136, 161; on third floor of No. 111, Alliance Lane, 53, 56, 57, 86, 87, 107; on threat of being sent to countryside, 74–75
Wang Anyi, 6, 141, 148–149, 217n17
Wang, Ban, 113
Wang family: in Alliance Lane No. 111, 33–39, 49, 52, 55–56, 87. *See also* Grandma Apricot

Wang Xiaoming, 147

Wang Yaqing (mother): and alleyway romance, 127; and Alliance Lane visit, 152; diary of, 113; education of, 122; family photograph, 58; friendship with Aunt Duckweed, 57; and Going Up the Mountain and Down to the Countryside movement, 75–76, 127; and grain bed in attic, 94; kindergarten attendance of, 70, 71; and peddlers, 150; photographs of, 108, 128; reading banned books, 127–128

Wang, Zheng, 63

Ward, Frederic Townsend, 220n4

Ward Road, 27, 49, 220n4

Warring States period, 19

White, Lynn, 224n49

White Hair, 117–118

Wolf, Margery, 144

women: Communist liberation of, 133; and concubines, 9, 35, 36, 52, 56, 87, 104, 155–156, 166, 170, 174, 176; as counterrevolutionary family members, 163–164; and domestic sphere, 62, 64, 102–103; dowries of, 50, 91–92, 119, 227n4; housewife mobilization, 62–64, 73–74; and private realm, 19; temporary work of, 164, 167, 168; and urban communes, 70; use of gossip in domestic conflicts, 147–148

Women of the Great Leap Forward (film), 73

workers. *See* model workers; silk factories

work units: and collectivity, 17, 72; and housing allocation, 9, 49, 56, 57, 61, 81, 83, 86, 176, 193, 223–224n42, 226n66; and political campaigns, 65, 75, 97, 111, 118–120, 176; as state control of society, 63, 64, 86, 148, 164, 193, 200; as welfare provider, 158

writing desk, palimpsest history of, 23, 90, 95–100, 95

Wu family, 69

Wu Yonggang, 145

Wubajin, 115

Xia Yan, 217n14, 226n70

Xinjiang, 76, 99, 130

Xintiandi, 10

Yan, Yunxiang, 15, 17, 196, 230n51

Yang, Mayfair, 86

Yangshupu (Yangpu) District, 4, 5, 26–27, 39, 41, 61, 192–193, 200, 213, 235n21

Yeh, Catherine, 145

Yeh, Wen-hsin, 217n16

Yeye (paternal grandfather): as accountant for China Textile Construction Company, 46–47; and Aunt Pearl's shanty, 78, 79, 80, 88, 225n60; book collection of, 96, 129, 212, 213; correspondence of, 99–100; cousins of, 96–98; death of, 209–210, 212; diploma for St. John's University, 1–2, 2, 3, 3, 44, 96, 115; domestic quarrels with Nainai, 156; family photographs, 63, 99; and Hundred Flowers Campaign, 66–67; and Japanese presence in China, 44; labor reform in Shanghai suburbs, 68, 75, 101–102; leaving something for posterity, 211–212; loss of housing to children, 80–84, 133; and Mao Zedong's portrait, 112; and No. 183, Pingliang Road, 4, 41, 47, 62, 68, 80–84, 82, 87, 88, 97, 209, 211–213; radios of, 109, 140; relationship with married children, 133–134; retiring to give job to Aunt Bean, 80; as Rightist, 66–70, 74, 75, 80, 81, 97, 98, 100, 112, 113, 114; and Three-Anti Five-Anti Campaign,

65, 97; writing desk of, 95–100, *95*;
written confessions of, 16, 66, 87, 96,
97–98, 211, 212

Yuan Muzhi, 9

Zarrow, Peter, 17
Zhang, Xudong, 10

Zhang, Zhen, 156
Zhang family: books of, 123, 125–127; on
first floor of No. 111 Alliance Lane, 53,
57, 108, 122–129; Mrs. Zhang's Bible,
125, *126*; photographs of, *122, 123*
Zhao, Chunlan, 29
Zheng Junli, 8, 226*n*70

CPSIA information can be obtained
at www.ICGtesting.com
Printed in the USA
LVOW08s0339290917

550391LV00006B/29/P

9 780231 167178